Industrial policy in Britain 1945–1951 is an archive-based study of the economic planning of the Attlee governments, in which the author seeks to analyse the interaction between the decisions of central planners and the micro-economic effects of those decisions. Throughout the book, Martin Chick pays particular attention to the level, pattern and quality of fixed capital investment. At the same time, there is a continuous concern with the struggle between politicians, economists and industrialists over the mix of pricing mechanisms and administrative orders which were to be used in this period. This struggle permeated all discussions of matters such as the organisation and structure of nationalised industries, the allocation of resources and the promotion of higher productivity. The author also asks what impact, if any, economic planning had on the productivity performance of the UK economy.

Industrial policy in Britain 1945–1951

Industrial policy in Britain 1945–1951

Economic planning, nationalisation and the Labour governments

Martin Chick

University of Edinburgh

CAMBRIDGE
UNIVERSITY PRESS

338.941
C53i

PUBLISHED BY THE PRESS SYNDICATE OF THE UNIVERSITY OF CAMBRIDGE
The Pitt Building, Trumpington Street, Cambridge CB2 1RP, United Kingdom

CAMBRIDGE UNIVERSITY PRESS
The Edinburgh Building, Cambridge CB2 1RP, United Kingdom
40 West 20th Street, New York, NY 10011–4211, USA
10 Stamford Road, Oakleigh, Melbourne 3166, Australia

First published 1998

Printed in the United Kingdom at the University Press, Cambridge

Typeset in Plantin 10/12 [CE]

A catalogue record for this book is available from the British Library

Library of Congress Cataloguing-in-Publication Data
Chick, Martin, 1958– .
Industrial policy in Britain, 1945–51: economic planning, nationalisation, and the
Labour governments / Martin Chick.
       p.   cm.
Includes index.
ISBN 0 521 48291 7 (hardback)
1. Industrial policy – Great Britain – History – 20th century.
2. Great Britain – Economic policy – 1945– .
3. Great Britain – Politics and government – 1945– .   I. Title.
HD3616.G72C47   1997   338.941′009′045–dc21   97–10272   CIP

ISBN 0 521 48291 7 hardback

JK

Hatty's book

Contents

Tables

Preface

The Attlee governments of the period 1945–51 are popularly associated with the establishment of the National Health Service, the implementation of the Beveridge Report, and the nationalisation of major industries. What is generally less well known is that the Attlee governments also presided over a period of economic planning unique in British peacetime history. While the postwar rationing of food remains a keen memory for many, and is a staple of popular television and radio documentaries, there is less awareness of other aspects of postwar planning. The duller details of the operation of price controls, import controls, and building licences are understandably less memorable. Yet, at the end of World War II, the potential ability to combine these and other controls into an effective system of economic planning occasioned much excitement in political circles. Economic planning and nationalisation appeared to offer an opportunity to reconstruct and modernise an economy more efficiently and effectively than the free market could ever do.

This book examines the development and effectiveness of economic planning and nationalisation during the Attlee governments. The particular concern is with industrial policy and the impact of economic planning on industrial fixed capital investment. There is a slightly anachronistic ring to 'industrial policy', a term more common today than in the 1940s. Yet, a system of economic planning which forced government to make decisions concerning the allocation of resources, also forced government in practice, if not in theory, to develop what we would now recognise as an industrial policy. Of particular interest are the decisions concerning the allocation of resources to industrial investment. Investment is commonly seen as an important source of economic growth and increased productivity, and as a measure of an economy's willingness to forego current consumption in the hope of enhanced consumption in the future. One of the most serious criticisms made of the Attlee governments has centred on the accusation that they failed to give sufficient priority to the needs of industrial investment, preferring instead to squander resources on their 'New Jerusalem' health, housing, and social security programmes. Such criticisms are examined in this book, as are the factors which influenced the resource allocation between industries. If complaints about the cost of the welfare state have long been the standard fare of noisy pubs and genteel dinner parties alike, then so too have criticisms of the performance of the nationalised industries. With much of the Attlee governments' nationalisation programme now unwound by privatisation, it is worth asking why anyone ever thought nationalisation was a good idea, and whether fundamental problems were inherent in the original structure and operating principles of the nationalised industries.

This book is organised into three sections. The first three chapters examine the early changes in the machinery of economic planning (chapter 1), the influence of economic planning on the level of industrial investment (chapter 2), and the criteria and factors which influenced the allocation of resources between competing industries (chapter 3). The second section of the book examines the nationalisation programme, in both its origins and structure (chapter 4) and the early arguments concerning the rules for pricing (chapter 5). This latter chapter proceeds from its initial concern with the specific arguments over marginal and average cost pricing in nationalised industries, to a wider discussion of the use made of pricing mechanisms in general. The purpose of this is to lead the discussion beyond the confines of central government, and out into the myriad of boardrooms and construction sites where economic planning and the market met.

In the third section of the book, the impact which economic planning had on the investment decisions made by industrialists is examined. Chapter 6 examines the plant choices made by mangers in the nationalised electricity and railway industries, while chapter 7 examines the attempts of planners to promote rationalisation and modernisation in the textile and iron and steel industries. In both of these chapters, attention is paid to the interaction between the aspirations and exhortations of politicians and planners, and the information and signals sent to managers through the system of economic planning. The question posed is whether the incentives offered to managers were likely to encourage them to act as planners intended, or whether economic planning sent out a confusing set of signals in which increased output was bought at the expense of productivity improvements. The final chapter of the book examines the drift away from economic planning and the discussions within government of which controls a Labour government might wish to retain. The book closes by considering the effects of economic planning on the productivity and growth performance of the British economy, and nudges the reader to speculate on whether the British experience of economic planning had much in common with the more durable experience of much of eastern Europe.

Acknowledgements

Many people have helped me during the writing of this book. Among the archivists who guided me through their collections, I am particularly grateful to Terry Whitehead, Andrew Burns (British Steel), Kalina Page (ICI), Richard Storey, Alistair Tough (Modern Records Centre, University of Warwick), P. Johnson (Courtaulds), Angela Raspin (British Library of Political and Economic Science), Michael Moss (University of Glasgow), Stephen Bird (Labour Party), Henry Gillett (Bank of England), and all the staff at the Trades Union Congress, the Chemical Industries Association, 3i, the Electricity Council and the Public Records Office, Kew. I never fail to be amazed by the apparently limitless willingness of archivists to go and fetch yet more boxes for me to trawl through.

These archives are scattered all over Britain, and my journeying was made easier by the friends and relatives who were prepared to accommodate me. Thanks again to Simon and Sarah Blandy, Mary and Tim Wood, Peter and Pat Chick, Peter and Verrall Dunlop, Margaret and Andrew Underwood, and Julie Bourke, all of whom have put me up and put up with me over many years.

In thinking and writing about the issues in this book, I have benefited greatly from discussions with historians and economists, some of whom were themselves at the centre of events in industry and government during the Attlee governments. Paul Addison, John Banasik, Sue Bowden, Duncan Burn, Sir Alec Cairncross, Roger Davidson, James Foreman-Peck, David Greasley, Trevor Griffiths, Leslie Hannah, Douglas Jay, John Kinross, Bob Millward, Neil Rollings, Jim Tomlinson, and Peter Vinter have all variously listened to my latest enthusiasm, answered my questions, or prompted me to think anew about the issues. I hope they think that this book was worth some of their trouble.

Finally, and mostly, I am quite unable to say how much I owe to Hatty, Freddy and Tom. At a practical level, I am extremely appreciative of the grace with which Freddy and Tom allowed me to commandeer their computer, when my ten-year-old machine expired, taking most of the book with it. Yes, I did have back-ups. I am also hugely grateful to Hatty for all the Saturday mornings that she has taken the boys to their various sporting and dramatic activities, leaving me to chase paper around the study. This book is dedicated to Hatty as a small and inadequate expression of my love and thanks.

Abbreviations

BEA	British Electricity Authority
BISF	British Iron and Steel Federation
BKEA	Bank of England archive
BLPES	British Library of Political and Economic Science
BOAC	British Overseas Airways Corporation
BSA	British Steel archive
CEB	Central Electricity Board
CEPS	Central Economic Planning Staff
FBI	Federation of British Industries
GDFCF	Gross domestic fixed capital formation
GPO	General Post Office
IPC	Investment Programmes Committee
IWP	Investment Working Party
LNER	London and North Eastern Railway
LPA	Labour Party archive
NCB	National Coal Board
NHS	National Health Service
NIC	National Investment Council
NSHEB	North of Scotland Hydro-Electric Board
OEEC	Organisation for European Economic Co-operation
PRO	Public Records Office, Kew
TUC	Trades Union Congress
UGA	University of Glasgow archive

1 Economic planning

'Peace-time planning, in any serious sense, began in the year 1947'.[1]
(E. A. G. Robinson, *Economic Planning in the UK*, p. 3)

A lot can happen during a three-week holiday in Cornwall. Returning from a holiday begun on 26 July 1945, the economist James Meade 'came back to a totally different world: the United Kingdom had a Labour Government with a huge majority; the future of the world had been totally altered by the dropping of two atomic bombs; and the war in the Far East was over. The situation when I got back was quite transformed.'[2] By the time of his return, the announcement of the general election results had brought to power a Labour government committed to nationalising the coal mines and the leading utilities, determined to effect improvements in health, housing, and welfare, and concerned to pursue low rates of unemployment. In a remarkable legislative programme the basis for both the postwar welfare state and increased government involvement in the economy was to be established. Much of what the later Thatcher governments sought to reorganise and reform had its origins directly in the legislative programme of the 1945–51 Attlee governments.

The immediate task confronting the government was to supervise the transition of the economy from a wartime to a peacetime footing. This had been effected once before, after World War I, and lessons were drawn from that experience. Then, the rapid release of controls was held to have contributed to an inflationary boom in 1919–20 followed by a slump in which unemployment had risen within a few months in the second half of 1920 from 4 to over 20 per cent. Inequity was held to

---

[1] E. A. G. Robinson, *Economic Planning in the UK: Some Lessons*, Cambridge University Press, 1967, p. 3.
[2] S. Howson and D. Moggridge (eds.), *The Collected Papers of James Meade: vol. IV, The Cabinet Office Diary, 1944–46*, London, Unwin Hyman, 1990, p. 114, entry for 26 August 1945. The general election was held on 5 July 1945 but the result was not announced until 26 July to allow time for the votes of those serving in the forces to be counted.

1

have accompanied the inflationary scramble for resources. Work by the historian Tawney and the economist Pigou provided academic confirmation of the perceived detrimental economic and distributive consequences of the early release of World War I controls.[3] Concerned to prevent a recurrence of an inflationary boom and slump, and equally concerned to secure 'fair shares' in the distribution of scarce resources, the Attlee government had few misgivings about retaining many of the wartime controls.[4] Whatever the arguments over rationing, there was a wide scepticism about the benefits alleged to proceed from the operation of free, uncontrolled markets.[5]

The retained controls varied in their range and longevity. Many of the most visible were intended to endure throughout the transition period, but then to be abolished as increased production reduced shortages. Many consumer controls fell into this category, consumer rationing controls covering less than one-third of consumer spending in 1948, and never more than one-eighth from 1949. In 1948 over half of consumer spending on food was not subject to rationing.[6] Many of these controls provided the bulk of Harold Wilson's 'bonfires' of controls from November 1948.

Beyond the controls which were most obviously designed to ease the transition from a wartime to a peacetime economy, there were two further important groups of controls. The first and increasingly important group of controls were those intended to promote exports and to restrain imports. The import controls covered four-fifths of food and raw-material imports and two-thirds of total imports, including manufactures, in 1946. On the export side, direct controls over steel, timber and scarce materials directed resources to leading export industries as well as giving priority to essential basic sector and bottleneck industries such as iron and steel, coal mining, and building materials. These controls were reinforced by building-licence controls, which also sought to ensure that priority was given to the building of

[3] R. H. Tawney, 'The Abolition of Economic Controls', *Economic History Review*, 13 (1943), pp. 1–30. A. C. Pigou, *Aspects of British Economic History, 1918–1925*, London, Macmillan, 1947, the research for which was undertaken during the war at the request of the wartime government. Papers from Tawney and Pigou were circulating around Whitehall towards the end of the war.
[4] LPA RDR 267 Post War Finance Sub-Committee, 'Full Employment and Financial Policy', April 1944. LPA RD 75 'Inflation', November 1947.
[5] Ina Zweiniger-Bargielowska, 'Bread Rationing in Britain, July 1946–July 1948', *Twentieth Century British History*, 4, 1 (1993), pp. 57–85. UGA, McCance Papers, Nuffield 24th Private Conference on 'The Government's Controls of Industry and Trade', 26 and 27 June 1948. Contribution by Sir John Woods.
[6] Alec Cairncross, *Years of Recovery: British Economic Policy, 1945–51*, London, Methuen, 1985; university paperback 1987, p. 334.

council houses and to investment in the traditionally depressed Development Areas. With the growing importance and awareness of the balance-of-payments problems, key controls retained their importance longer than originally expected, some gaining an added lease of life during the Korean War rearmament programme. Direct controls on most steel, which had been scrapped in May 1950, were reinstated in February 1952 before finally expiring in May 1953.[7]

The other set of controls were those intended to contribute to the planning of an economy in which approaching unemployment was counteracted by government manipulation of fixed capital-investment activity.[8] Such thinking, with its deep Liberal Party roots, emanated in the 1930s from groups such as the XYZ group and the New Fabian Research Bureau, many of whose discussions became familiar to a future generation of government ministers and advisers, including Hugh Gaitskell, Douglas Jay, James Meade, Hugh Dalton, and Evan Durbin.[9] Dalton, the Attlee government's first Chancellor of the Exchequer, was keen to give physical embodiment to attractive ideas, and in January and February 1946 he began to organise the establishment of the National Investment Council (NIC). Drawing on established counter-cyclical trade theory, the NIC was to prepare a 'shelf' of projects which could be held in readiness for implementation when downturns in the trade cycle began to manifest themselves.[10] Dalton was chairman of the NIC, whose membership included a mix of friends and XYZ members.[11] Established with typically ebullient apparent self-confi-

---

[7] Cairncross, *Years of Recovery*, p. 338–9. The controls of sheet steel and tinplate were not lifted in May 1950.

[8] PRO CAB 134/982, 'Investment in 1953 and 1954', Report by the Investment Programmes Committee, 3 January 1953, p. 5, para. 2. 'It was contemplated in the 1944 White Paper on Employment Policy that the Government's power to influence the level of investment should be used to maintain the level of employment.'

[9] S. Howson, *British Monetary Policy 1945–51*, Oxford, Clarendon Press, 1993, p. 63.

[10] J. C. R. Dow, *The Management of the British Economy, 1945–60*, Cambridge University Press, 1970, p. 214. PRO 134/982, 'Investment in 1953 and 1954', Report by the Investment Programmes Committee, 3 January 1953, para. 2. PRO T288/81, Letter from Hugh Dalton to Sir Clive Ballieu, 17 January 1946. BKEA G1/247, Letter from Dalton to Lord Catto, 15 January 1946.

[11] The members 'chosen for their wide knowledge and experience of financial, economic and industrial questions' included Lord Catto (Governor of the Bank of England); William Piercy, the first chairman of the newly established Industrial and Commercial Finance Corporation, which was to assist in improving the supply of capital to small and medium-sized companies; Sir Robert Pearson (Chairman of the Stock Exchange); Lord Kennet (Chairman of the Capital Issues Committee); Sir Albert Gladstone (Chairman of the Public Works Loan Board); Lord Hyndley (Chairman of Finance Corporation for Industry, before leaving to become chairman of the National Coal Board); C. E. Prater (Co-operative movement); Sir Clarence Sadd (Midland Bank); Sir Clive Baillieu (President of the Federation of British Industries); Nicholas Davenport, and George Gibson. PRO T288/81, letters from Hugh Dalton to Sir Clarence Sadd,

dence, the achievements of the NIC must have proved a disappointment to Dalton. Its fundamental *raison d'être* was undermined by the failure of the expected slump to materialise and in its short life, prior to being wound up by Stafford Cripps in December 1948, it tended to discuss rather marginal issues such as relaxing the wartime ban on companies issuing bonus shares.[12]

The fate which befell Dalton's ambitions for the NIC also attended his complementary approach to planning in which capital issues controls assumed a central position. The NIC and the 'control of demands on the capital market' through the Capital Issues Committee formed the basis of Dalton's 'planning of investment' and his anti-slump measures.[13] Whatever the long-term potential of such instruments, Dalton's claim in 1946 that these financial controls provided the basis for 'effective planning' in an economy in which companies often had high levels of accumulated savings seems overly sanguine. To Meade, Dalton's claim was 'absurd' and 'pure eye-wash', being 'no more a proper control of investment than anything we had before the war'.[14]

The real constraint on investment activity was the shortage of building materials, steel, timber, and labour.[15] Indeed, it was the predominance of physical-resource shortages, and the secondary importance of finance, which in part allowed Dalton to operate the cheap money policy with which he is so closely identified.[16] Cheap money had many attractions for government. It reduced the cost of servicing the national debt of around £25,000 million, with a floating debt component of £7,000 million; it was consistent with the aim expressed in the coalition government's 1944 White Paper on employment policy of avoiding 'dear money in the Reconstruction'; it was held to be in keeping with the longer-term anti-slump measures; and it reduced the cost of raising money for the reconstruction and nationalisation programme.[17] The stock issue in compensation for the railways was

Lord Hyndley, and Lord Piercy, 17 January 1946. M. Chick, 'William Piercy', in D. Jeremy (ed.), *Dictionary of Business Biography*, vol. IV, London, Butterworth, 1985. BKEA G1/247, 'National Investment Council, Members', 5 February 1946.

[12] Howson, *British Monetary Policy*, p. 121.

[13] PRO T288/81, National Investment Council, Paper 5, 'Note on the Work of the Investment Working Party', November 1946, para. 5. BKEA G1/247, letter from Dalton to Lord Catto, 15 January 1946.

[14] Meade, *Diary*, 2 December 1945.

[15] PRO CAB 134/440, IPC(49)3, Cabinet, Investment Programmes Committee, *Report on Capital Investment in 1950–1952*, para. 61.

[16] For a detailed analysis of Dalton's cheap money policy, see S. Howson, *British Monetary Policy*.

[17] PRO T233/299, Paper on 'Cheap Money' by H. A. Copeman, 17 March 1947, paras. 1, 3, and 4. For a critique of Keynes' *General Theory* and the cheap money policy see

expected to amount to over £1,000 million, that for electricity to around £350 million, while the housing programme was thought likely to require that the government borrow £500 million.[18] Dalton was understandably keen to pursue cheap money. Loans raised at higher rates of interest would form correspondingly high capital charges on the assets represented by the loans, and in turn would require the rents of new houses and the prices charged by the National Coal Board (NCB) and other public corporations to be increased. Since increased prices were held to contribute to inflationary tendencies, cheap money could be presented as being anti-inflationary.[19] This contrasted with the view articulated in some sections of the Conservative Party that interest rates should be raised precisely so as to dampen inflationary tendencies. What was not clear was how high interest rates would have to go to have any such effect. If the intention was to take immediate measures to dampen demand and to promote savings, then a more direct option was to run a budget surplus. Compared with the potential impact of a budget surplus, dearer money was dismissed by planners, such as Alec Cairncross, at the Board of Trade, as 'largely a red herring'.[20]

Before a move could be made to attempt to balance income and expenditure by such means as a budgetary surplus, a number of major adjustments had to be made to the structure and assumptions of immediate postwar economic planning. It had to be recognised that excess rather than deficient demand was the principal persistent problem, and that budgetary techniques offered at least as much scope for managing excess demand as the phalanx of price controls and allocating committees. Such a shift in perspective would require central, physical planners such as the Lord President, Herbert Morrison, to step to one side and allow the Treasury a greater role in 'economic planning'. Such significant changes were never likely to be conceded easily, and it was only on the back of the two crises of 1947

BKEA ADM 14/16, 'Cheap Money: A Criticism of Lord Keynes' Theory and an Alternative View' by Lucius P. Thompson-McCausland, March 1945. His criticism that Keynes' *General Theory* was too concerned with the outlook of the speculative investor rather than that of businessmen was supported by Dennis Robertson. BKEA ADM 14/16, Letter to L. P. Thompson-McCausland from Henry Clay, Warden, Nuffield College, Oxford, 11 April 1945. BKEA ADM 14/16, Letter to L. P. Thompson-McCausland from James Meade, 23 April 1945. Letter to Thompson-McCausland from D. H. Robertson, 19 March 1945.

[18] For possible alternative bases for compensation see Frederick Geidt, 'Taking over Railways: an Annuity Plan', letter, *Financial Times*, 29 November 1946.

[19] PRO T233/299, paper on 'Cheap Money' by H. A. Copeman, 17 March 1947, para. 4.

[20] PRO T230/25, letter to R. Tress (Economic Section) from Alec Cairncross (Board of Trade), 19 June 1947.

that substantial changes to the machinery, personnel and outlook of postwar economic planning were effected.

The two major crises of 1947 were the fuel crisis in February and the convertibility crisis in August. While a counterfactual £200 million exports were lost, the political importance of the fuel crisis was probably much greater than its economic significance, since it raised clear suggestions of incompetence at the centre of government and cruelly broke any confidence in the omniscience and effectiveness of planning. As Dalton remarked, after the fuel crisis it was 'never glad, confident morning again'.[21] Indeed, it is difficult to refute accusations of incompetence and weak management at the centre of government. There was clearly a fundamental excess demand for coal, and, if it were allowed to continue, a crisis of some sort was entirely predictable. Eight months before the fuel crisis, James Meade, the Director of the Economic Section, wrote to Morrison warning him that not only was it 'difficult to exaggerate the urgency of radical action to increase coal production', but that it was not at all 'impossible that shortage of coal this winter may so interfere with supplies of fuel for industry as to cause widespread unemployment and a failure to maintain our economic targets, including our export drive, and may make it difficult to keep our homes warm. Such a development, coming on top of the present food situation, would clearly be disastrous'.[22] Counter-arguments made by Emanuel Shinwell, the Minister of Fuel and Power, that 'the worst is over' were regarded by Douglas Jay as 'too optimistic', and that

in fact, as things are going at present, industry, transport and domestic consumption is bound to be dislocated on a wide and uncontrollable scale by December or a little later. This easily predictable and avoidable disaster is likely to occur at exactly the moment when the National Coal Board takes over the first great nationalised industry in this country. The discredit to the Government would be as devastating as the dislocation to industry.[23]

That the predicted fuel crisis did occur highlighted the ability of planners to extrapolate from existing consumption and production trends and to forewarn politicians of approaching problems. That, despite such warnings, the fuel crisis occurred also pointed to the insufficiency of information alone; in a planning structure there also had to be at least a commensurate willingness on the part of political leaders

[21] H. Dalton, *High Tide and After*, London, Frederick Muller, 1962, p. 205.

[22] PRO CAB 124/706, CP(46)232, note from J. Meade to Lord President, 'Output, Recruitment and Conditions of Employment in the Coal-mining Industry, memorandum by the Minister of Fuel and Power', 19 June 1946, para. 1.

[23] PRO CAB 124/706, note entitled 'Coal Crisis' from D. Jay to J. A. R. Pimlott, 19 June 1946, paras. 1–3.

to act on the information. The tale of Attlee confronting Shinwell with the statistics only to be told in reply that he should not 'be led up the garden path by the statistics', and that rather he 'should look at the imponderables' did not bode well.[24]

The political response to the fuel crisis was to replace Shinwell with Gaitskell as Minister of Fuel and Power, with Gaitskell also being appointed chairman of the newly established Fuel Allocations Committee. To strengthen the credibility of the wider planning structure, the establishment of the Central Economic Planning Staff (CEPS) and the Economic Planning Board was announced during a three day debate on the economy between 10 and 12 March 1947. These were rushed creations, the Economic Planning Board being a rather cosmetic, tripartite talking shop whose members were not appointed until July. Of much more importance was the CEPS headed by Sir Edwin Plowden, which, again, did not take up its duties until the summer of 1947 but which did mark a sharp move towards strengthening the centralised administrative balancing of supply and demand within the planning structure.[25] The establishment of the CEPS was both a reflection of the growing concern about the persistence of excess demand and an implicit acknowledgement that the existing planning structure was experiencing considerable difficulties with operating in such conditions. For all of Morrison's boasts of planning, and his self-regard as the 'central economic co-ordinator', his department had little supervisory central control over the issue of steel approval forms and building licences by other departments such as the Ministry of Works.[26]

There were also pockets of the economy where 'co-ordination' was conspicuously absent. In a reconstructing economy, resources became too thinly spread over a growing number of construction projects, few of which were completed. By 1947, in the Development Areas, which accounted for half of all the factory building authorised since 1944, only 40 per cent had been started and a mere 6 per cent completed. In the North West region alone, only 38 per cent of all licensed industrial building jobs costing over £10,000 were more than one-quarter complete.[27] For all of the government's insistence on learning from the experience of the economic reconversion after World War I, this over-

[24] D. Jay, *Change and Fortune*, London, Hutchinson, 1980, p. 149.
[25] D. N. Chester, 'Machinery of Government and Planning' in G. D. N. Worswick and P. H. Ady (eds.), *The British Economy 1945–50* Oxford, Clarendon Press, 1952, pp. 344–5.
[26] Herbert Morrison, *Economic Planning*, London, Institute of Public Administration, 1946. Paper read before a meeting of the Institute of Public Administration, 17 October 1946, p. 8. BLPES, Meade papers, 1/4. Diary, 26 August 1945.
[27] PRO CAB 134/437, IPC(47)9, Cabinet, Investment Programmes Committee, *Report*, 8 October 1947, p. 5, para. 12.

starting of building work replicated that previous experience. In housing, completion rates were low as the excessive start authorisations exacerbated the problem of resource allocation. By 1947, there was a growing stock of unfinished houses and houses under contract, numbering 360,000.[28] By 1947, the wider effects of excess demand were manifesting themselves in crucial sections of the planning system, with the steel-allocation system steadily breaking down as paper authorisations ran ahead of steel supplies, which had become 'chaotically distributed'.[29]

These specific failures in allocation and co-ordination were products of the fundamental problem of excess demand. Various economists, such as Michal Kalecki, Christopher Dow and David Worswick, made estimates of the size of this excess demand, and all seemed broadly agreed that it was likely to persist for five to six years after the end of World War II. While the general problem of excess demand had been well understood for a long time and had, of course, underpinned the decision to retain many of the wartime controls, the events of 1947 increased the political willingness to address the immediate problems of excess demand rather than worry about the longer-term potential problem of demand deficiencies.[30] By September 1947, Nicholas Davenport, the founder of the XYZ group and a keen member of the

[28] PRO CAB 134/437, IPC(47)9, Cabinet, Investment Programmes Committee, *Report*, 8 October 1947, p. 5, para. 11
[29] PRO CAB 134/437, IPC(47)9, Cabinet, Investment Programmes Committee, *Report*, 8 October 1947, Appendix 2, para. 1. N Rosenberg, *Economic Planning in the British Building Industry, 1945–9*, Philadelphia, University of Pennsylvania Press, 1960, p. 39.
[30] PRO T230/26, EC(S)(47)27, Economic Section, 'Hyper-demand', paper by J. C. R. Dow, 17 July 1947, paras. 5 and 6. PRO CAB 134/503, MEP (46)5, Cabinet, Ministerial Committee on Economic Planning, 'Economic Survey for 1946/47; Report by the Economic Survey Working Party', 11 July 1946, para. 29.

During the war, savings of £5,000 million had accumulated, while capital maintenance of £2,000 million and net investment of £4,000 million were foregone in war. A total of £1,200 million was sitting in unspent maintenance allowances, to which could be added War Damage compensation payments, Excess Profits Tax refunds, and funds released by wartime depletion of working stocks which had not yet been re-absorbed. Clearly, although about £4,000 million of the consumption foregone would never be recovered – 'the eggs of yesteryear will never be eaten' – it was clear that there was a large accumulated spending power. Much of this was held in relatively liquid form, whether as cash, bank deposits, or, as was most common, in the form of government-sponsored 'small savings' (i.e. Post Office and Trustee Savings Banks deposits, National Savings Certificates, and Defence Bonds) which between 1939 and 1945 increased by more than £3,800 million. While price rises had depreciated some of the real value of these holdings, the cheap money policy reduced the opportunity cost of consumption. LPA RD1, 'A Labour Policy for Privately Owned Industry', by G. D. N. Worswick, September 1945. Refers to M. Kalecki, 'Employment in the United Kingdom During and After the Transition Period', *Bulletin of the Institute of Statistics*, December 1944. David Worswick reckoned the 'piled-up demand' for consumption at about £1,700 million, in terms of 1938 retail prices.

NIC, was urging that 'counter-inflation action today must be more direct than the monetary measures of the past', and that the government should reduce excess purchasing power through such means as running a budgetary surplus, cutting defence expenditure severely, and, possibly, reducing food subsidies.[31] Added urgency was provided by the convertibility crisis and the renewed emphasis on increasing exports. The wartime sale of over £1,000 million of investments and the accumulation of sterling and dollar liabilities of £3,500 million, produced a net change on the capital account across the war of £4,700 million, giving Britain the largest external debt in its history.[32] It had been recognised long before the end of the war that with exports at 30 per cent of their pre-war level, a major postwar export drive would have to be launched with the aim of achieving a very substantial excess of between 50 per cent and 75 per cent over the pre-war volume of exports.[33]

In general quantitative terms, the export drive could be considered a success. In 1946, exports increased by 70 per cent in volume over 1945 and to a higher level than before the war.[34] At £960 million in 1946, exports had climbed to £2,735 million by 1951.[35] Yet, despite this performance, the government was dogged by biennial balance-of-payments problems, which were not fully understood by most ministers and officials. The end of the war had brought to an abrupt end the Lend-Lease arrangement with the United States. The convertibility problem – which arose out of US insistence during the negotiations on the postwar loan that sterling become convertible – was dramatic, but only in the sense that it was a very visible manifestation of a complex problem. A dollar drain preceded convertibility, and convertibility itself did not add substantially to the current dollar deficit in the first half of 1947. It was not the suspension of convertibility but rather the cuts which followed in its wake which ended the dollar drain.[36]

What was difficult for politicians to understand was why balance-of-payments difficulties should coexist with a favourable balance of trade position. It had been expected that the trade and gold-dollar position would move roughly in line with each other, and that the postwar balance-of-payments problems would not endure for long. Discussing

---

[31] BKEA G1/247, National Investment Council, NIC Paper 16, Memorandum by Nicholas Davenport on Counter-Inflation Measures, 22 September 1947.

[32] Alec Cairncross, *Years of Recovery*, p. 7.

[33] Cairncross, *Years of Recovery*, pp. 6–7.

[34] R. Clarke, *Anglo-American Collaboration in War and Peace 1942–49*, Oxford, Oxford University Press, 1982, pp. 40–1. Cairncross, *Years of Recovery*, pp. 26–7.

[35] Central Statistical Office, *Economic Trends, Annual Supplement*, London, HMSO, 1996, Table 1.17.

[36] Cairncross, *Years of Recovery*, pp. 163–4.

the severity of the balance-of-payments position in 1944, both Richard Clarke and James Meade expected the problem to be resolved within five years. In the event, this did not happen. In June 1948, Meade acknowledged that 'there is one thing, of course, that is much worse now than one had reason to expect it might be three years after the end of the war: I mean our balance of payments position'.[37] The development of the almost separate problem in the gold and dollar reserves presented planners with balance-of-payments difficulties of an unanticipated character and durability. What was clear, however, was that the balance-of-payments problems heightened the need to increase exports, to constrain or substitute imports, and that increased exports would add even more to the problem of excess demand within the domestic economy. If excess demand was not reduced then the increased competition for resources was likely to result in even more unfinished projects and implosions within the machinery of economic planning. Necessity, aided by illness, crisis, and blunder, impelled changes to the structure of economic planning.

The illness was the thrombosis of Morrison, which removed him from the centre stage of economic planning between January and May 1947, and allowed Stafford Cripps and Dalton to step into his place. The crisis was the convertibility crisis, following which Cripps was appointed Minister of Economic Affairs, and Morrison's role as economic co-ordinator effectively ended. The blunder was Dalton's budget leak in November 1947, which occasioned his resignation and allowed Cripps to succeed him and amalgamate the posts of Chancellor and Minister of Economic Affairs. Two years after the end of the war the Treasury was back at the centre of economic policy-making, and domestic and external policy came much closer together. This marked a turning-point in the arguments over the practice of planning and the role of the Treasury in the planning structure. Coincidentally, drawing on his work with Richard Stone on the development of national-income accounting, Meade pushed for the gap between supply and demand to be presented on an income–expenditure basis. This approach was opposed by Morrison, who, like many politicians, preferred 'gaps' to be measured in physical, usually manpower, terms.

In the wake of the convertibility crisis, significant changes were made to the planning structure. The establishment of the Investment Programmes Committee (IPC) was a move towards the tighter screening of departmental investment programmes.[38] To an extent, the

[37] UGA McCance Papers, Nuffield 24th private conference on 'The Government's Controls of Industry and Trade', 26 June 1948. Contribution by James Meade.
[38] PRO CAB 129/20, CP(47)231, Cabinet, 'Investment Programmes Committee, Note

IPC picked up on some of the earlier work of the Investment Working Party (IWP), which, prompted by Peter Vinter at the Treasury, Douglas Jay and the Economic Section, had already begun to move towards examining the investment programmes of departments, both in response to the Economic Survey considered by the Cabinet in February 1946 and as part of its efforts to prepare a shelf of anti-slump projects.[39] However, the IWP, reflecting the structure of the early planning administration, had concentrated on the 'physical' aspects of investment, such as the availability of labour, materials and capacity, and had tended to ignore its financial aspects, paying almost no attention to interest rates, variable grants-in-aid, taxes and subsidies.[40] The IPC now attempted to integrate both the financial and the physical aspects of investment, in keeping with the greater emphasis given to financial and budgetary means of acting on demand.

The determination to reduce excess demand was evident in Dalton's budget of November 1947. While the budget had swung from a deficit of £2,207 million in 1945–6 into a surplus in 1947, largely due to demobilisation and a reduction in public expenditure, the importance of the November 1947 budget was that it marked a deliberate attempt to reduce excess demand using budgetary techniques. The budget hit a peak surplus of £831 million in 1948–9.[41] A high level of taxation was maintained and cuts sought in public expenditure, which, as in World War I, had risen during World War II. From 9.9 per cent of total domestic expenditure in 1935, public authorities' current expenditure on goods and services had peaked at 46 per cent in 1944, before falling to 14.7 per cent in 1948, but rising again to 18.2 per cent in 1952.[42] War appeared to have had a once-and-for-all ratchet effect on public expenditure, which, once increased, never returned to its pre-war level.

Among the components of public expenditure, what caught the eye of contemporaries was the subsidy bill. As a share of central government expenditure, total subsidies climbed from 2.7 per cent in 1939 to 4.2

by Secretary of the Cabinet'. PRO CAB 128/10, CM(47)68th Conclusions (2) and (3). Meade, *Diary*, entry for 27 January 1946, p. 204.

[39] PRO T288/81, National Investment Council, Paper 5, 'Note on the Work of the Investment Working Party', November 1946 para. 5. PRO CAB 134/188, IWP(46)4 (Revise), 'First Report by the Investment Working Party', 12 March 1946. para. 7. Meade, *Diary*, 10 February 1946, pp. 212–13.

[40] PRO T288/81, National Investment Council, Paper 5, 'Note on the Work of the Investment Working Party', November 1946, para. 1.

[41] Cairncross, *Years of Recovery*, pp. 420–1

[42] C. H. Feinstein, *Statistical Tables of National Income, Expenditure and Output of the UK, 1855–1965*, Cambridge, Cambridge University Press, 1972, Table 2. R. Middleton, *Government versus the Market: The Growth of the Public Sector, Economic Management and British Economic Performance, 1890–1979*, Cheltenham, Edward Elgar, 1996, pp. 497–509.

per cent in 1944, but then continued to climb after the war, peaking at 16.9 per cent in 1948, before beginning to fall slowly to 11.4 per cent in 1951.[43] Introduced in 1941 to help control wartime inflation, by June 1945, food subsidies alone were costing £250 million per annum and rising.[44] Keynes and the Economic Section, regarded the food subsidies in particular as 'very inflationary' inasmuch as they reduced or enlarged the budget surplus or deficit, and of questionable importance in combating wage inflation.[45] In September 1947, Nicholas Davenport was wondering whether 'some part of the food subsidies might be passed on without exciting wage claims' and whether

perhaps more could be done about the wheat subsidy by adopting the simple expedient of selling a white loaf at its true economic price. Seeing that a large proportion of the working population appears to suffer from gastric trouble there should be no class reaction to this simple plan. All gastric sufferers in every walk of life would willingly pay more for a white loaf and their peace of digestion.[46]

If one of the aims of food subsidies was to assist low-income households, Meade argued that could be done more efficiently, not by subsidising prices of items consumed by all households but by increasing the incomes of households with children through increasing family allowances.[47]

Although the size and targeting of food subsidies were attacked, it was not clear whether there was much scope for reducing consumers' expenditure in general. Consumer expenditure as a share of total domestic expenditure was on a trend decline, as public authorities' current expenditure on goods and services, gross domestic fixed capital formation and, above all, exports increased their share.[48] While consumer expenditure per capita recovered its 1939 level in 1946, its 1938 level was not reached until 1949.[49] Over the years 1946–51, consumption per head rose by only 1 per cent per annum.[50] Rationing continued into the postwar period, being introduced for the first time on bread in 1946 and potatoes in 1947. This was not what a victorious, fully employed working population, which uniquely among workers in the European belligerent countries had enjoyed a wartime increase in

[43] C. H. Feinstein, *Statistical Tables*, Table 12.
[44] Cairncross, *Years of Recovery*, p. 39.
[45] Meade, *Diary*, pp. 271–2, 281, 7 June 1946.
[46] BKEA G1/247, National Investment Council, NIC Paper No. 16, Memorandum, by Nicholas Davenport on Counter-Inflation Measures, 22 September 1947.
[47] Meade, *Diary*, pp. 249, 259, 6 and 27 April 1946.
[48] C. H. Feinstein, *Statistical Tables*, Table 2.
[49] C. H. Feinstein, *Statistical Tables*, Table 17, Column 3.
[50] Cairncross, *Years of Recovery*, p. 23.

real earnings, had necessarily expected in the postwar years. Certainly, as the years passed, the willingness of the population to 'Shiver with Shinwell and Starve with Strachey' declined.

It was of little comfort, or relevance, that others were faring worse. In terms of calorific intake, British people were faring better than most other countries, if not consuming at pre-war levels. Statistically, the daily per capita intake of 2,970 calories in the UK in 1947/8, was second only to the 3,240 of the USA and certainly higher than the 2,550 in France, 2,180 in Austria, 2,150 in the Western Zones of Germany and 1,900 in the Soviet Zone of Germany.[51] However, by 1948/9 the UK calorific intake of 3,030 had not recovered its 1934–8 level of 3,100. Moreover, what these statistics did not capture was the dissatisfaction with the quality and monotony of the food available. In December 1946, this inability of bare quantitative statistics to reflect qualitative changes in what was available for consumption was noted by the steering committee charged with preparing the Economic Survey for 1947:

A pint of beer at the moment is not of the same quality as a pre-war pint, nor is a railway journey, standing in a crowded corridor, the same as a pre-war journey seated in a half-empty railway carriage. Nor are retail purchases obtained after considerable difficulty standing in a queue the same thing as an easy last-minute purchase of the same goods nicely packed and delivered.[52]

Despite the ambitions of planning, there also appeared to be inequity in patterns of consumption. While consumption (by richer groups) of motor vehicles, hardware, furniture and travel increased, the consumption of basic items such as food, clothing, coal, beer, and tobacco did not. In 1946, the targets for food and clothing were still low compared with 1938, food consumption being 91 per cent of its pre-war level and clothing 76 per cent.[53] Controls fell on areas where increased consumption was likely to draw manpower away from other, higher-priority industries and, conversely, were absent where this did not occur. Thus, while food and clothing were severely rationed, there was a large increase in expenditure on travel and entertainment, which involved the full utilisation of existing capital and comparatively little labour. While from 1940–5, consumption in real terms had been 80–90 per cent of its 1938 level, the consumption of clothing and household goods had been

51 Department of Economic Affairs, *Economic Survey of Europe in 1949*, Geneva, United Nations, 1950, Table 21, p. 27.
52 PRO CAB 134/503, Cabinet, Ministerial Committee on Economic Planning, 'Economic Survey for 1947: Covering Memorandum by the Steering Committee', 21 December 1946, para. 62.
53 PRO CAB 134/188, 'Economic Survey for 1946–7: Draft Report', July 1946, para. 6.

curtailed much more severely to less than 60 per cent of its peacetime rate.[54] By changing the pattern of consumer expenditure, the fall in the standard of living had been alleviated more than would otherwise have been possible without inflation.[55]

Public dissatisfaction with the quantity and quality of food posed political and economic problems for the government. Politically, it was damaging that three years after the end of the war, the Minister of Food, John Strachey, was still quoting the findings of a Gallup Poll which asked readers of the *News Chronicle* which of their problems they would most like to sit down and discuss with the Prime Minister: 17 per cent of the respondents said food; 13 per cent, the high cost of living; 12 per cent, housing; 6 per cent, fear of war; 3 per cent, clothing; 3 per cent, cigarettes; 2 per cent, household goods; 1 per cent, petrol; 1 per cent, household fuel; and all others less than 3 per cent. Economically, workers were complaining that food shortages were adversely affecting their ability and incentive to work hard. If anything, people seemed to feel that they had been fed better during the war. According to the government's own 'Social Survey' of April 1948, 55 per cent of respondents felt that they were not getting enough food to keep them in good health, compared with a figure of 28 per cent of people in 1942, while 5 per cent of all workers and 66 per cent of all manual workers felt that they would be able to work harder if they had more and better food. That there may have been a higher tolerance of shortages during the war was of little comfort to a government at the receiving end of public discontent. Public exhortations to work harder, 'to export or die', and warnings that 'Britain's bread hangs by Lancashire's thread', were of diminishing impact. As Strachey remarked, 'I am convinced that we now have to deal with a state of mind which is largely immune to "public relations" unaccompanied by food.'[56]

By the autumn of 1947, with the CEPS and the IPC in place, with Morrison's Office of Lord President displaced by the Treasury, with Dalton's November 1947 budget to come, and with a shift towards viewing the excess demand 'gap' in terms of national income and expenditure, the machinery of economic planning was significantly different from the collection of wartime controls and ambitions which

[54] PRO CAB 134/503, MEP(46)5, Cabinet, Ministerial Committee on Economic Planning, 'Economic Survey for 1946/7: Report by the Economic Survey Working Party', 11 July 1946, para. 29.
[55] PRO T230/25, Letter to Ronnie Tress from Alec Cairncross (Board of Trade), 19 June 1947.
[56] PRO CAB 134/219 Economic Policy Committee, EPC(48) 82, 10/9/48, 'Food Consumption Levels Proposed for the Next Four Years', memo by the Minister of Food, John Strachey, citing Gallup Poll in the *News Chronicle* of 23 August, paras. 3–4.

had been retained in 1945. Although there was still anxiety about the return of depression and unemployment at some time in the future, this concern was now at least matched by the more immediate wish to address the problem of excess demand. If the export drive was to be continued, then cuts would have to be sought in other programmed expenditure. The age-old political process of bargaining was to become more explicit and formalised in the economic planning structure from 1947.

2 New Jerusalem?

The establishment of the CEPS and the IPC put in place a central administrative machinery charged with reviewing the plans of departments and matching them with the resources likely to be available. Conceived amidst a rising concern with excess demand, these new instruments of planning would almost inevitably be perceived as miserable rejecters, trimmers, and cutters of departmental programmes. In each biennial year of crisis, 1947, 1949, 1951, the rhetoric of cuts was predominant. At the time, industrialists complained that the needs of industrial investment were particularly badly hit in this process and almost ever since there have been general accusations that the 'New Jerusalem' policies of the Attlee governments involved excessive expenditure on welfare, health, and housing programmes at the expense of industrial investment and modernisation, and the development of such programmes as technical education. In short, it is argued that the Attlee governments got their priorities wrong.[1] The predominant concern of the CEPS and the IPC was with this very issue of priorities. Just how should resources be distributed between the competing needs of consumption, exports, investment, defence, and the 'New Jerusalem' programmes? The CEPS and the IPC were established to produce recommendations on just these issues, and their proposals would then be considered by Cabinet and final decisions made. The planning structure required priorities to be articulated, and thus provides a basis on which to test the claims that the Attlee governments were insufficiently mindful of the needs of industrial investment and thereby pawned the relative economic growth of Britain for the sake of excessive social-welfare programmes.

In each biennial year of crisis, the IPC and the Cabinet did seek to reduce the rate of gross domestic fixed capital formation. In its first report, the committee sought to reduce the mid-1947 rate of £1,500 million per annum to £1,300 million by the end of 1948. Reducing the

---

[1] C. Barnett, *The Lost Victory: British Dreams, British Realities, 1945–1950*, London, Macmillan, 1995. Chapter 13 is entitled 'A Disastrous Choice of Priorities'.

rate was expected to reduce the total of gross domestic capital investment formation completed by the end of 1948 from £1,600 million to £1,400 million, a cut of 12.5 per cent.[2] One-third of this cut was thought likely to fall on new investment. In October 1949, in the wake of the devaluation of sterling, the Cabinet sanctioned total cuts of £280 million, to free more resources for exports.[3] In November 1949, the Cabinet decided that these cuts should be shared equally between government expenditure and capital investment.[4] Expectations of rising investment were dashed again in 1951, as the rearmament requirements of the Korean War led the IPC's *Report* of 17 March 1951 to envisage civil investment in 1951 being £46 million lower than in 1950, and £140 million less in 1952 than in 1950.[5]

The initial dismal aspect of these biennial cuts fades on closer inspection. Although the vocabulary of the reports of the IPC was that of cuts and constraints, one of the main purposes of making cuts was actually to allow more investment to be completed. A leading reason for the cuts in 1947 was to ensure that 'no more work is started than can be completed at the proper speed' and by concentrating resources on existing half-built projects to accelerate their completion.[6] Tracing the impact of cuts in the rate of investment is difficult, just as cutting investment was always going to be an approximate activity in a economy with so much work already in progress and with an overloaded building-licence system.[7] Despite the cuts of 1947, investment continued its postwar increase in 1948, albeit at a slightly slower pace. By 1951,

---

[2] PRO CAB 134/437, IPC(47)9, Cabinet, Investment Programmes Committee, *Report on Capital Investment*, 8 October 1947, para. 7. The forecast of gross capital investment of £1,600m in 1948 was made in the draft Economic Survey for 1948–51. Most of the data on gross domestic fixed capital formation in this period include estimates for 'current repairs to buildings and works'. From March 1952, this item was excluded from 'gross fixed capital investment', as is explained in the notes to Table 8 of the *Preliminary National Income and Expenditure Estimates, 1948 to 1951* (March 1952, Cmd 8486). This reduced gross domestic fixed capital formation by about £600 million, to which a new item for expenditure on legal fees, stamp duties, etc., worth about £50 million was added.

[3] PRO CAB 134/440, IPC(49)3, Cabinet, Investment Programmes Committee, *Report on Capital Investment in 1950–1952*, 12 May 1949, p. 3.

[4] Cairncross, *Years of Recovery: British Economic Policy 1945–51*, London, Methuen, 1985, university paperback, 1987, pp. 191–5. The final total cuts were reduced to £260 million. PRO CAB 134/441, IPC(50)2, *Report on Capital Investment in 1951 and 1952*, 24 April 1950, p. 5, para. 10.

[5] PRO CAB 134/442, IPC(51)1, Cabinet, Investment Programmes Committee, *Report on Capital Investment in 1951, 1952 and 1953*, 17 March 1951, paras. i and xvii.

[6] PRO CAB 134/437, IPC(47)9, Cabinet, Investment Programmes Committee, *Report on Capital Investment*, 8 October, 1947, para. 2.

[7] PRO CAB 134/440, IPC(49)3, Cabinet, Investment Programmes Committee, *Report on Capital Investment in 1950–1952*, 12 May 1949, p. 3.

investment was 45 per cent higher in volume than in 1946.[8] The bark could often be worse than the bite. As Cairncross notes, of the post-devaluation cuts of £280 million in investment and government expenditure, these probably did little more than aim at restoring the pressure of demand to what had been contemplated in the previous spring.[9] Certainly, the cuts in the programme were not visible in the total fixed investment for 1950 which increased by £100 million, exactly as had been originally expected.[10]

Whatever the retrospective evidence of the aggregate statistics, the spectacle of the government making cuts in programmed investment provoked protests from industrial groups, who claimed that in a centralised planning structure the needs of industrial investment suffered from inadequate political representation. Industrial investment was often characterised as being a residual legatee, picking over its meagre share after smugger relatives had left the room. Compared with the housing, defence, consumption, and welfare programmes, industry felt itself to be conspicuously short of powerful ministerial representatives within the Cabinet. Few in the Cabinet would tolerate cuts in personal consumption. The Prime Minister, the Minister of Defence, and the Foreign Secretary all supported the defence programme. In Aneurin Bevan, health and housing had a highly articulate and formidable personality defending its interests. By contrast, none of the leading industrial sponsoring departments, such as the Board of Trade, the Ministry of Supply, and, after 7 October 1947, the Ministry of Fuel and Power, even had a seat at the Cabinet table. Instead, especially from 1947, industrial matters tended to be spoken to by the Treasury, which was the very department seeking cuts. To be represented by the axeman when cuts were being sought was regarded as unpropitious.

One such set of industrial complaints appeared in *The Times* on 15 and 16 October 1948. These two articles on the 'Re-equipment of Industry' calculated that, although there had been industrial net investment of £250 million (at 1947 prices) in 1938, there had been net disinvestment of £200 million in 1946, and only £200 million and £300 million of net investment in 1947 and 1948 respectively.[11] Not

---

[8] C. Feinstein, *Statistical Tables of National Income, Expenditure and Output of the UK, 1855–1965*, Cambridge, Cambridge University Press, 1972, table 5.

[9] Cairncross, *Years of Recovery*, p. 191.

[10] Dow, *Management of the British Economy, 1945–60*, Cambridge, Cambridge University Press, 1970, p. 46n. The cuts in housing were revoked within six months, and investment in new dwellings in 1950 fell by no more than it had in 1948 or in 1949. It is possible that some of the cuts (e.g. in power and transport) did take effect, partly in 1949 and partly in 1950.

[11] PRO T229/464, 'Industrial Investment', paper by Peter Vinter, 2 November 1948, para. 2.

only was it asserted that net investment in industry was too low, but that it was overly concentrated on the basic industries of fuel, power, transport, steel and chemicals, with engineering left as the Cinderella among industries. These points were repeated by Sir Norman Kipping, Director-General of the Federation of British Industries (FBI) to Sir Edwin Plowden in a subsequent meeting.[12]

Such use of net investment data, extracted from gross investment statistics and including the problematic item of stocks, was difficult. Responding to the attack in *The Times*, Peter Vinter felt that, in estimating the 1946 change in stocks at £200 million, *The Times* was on 'shaky ground'. The Central Statistical Office estimate for the movement of stocks in 1946 showed no net change and, as Vinter remarked,

this factor alone is sufficient to undermine any argument which proceeds from global total investment to argue about net investment in productive industry. If the margin on which the argument turns is of the order of £100 million, a doubtful factor of £200 million, plus any other margins of error, may demolish the whole statistical apparatus . . . *The Times* may be right; equally it may not.

There were also arguments about what should be included in the category of 'industrial investment', with the FBI proposing that iron and steel, and shipbuilding should be excluded. Contrary to the pleading of the FBI, Vinter considered that as a proportion of total investment 'the industrial share is still very large'.[13]

Contrary to what industrial groups might have thought, there was a very real concern within government with what was happening to net investment, in both current and historic terms. However, estimating net investment and then making historic comparisons was fraught with problems. In the Economic Survey for 1946 it was suggested that of a likely total of £1,595 million of gross domestic fixed capital investment in 1946, £1,055 million would consist of net investment and £540 million of depreciation and maintenance.[14] With national income estimated at £8,120 million, this would produce ratios of 19.6 per cent for gross domestic fixed capital investment and 13.0 per cent for net

---

[12] PRO T229/464, 'Industrial Investment', Paper by Peter Vinter, 2 November 1948, paras. 1, 4.

[13] PRO T229/464 'Industrial Investment', paper by P. Vinter, 2 November 1948, paras. 3, 4, 7, 8. While there was a reported reduction of some £60 million in investment in plant and machinery between 1948 and 1949, this was largely accounted for by a small reduction in shipbuilding, falls in transport and communications, and 'other industry'.

[14] PRO CAB 134/188, IWP/46/1, 'Investment Working Party, Memorandum by the Treasury', 6 February 1946, para. 2. Government net investment was estimated at £345 million and private net investment at £710 million. The estimates for depreciation and maintenance for government and the private sector were £140 million and £400 million respectively.

investment.[15] On this basis, whereas gross investment was some 5 per cent higher than in 1938, net investment was 40 per cent above the 1938 level.[16] However, the apparent increase in the proportion of the national income devoted to net investment (7.7 per cent in 1938, 11.7 per cent in 1946/7) and the decline in the proportion put aside for maintenance and depreciation (10.3 per cent in 1938, 7.3 per cent in 1946/7) was understood to be 'more apparent than real' because of the practice of depreciating the original rather than the replacement costs of assets.[17] With costs rising, historic-cost accounting fell short of replacement costs and flattered net investment. None the less, the interest in what was happening to net investment was clear.

Similarly, to improve historic comparisons, efforts were made to improve estimates of pre-war investment. In May 1949, the IPC's *Report on Capital Investment in 1950–1952* reported a tentative comparison made by Russell Bretherton between gross fixed investment before the war and in 1948. Bretherton, using the earlier work of Colin Clark, estimated that over the decade 1929–38, gross fixed investment at home averaged about £653.5 million a year at 1937/8 prices, equivalent to perhaps about £1,530 million at 1948 prices.[18] To offset the effects of the depression years in this decade, the average for the five years 1934–8 was also calculated, being almost £100 million higher at £744 million at 1937/8 prices, equivalent to about

[15] PRO CAB 134/188, IWP/46/1, 'Investment Working Party, Memorandum by the Treasury', 6 February 1946.

[16] PRO CAB 134/188, IWP/46/1, 'Investment Working Party: Memorandum by the Treasury', 6 February 1946 para. 3(ii). These figures should also be compared with wartime disinvestment and physical destruction at home, which together were reckoned at £3,000 million. (Overseas disinvestment was put at £4,200 million). PRO T288/81, 8 October 1946, paper on 1938 and 1946/7 Domestic Fixed Capital Formation by Mr Vinter and Mr Proctor, for consideration by National Investment Council (NIC) para. 3. In October 1946 Vinter and Proctor estimated gross fixed investment formation as 18% in 1938 and as likely to be 19% of net national income in 1946/7.

[17] Vinter and Proctor have this as 10.2 per cent, but it is in fact 10.3%. PRO T288/81, 8 October 1946, paper on 1938 and 1946/7 Domestic Fixed Capital Formation by Mr Vinter and Mr Proctor, for consideration by National Investment Council, para. 3.

[18] PRO CAB 134/440, IPC(49)3, Cabinet, Investment Programmes Committee, *Report on Capital Investment in 1950–1952*, 12 May 1949, para. iii. Colin Clark, 'National Income at its Climax', *Economic Journal*, 47 (June 1937) pp. 308–20, and 'Determination of the Multiplier from National Income Statistics', *Economic Journal*, 48 (September 1938), pp. 435–48. These were assembled and slightly adjusted, together with other estimates, in R. Bretherton, F. Burchardt, and R. Rutherford (eds.), *Public Investment and the Trade Cycle in Britain*, Oxford, Clarendon Press, 1941, pp. 399–404, Tables 1–7. In the calculations made in 1949, the figures for 'gross fixed investment at home, excluding warships, aeroplanes and munitions' from Table 4 were used for the years 1929–37, and an estimate for 1938 was added. Correction to 1937/8 prices was made using Clark's Index of Prices of Capital Goods. PRO T230/346, 'Pre-War Investment in the United Kingdom', note by R. F. Bretherton, 12 May 1949, para. 1.

£1,749 million at 1948 prices,[19] as compared with the rough estimate of £2,000 million for gross fixed investment of all kinds achieved in 1948, thus representing a rise of nearly one-third on the average of the pre-war decade, and of about one-seventh on the average of the years 1934–8.[20] When this was reported in the IPC's *Report on Capital Investment in 1950–1952*, it was suggested that at 'the remarkably high level' of £2,000 million in 1948, accounting for 20 per cent of Gross National Product (GNP), and probably exceeding the average invest-ment of the pre-war decade by about one-third, and that of the years 1934–8 by about one-seventh', if anything gross fixed investment might be too high.[21]

Given these investment estimates, it was difficult for planners to see the evidence for claims that the needs of industrial investment were being neglected. Gross domestic fixed capital formation was rising, both in absolute terms and as a proportion of GNP (see Tables 2.1 and 2.2). As a proportion of gross domestic fixed capital formation, the share of manufacturing investment (including construction) climbed to 31 per cent in 1951, a proportion never regained in later years.[22] Claims that investment was being deliberately squeezed by the government seemed difficult to demonstrate at a time when the IPC was reporting that in 1948 'almost the whole of the increment in the national income over the previous year went to increase either investment or exports. To permit this large volume of investment to be carried out without inflation, voluntary savings had to supplemented by forced savings secured through a large budget surplus.'[23] Moreover, as the IPC noted, 'this rising trend in civilian investment might well have continued had it not been for the large additional commitments which have now arisen for defence.'[24] It was only after 1950, when the rearmament programme cut across any further expansion, that for the next two years fixed investment marked time (see Table 2.2). In terms of constant prices,

[19] PRO T230/346, 'Pre-War Investment in the United Kingdom', note by R. F. Bretherton, 12 May 1949, paras. 3–4.
[20] PRO T230/346, 'Pre-War Investment in the United Kingdom', note by R. F. Bretherton, 12 May 1949, para. 1. PRO CAB 134/188, IWP/46/1, 'Investment Working Party: Memorandum by the Treasury', 6 February 1946, for estimates of total gross capital formation of £2,295 million. This comprised the total increase in working capital (£700 million) and total gross domestic fixed capital investment (£1,595 million).
[21] PRO CAB 134/440, IPC(49)3, Cabinet, Investment Programmes Committee, *Report on Capital Investment in 1950–1952*, 12 May 1949.
[22] Cairncross, *Years of Recovery*, p. 455.
[23] PRO CAB 134/440, IPC(49)3, Cabinet, Investment Programmes Committee, *Report on Capital Investment in 1950–1952*, 12 May 1949, para. iii.
[24] PRO CAB 134/442, IPC(51)1, Cabinet, Investment Programmes Committee, *Report on Capital Investment in 1951, 1952 and 1953*, 17 March 1951, para. 2.

Table 2.1. *Gross domestic fixed capital formation as a percentage of GNP,*
1938–53

Year	per cent	Year	per cent
1938	11.4	1946	10.4
1939	9.9	1947	12.7
1940	7.6	1948	13.5
1941	6.1	1949	14.2
1942	5.3	1950	14.5
1943	4.0	1951	14.6
1944	3.3	1952	15.0
1945	4.0	1953	15.7

(*Source:* C. H. Feinstein, *Statistical Tables of National Income, Expenditure and Output in the*
UK, 1855–1965, Cambridge, Cambridge University Press, 1972, Table 2)

Table 2.2. *Gross domestic fixed capital formation at constant market prices,*
1938–52 (1913 = 100)

1938	1939	1940	1941	1942	1943	1944	1945
219.3	195.3	169.3	136.2	118.0	81.1	62.5	70.0

1946	1947	1948	1949	1950	1951	1952	
176.8	206.1	222.1	242.8	255.9	256.8	257.9	

(*Source:* C. H. Feinstein, *Statistical Tables of National Income, Expenditure and Output in the*
UK, 1855–1965, Cambridge, Cambridge University Press, 1972, Table 7)

investment in manufacturing industry rose throughout the Attlee
governments' period in office (it fell in 1953).[25] The government's aim,
as set out in the Long-Term Programme submitted to the Organisation
for European Economic Co-operation (OEEC), of maintaining industrial investment at a higher level than the previous peacetime peak in
1937, as well as above the level of any previous four-year period, was
successfully pursued.[26] If anything, the worry was that too much was
being sunk into capital investment, at the expense of consumption, with
a detrimental effect on incentives to work. As ministers confirmed in
May 1949 that investment for the re-equipment and modernisation of
export and basic industries was to 'take precedence over investment

[25] Central Statistical Office, *National Income and Expenditure,* London, HMSO, 1960,
Table 53.
[26] PRO CAB 134/440, IPC(49)3, Cabinet, Investment Programmes Committee, *Report*
on Capital Investment in 1950–1952, 12 May 1949, para. 45. Cmd 7572. *European Co-*
operation: Memoranda Submitted to the Organisation for European Economic Co-operation
Relating to Economic Affairs in the Period 1948 to 1953, London, HMSO, 1948.

Table 2.3. *Gross domestic fixed capital formation in new buildings and works, 1948–51* (per cent)

	1948	1949	1950	1951
Manufacturing industry	14.2	14.3	15.2	14.6
New housing	55.5	49.8	45.7	46.1
Education	3.5	5.2	6.6	7.1
Health	1.5	1.5	1.5	1.3
Electricity	4.0	5.4	5.0	4.7
Total new building and works (per cent of total GDFCF)	44.5	43.7	43.4	39.8

(*Source:* Central Statistical Office, *National Income and Expenditure 1946–1952*, London, HMSO, August 1953, Table 43)

designed solely or mainly to increase consumption standards', the economist Roy Harrod was not alone in asking whether such hardships for the sake of capital investment were really necessary.[27] The view that gross domestic fixed capital formation was not accorded a low priority by the Attlee governments sits somewhat uncomfortably beside international comparisons of gross and net investment as proportions of GNP. That these were low in the UK was not peculiar to the 1945–51 period, being true across much of the twentieth century. Measures of net investment were always precarious, especially when depreciation practices varied between economies. None the less, the unflattering comparisons between UK net investment at 5 per cent of the net national product in 1950 and 1951, as against 14 per cent in West Germany, 7–8 per cent in France, and 21–22 per cent in Finland, did provide ammunition for critics who wished to attack the British economic performance.[28] Contemporary data on gross domestic capital formation as a percentage of GNP showed the usual picture of the UK's share lagging that of most of its competitors.[29] This ranking would not have surprised the planners in the Attlee governments, who were well aware that, by international standards, UK investment/ national income ratios were not remarkable. The revised Economic Survey for 1948, estimating total gross investment at around 22 per

---

[27] PRO CAB 134/440, IPC(49)3, Cabinet, Investment Programmes Committee, *Report on Capital Investment in 1950–1952*, 12 May 1949, para. 47. R. Harrod, *Are these Hardships Necessary?*, London, Rupert Hart-Davis, 1947.

[28] PRO T230/346, Treasury paper, 'Estimated Capital Accumulation in Western European Countries: Net Fixed Investment as a Percentage of Net National Product', April 1956, Table 2.

[29] Organisation for European Economic Co-operation (OEEC), *Statistics of National Product and Expenditure, 1938, 1947 to 1952*, Paris, 1954, Tables 1, 2, and 3.

cent of national income, recognised that 'this would not be an exceptionally large figure'. Although higher than the gross investment estimates of 17 per cent of national income in 1938, this had to be compared with 24 per cent in the USA during 1925–9; with planned investment in the postwar French Monnet Plan of 25 per cent; and of around 22.5 per cent in the USSR under the existing Four-Year Plan.[30] What concerned planners was not so much the total of gross domestic capital formation, but rather whether within that total a greater share could be shifted towards industrial investment.

The major programme identified by planners as a possible source of additional resources for industrial investment was house construction. As the largest single field of investment under government control, Bevan's housing programme was an immediate and persistent target for attacks by the CEPS and the IPC.[31] This is what Bevan had feared when opposing the establishment of the IPC.[32] In the biennial rounds of recommended cuts, the IPC frequently commented that, apart from housing, they could 'see no other field where a reduction can be secured which would be sufficient to enable the programme as a whole to be reduced to the level required'.[33] While it is true that, as a share of GNP, investment in housing may have accounted for no more in 1920–38 than in 1945–51, in the post-World War II period the opportunity costs of directing scarce construction resources to the housing programme may well have been higher.[34] Construction investment resources not absorbed by housing could probably be used by other industries, which were short of such resources and plagued by long construction times. The impact of the housing programme was reflected not so much in its general share of gross domestic fixed capital formation, but rather in its specific share of investment in new buildings and works. Between 1948 and 1951, total investment in new buildings and works constituted 43.5 per cent of total gross domestic fixed capital formation. Of investment in new buildings and works, 49

[30] PRO CAB 134/191, ED(48)3, Cabinet, Official Committee on Economic Development, 'Economic Survey for 1948', revised version, 2 February 1948, p. 29.

[31] PRO CAB 134/441, IPC(50)2, Cabinet, Investment Programmes Committee, *Report on Capital Investment in 1951 and 1952*, 24 April 1950, paras. 71, 209.

[32] PRO CAB 134/190, ED(47), 5th meeting, Official Steering Committee on Economic Development, 26 February 1947. PRO CAB 134/442, IPC(51)1, Cabinet, Investment Programmes Committee, *Report on Capital Investment in 1951, 1952, and 1953*, 17 March 1951, p. 3 (vi) and para. 73.

[33] PRO CAB 134/441, IPC(50)2, Cabinet, Investment Programmes Committee, *Report on Capital Investment in 1951 and 1952*, 24 April 1950, para. 209.

[34] R. Middleton, *Government versus the Market: the Growth of the Public Sector, Economic Management and British Economic Performance, 1890–1979*, Cheltenham, Edward Elgar, pp. 526–7. R. Matthews, C. Feinstein, and J. Odling-Smee, *British Economic Growth, 1856–1973*, Oxford, Clarendon Press, 1982, Table 136, p. 409.

per cent went into new housing, this single programme therefore accounting for 21.3 per cent of total gross domestic fixed capital formation[35](see Table 2.3). The resource demands of the new housing programme were varied. Measured in terms of the amount of steel which each industry required for each £1 million of investment (excluding maintenance) which it completed, then the requirements of housing were low. While the new house-building programme required 250 tons of steel for each £1 million of work done, the iron and steel industry required 10,000. On this basis other large users included: the railways executive (6,000 tons); electricity (BEA), petroleum, and the Admiralty (5,000 tons each); manufacturing industries sponsored by the Ministries of Health, Supply, Food, and Works (3–4,000 tons); manufacturing industries sponsored by the Board of Trade and the Ministry of Materials; gas; the Scottish Hydro; the Post Office; and water and sewerage (2–3,000 tons); deep-mined coal and education (1,250–2,000 tons each); and health services 500 tons.[36] However, when this low rate of steel use was multiplied by the size of the housing programme, then the latter emerged as the third largest departmental user of steel required for building and civil engineering (other than maintenance), requiring 98,000 tons.[37] However, of the total steel used for all purposes, the allocation of steel to housing and the entire social-investment programmes was low. In 1949, when steel supplies were identified as the prime determinant of the rate of investment activity, of a suggested distribution of 6,335,000 tons of steel for home investment, only 215,000 tons (3.4 per cent) were allowed for the housing, education and health programmes.[38]

Although making a proportionately low use of steel, the new housing programme did make further demands on timber, softwoods, bricks, cement and labour.[39] About one-third of the total annual usage of softwood was for housing, with more than half the total supplies in

[35] Central Statistical Office, *National Income and Expenditure 1946–1952*, London, HMSO, August 1953, Table 43.

[36] PRO CAB 134/442, IPC(51)1, Cabinet, Investment Programmes Committee, *Report on Capital Investment in 1951, 1952, and 1953*, 17 March 1951, Annex I.

[37] PRO CAB 134/442, IPC(51)1, Cabinet, Investment Programmes Committee, *Report on Capital Investment in 1951, 1952, and 1953*, 17 March 1951, Annex I. The larger users of steel for investment purposes were the British Electricity Authority (180,500 tons) and the iron and steel industry (140,000 tons).

[38] PRO CAB 134/439, *Capital Investment in 1949*, p. 13, Table 2.

[39] PRO CAB 134/437, IPC(47)9, Cabinet, Investment Programmes Committee, *Report on Capital Investment*, 8 October 1947, para. 5.

1950 coming from Russia or Russian-controlled countries, and some 12 per cent being obtained for dollars.[40] Shortages of softwood timber led to the production of substitute materials, the use of solid ground floors, and consideration of the use of pre-stressed concrete for first floors. The use of pre-stressed concrete was in its early stages, however, and was not without its problems, neither then nor later.[41] The housing programme also made demands upon the supply of building labour. At the end of June 1947, of the building labour ceilings for 1947, housing alone accounted for 59.9 per cent, with miscellaneous housing works taking another 3.6 per cent.[42] Considering investment in 1952 and 1953, the IPC argued that if a programme of 230,000 houses in 1952 was adopted, then this would mean that the labour for at least 18,000 houses would have to be drawn away from other new building work.[43] The supply of building labour was inelastic in the short term. Increasing the existing force of about 1 million building and civil engineering operatives was difficult, principally because of the difficulty of training a sufficient number of new skilled craft labour. The adult training schemes launched after the war, with grudging help from the industry, were ended in 1947 as part of the investment cuts, and partly in response to growing opposition from sections of the industry who were worried that an over-supply of skilled labour might reduce their bargaining power and lead to the existing stock of work being completed too quickly, thereby advancing the return of unemployment to the industry. Instead, reliance was placed on the apprentice system, but its contribution was limited, the annual entry being 14,000 compared with 22,000 required to maintain the industry at its existing level.[44]

Warfare was estimated to have destroyed 6–9 per cent (0.25 million dwellings) of the housing stock, roughly similar to proportionate damage in Belgium, the Netherlands, Austria, and France, but much

---

[40] PRO CAB 134/441, IPC(50)2, Cabinet, Investment Programmes Committee, *Report on Capital Investment in 1951 and 1952*, 24 April 1950, para. 72.

[41] PRO CAB 134/439, IPC(48)8, Cabinet, Investment Programmes Committee, *Report on Capital Investment in 1949*, 16 July 1948, para. 292.

[42] PRO CAB 134/437, IPC(47)9, Cabinet, Investment Programmes Committee, *Report on Capital Investment*, 8 October 1947, para. 15. Civil licence building took 4.8% and direct building took 2.3%. Other users included Board of Trade industrial building 7.1%, education 3.5%, coal 3.1%, industrial building for the Ministry of Supply 3.7%, health 2.8%, agriculture 1.9%, electricity 1.2%, food industrial building 1.5%, and Ministry of Transport industrial building 1.9%.

[43] PRO CAB 134/442, IPC(51)1, Cabinet, Investment Programmes Committee, *Civil Investment in 1952 and 1953*, 17 December 1951, para. 18.

[44] PRO CAB 134/440, IPC(49)3, Cabinet, Investment Programmes Committee, *Report on Capital Investment in 1950–1952*, 12 May 1949, para. 35.

less than the 20 per cent of pre-war housing stock lost in Germany, Poland, and Greece.[45] By international standards the British were not overcrowded, and the existence of a large housing stock in Britain meant that the new flow of house-building added only 1.5 per cent to the existing stock. The British housing programme reflected a genuine political wish to expand and improve the housing stock, not least as one means of honouring previous postwar promises to provide 'homes fit for heroes'. Apart from food supplies and the cost of living, concern with housing was the only other issue on which more than 10 per cent of Gallup Poll respondents said they would like to question the Prime Minister. The demand for housing arose partly as a result of the 2 million increase in population size since 1939, equivalent to 530,000 separate families, and the rise in the marriage rate. More vaguely, but no less importantly, public expectations seem to have risen as a result of total war. In consequence, the wartime estimate that 750,000 new houses and flats would be required to provide a separate home for each family was revised upwards by the Ministry of Health, which now envisaged an eight-year house-building programme of 150,000 houses per annum being required to meet the demand from families without a separate home in England and Wales. Not only was the programme intended to provide 'a separate home for every family in the country' to the minimum accommodation standards of the 1935 Housing Act, but it was also proposed to address such issues as overcrowding, particularly in the East End of London, industrial Scotland, the north-east coast and parts of the Black Country.[46] The extent of overcrowding depended upon the definitions employed. Using the minimum standard of the Housing Act 1935, which permitted roughly two persons for each habitable room, then overcrowding was probably low in most areas, although high in certain black spots. However, if, as in a sample survey in April 1947, the higher standard of one person per habitable room was employed, then around 23 per cent of all households were over-crowded.[47] As well as tackling overcrowding, there was also a general intent to improve the housing stock of 12–13 million houses in use, more than 25 per cent of which were at least 70 years old. Again, black-spots such as Glasgow tenements, the back-to-back houses of the North of England, and many 'primitive and even insanitary' agricultural

[45] United Nations, Department of Economic Affairs, *Economic Survey of Europe since the War*, Geneva, 1953, p. 5.
[46] PRO CAB 134/439, IPC(48)8, Cabinet, Investment Programmes Committee, *Report on Capital Investment in 1949*, 16 July 1948, para. 282.
[47] PRO CAB 134/440, IPC(49)3, Cabinet, Investment Programmes Committee, *Report on Capital Investment in 1950–1952*, 12 May 1949, para. 240.

cottages were identified.[48] Some additional housing was also required to provide accommodation where there were labour shortages such as in the traditional coal-mining and agricultural areas, and for new and expanded industrial projects such as the Stewart & Lloyds works at Corby.[49]

Suggestions from Meade that some demand might be choked off by raising rents, and unwinding some of the rent controls and subsidies were not welcomed.[50] Nor was there much warmth shown for IPC suggestions that housing specifications be relaxed, including the postponement of some of the less immediately necessary amenities such as the out-building, the secondary lavatory, or part of the hot-water system. Savings could also be effected by building smaller houses, the domination of three-bedroom houses doing little for childless couples and the increasing number of elderly people living alone, and by dividing a greater proportion of houses into flats, along the lines of the 'Duplex' houses which were accepted by many local authorities.[51] More use might also have been made of conversions, the 1949 Housing Act making subsidies available to individuals for house improvements or for conversion into two or more houses or dwellings. However, restrictions imposed on the licensing of repairs and altera-

---

[48] PRO CAB 134/441, IPC(50)2, Cabinet, Investment Programmes Committee, *Report on Capital Investment in 1951 and 1952*, 24 April 1950, para. 203.

[49] PRO CAB 134/440, IPC(49)3, Cabinet, Investment Programmes Committee, *Report on Capital Investment in 1950–1952*, 12 May 1949, para. 240. PRO CAB 134/437, IPC(47)9, Cabinet, Investment Programmes Committee, *Report on Capital Investment*, 8 October 1947, Appendix 13.

[50] PRO CAB 134/440, IPC(49)3, Cabinet, Investment Programmes Committee, *Report on Capital Investment in 1950–1952*, 12 May 1949, para. 240. PRO CAB 134/441, IPC(50)2, Cabinet, Investment Programmes Committee, *Report on Capital Investment in 1951 and 1952*, 24 April 1950, para. 203. Meade, *The Collected Papers of James Meade: Vol. IV, the Cabinet Office Diary, 1944–46*, London, Unwin Hyman, 1990, p. 249, 6 April 1946:

> I have, by the way, conceived the idea that we should get rid of the subsidies to the cost of living and to housing (and should modify rent restriction so as to let rents rise to a level which would cover the costs of housing) and should use the funds to pay increased family allowances. If my arithmetic is correct this should allow us to pay allowances of about £2 10s 0d [£2.50] instead of 5/- [25p] a child after the first child. (And if the allowances were paid free of tax, it would represent an income of some £6,000 a year per child to a man who pays 19s 6d [97.5p] in the pound on his marginal income.) There is no doubt that the population problem is soluble if we like to remove such advantages as those of cheap food and houses which are given to everyone and concentrate the resources on family allowances.

[51] PRO CAB 134/440, IPC(49)3, Cabinet, Investment Programmes Committee, *Report on Capital Investment in 1950–1952*, 12 May 1949, para. 251. PRO. CAB 134/437, IPC(47)9, Cabinet, Investment Programmes Committee, *Report on Capital Investment*, 8 October 1947, Appendix 1, para. 8.

tions to houses at the end of 1949 limited the practical application of these legislative provisions.[52]

The resource costs of the housing programme were not restricted to the specific cost of constructing each house, but also extended to the cost of providing the services and facilities which the new residents would require. The working estimate was that a housing programme of 200,000 houses would require a further £50 million per annum of investment in water, sewerage, electricity, schools, roads, railway facilities, postal and telephone work, churches, shops, public houses, and health-service buildings.[53] The extreme example of new housing programmes requiring considerable associated investment were the proposed New Towns, which required an almost complete infrastructure to be provided. Economists and economic planners enjoyed some success in limiting the development of this programme. The programme was attacked in June 1946 by Meade, who complained to Dalton about Jay's proposals for building New Towns in the Development Areas. In Meade's view this was to begin building houses in areas where there was already a superfluity of social capital (housing, drainage, etc.), but a great lack of suitable new factories. Instead, Meade proposed, why not build factories in these areas and take the work to the people, rather than vice versa?[54] Being less politically important than the mainstream housing programme, New Towns were more vulnerable to cuts. While some smaller schemes intended to meet immediate industrial needs, such as in East Kilbride and in the new mining areas such as Aycliffe, were sanctioned, work was slowed on projects designed to take the overspill from large cities, and from London, in particular. London's Green Belt was loosened, with the Ministry of Town and Country Planning agreeing to an additional 100,000 people being housed in former Green Belt areas, and for at least 18 months, from the beginning of 1948, most London Town Corporations were restricted to small sewerage and water works employing 150 men each. Exceptions were made for Stevenage and Harlow, where large water and sewerage services were required, although work at Stevenage was postponed until 1949.[55]

Given the resource costs of housing, it was unsurprising that planners pushed for cuts in what was overwhelmingly a public housing

[52] PRO CAB 134/442, IPC(51)1, Cabinet, Investment Programmes Committee, *Report on Capital Investment in 1951, 1952, and 1953*, 17 March 1951, para. 103.

[53] PRO CAB 134/442, IPC(51)7, Cabinet, Investment Programmes Committee, *Civil Investment in 1952 and 1953*, 17 December 1951, para. 13.

[54] Meade *Diary*, 27 June 1946, p. 276.

[55] PRO CAB 134/437, IPC(47)9, Cabinet, Investment Programmes Committee, *Report on Capital Investment*, 8 October 1947, Appendix 13.

programme. Some 90 per cent of all the new houses built under the Attlee governments were built for local authorities, with private construction struggling to exceed 42,000 houses only in 1953. Local authorities were able to sell 1 in 5 of their houses to owner occupiers, although in practice they tended to authorise a ratio of 1:6. However, when cuts were sought in the house-construction programme, Bevan insisted that any cuts fall as much as possible on houses built for private owner occupation. In October 1949, Bevan was only prepared to accept a proposed cut of £35 million in the housing programme, if the cut fell outside the local authority programme. If the rate of construction had to be cut from 200,000 to 174,000 houses per annum, Bevan intended to arrange that only 1 in 10 of those built would be houses for sale, thus securing that there was no serious reduction in the number of houses being built for rental by the local authorities.[56] It was only from 1953 onwards that the number of new local authority houses fell off while privately built houses increased rapidly.

One of the objectives of cutting the size of the housing programme was to accelerate the speed of house construction. Like factory building, house construction fell foul of the early planning difficulties in securing an effective balance between the issuing of licences to begin work and the allocation and delivery of resources to enable that work to proceed quickly. If anything, the planning problems in housing were worse than those for factory building, since housing did not come under the starting-date procedure, in part because local authorities could use their own direct labour.[57] It was only in 1947 that, 'painfully and with difficulty', some balance was struck between resources available and the load of work.[58] Until then new houses had been approved at twice the rate of completion, and in July 1947 completions of 12,500 compared with approvals of 17,500. The inevitable result was an increase in the stock of unfinished houses, which increased from 134,000 in July 1946 to 210,000 in January 1947, and to 249,000 in July 1947.[59]

Locking up scarce resources in unfinished houses was clearly undesirable, not least because the low completion rates caused political difficulties for the government. Paradoxically, more progress was likely to be made in completing houses if fewer were started. In 1947, when

---

[56] PRO CAB 134/220, EPC(49)35, Cabinet, Economic Policy Committee, 14 October 1949, p. 3.

[57] PRO CAB 134/442, IPC(51)7, Cabinet, Investment Programmes Committee, *Civil Investment in 1952 and 1953*, 17 December 1951, paras. 4, 19.

[58] PRO CAB 134/440, IPC(49)3, Cabinet, Investment Programmes Committee, *Report on Capital Investment in 1950–1952*, 12 May 1949, para. 39.

[59] PRO CAB 134/437, IPC(47)9, Cabinet, Investment Programmes Committee, *Report on Capital Investment*, 8 October 1947, Appendix 1.

the Investment Programmes Committee recommended reducing the starting rate of new houses from 15,000 to 5,000 a month (mainly for mining and farming areas) for at least a year, it was in part to reduce the large and growing stock of 360,000 unfinished houses under contract.[60] Cutting new work would enable more resources to be allocated to finishing existing projects. Advised that work-in-progress could be stopped by the cancellation of licences without incurring legal penalties, the Committee initiated the revocation of 269 licences in 1947, mainly for houses in the early stages of building work prior to the steel-erection stage.[61] Politically, this paradox of making cuts so as to get more was extremely difficult for Bevan to accept, his political instinct in the face of low completion rates being to announce ever-increasing numbers of housing starts. The problems in building houses reflected deeper problems in the construction industry in general. At the time, the high turnover and increasing age of the building labour force, exceptionally bad weather, the overloading of the industry during 1946 and 1947, and shortages of steel-reinforcing rods were all variously blamed. Yet, when such problems had eased by the 1950s, productivity did not improve significantly and construction costs continued to rise.[62]

The efforts of the IPC and the CEPS to reduce the housing programme were consistently resisted by Bevan and his Ministry.[63] Ultimately, on 17 April 1950, after sustained departmental guerrilla activities, a compromise of sorts was struck in Cabinet in which it was agreed that for 1950–2 the housing programme for Britain would be stabilised at 200,000 per annum. Although more severe cuts had been sanctioned by Cabinet on 21 October 1949, Bevan had subsequently invoked the housing needs of families, industry, married personnel in the Services and police to push for authority to reverse these cuts.[64] The

---

[60] PRO CAB 134/437, IPC(47)9, Cabinet, Investment Programmes Committee, *Report on Capital Investment*, 8 October 1947, para. 11.

[61] PRO CAB 134/442, IPC(51)7, Cabinet, Investment Programmes Committee, *Civil Investment in 1952 and 1953*, 17 December 1951, para. 20.

[62] PRO CAB 134/440, IPC(49)3, Cabinet, Investment Programmes Committee, *Report on Capital Investment in 1950–1952*, 12 May 1949, paras. 37, 41. PRO CAB 134/982, Cabinet, Investment Programmes Committee, *Investment in 1953 and 1954*, para. 5, Table 1. Central Statistical Office, *National Income and Expenditure 1946–1952*, August 1953, Table 42.

[63] PRO CAB 134/439, IPC(48)8, Cabinet, Investment Programmes Committee, *Report on Capital Investment in 1949*, 16 July 1948, para. 404.

[64] PRO CAB 134/441, IPC(50)2, Cabinet, Investment Programmes Committee, *Report on Capital Investment in 1951 and 1952*, 24 April 1950, para. 70. PRO CAB 129/39, CP(50)67, 'The Housing Programme (England and Wales)', memorandum by the Minister of Health, 13 April 1950. It was intended to reduce the allocation of new houses to local authorities in England and Wales for 1951 to 120,000, as compared with 148,000 for 1950 and 170,000 for 1949.

compromise proposed in the Cabinet by the Chancellor of the Exchequer on 17 April 1950 of a completion rate of 200,000 (175,000 for England and Wales, and 25,000 for Scotland) houses a year in the three years 1950–2 was warmly supported. This represented a return to the rate originally envisaged for 1950 before the Cabinet cuts of 21 October 1949, and in financial terms it fixed the housing programme for 1950 at £253 million, of which £215 million was for England and Wales and £38 million for Scotland.[65] Thus, housing became a fixed priority in the capital-investment programme for 1950–2, and any necessary cuts in the total volume of investment would have to fall on other parts of the programme.[66] In 1951, when reviewing departmental investment proposals, the IPC recognised that they were 'precluded from making any reduction in the new housing programme'.[67] This political unwillingness to cut the housing programme fed the growing tension between the planners on the IPC and the politicians in the Cabinet. While the IPC consistently identified the housing programme as the one area where significant cuts could be made, ministers continued to protect the programme and, on occasions, even asked the Committee if more resources could be directed towards housing.[68]

Politically constrained in their ability to reduce the housing programme, the IPC moved to ensure that the entire social-investment programme (health, housing, and education) was held within bounds. In 1948, the Committee urged that where increases were made to the individual social investment programmes for 1949, 'there should be a corresponding reduction of another part of social service investment'. Thus, in attacking the housing programme, the Committee was seeking not just to free resources in general, but in particular to allow more resources to be provided for the building of schools and hospitals.[69] In 1949, the Committee explicitly stated that 'by stabilising capital expenditure on new housing at the level approved for 1949, it is possible to make room within the total recommended for substantial increases in the other social services'.[70] Conversely, in 1951, in order to facilitate the new housing programme sanctioned by the Cabinet, severe cuts

---

[65] PRO CAB 134/441, IPC(50)2, Cabinet, Investment Programmes Committee, *Report on Capital Investment in 1951 and 1952*, 24 April 1950, para. 204.

[66] PRO CAB 128/17, CM 21(50), 17 April 1950, para. 2.

[67] PRO CAB 134/442, IPC(51)1, Cabinet, Investment Programmes Committee, *Report on Capital Investment in 1951, 1952 and 1953*, 17 March 1951, para. 103.

[68] PRO CAB 134/441, IPC(50)2, Cabinet, Investment Programmes Committee, *Report on Capital Investment in 1951 and 1952*, 24 April 1950, paras. 69, 209.

[69] PRO CAB 134/439, IPC(48)8, Cabinet, Investment Programmes Committee, *Report on Capital Investment in 1949*, 16 July, 1948, paras. 30, 293.

[70] PRO CAB 134/440, IPC(49)3, Cabinet, Investment Programmes Committee, *Report on Capital Investment in 1950–1952*, 12 May 1949, para. 57.

were imposed on other planned social investment. As full funding was proposed for the new housing programme, the much smaller departmental proposals for health and education were trimmed further. In response to proposed investment for health services of £27.5 million in 1951, £33.2 million in 1952, and £35.2 million in 1953, funding levels of 90 per cent in 1951, 73.2 per cent in 1952, and 69.0 per cent in 1953 were recommended. Education departmental proposals of £62.6 million in 1951, £69.4 million in 1952, and £72.8 million in 1953, received respective funding recommendations of 90.4 per cent, 86.3 per cent, and 92.2 per cent.[71]

Requests for health programmes were treated more harshly than those for education, as the health service was thought more able to cope with a restricted investment programme. During the Attlee government, relatively little investment was undertaken in the NHS (see Table 2.4). The early NHS operated on a patch-and-mend basis, with the volume of work in 1949 being only about 25 per cent of immediate pre-war estimates of likely post-war activity.[72] Although plans were laid for the building of new hospitals, with sixteen areas, including South West Essex, Coventry, Harrow, and Tooting, being classified as urgent, during 1945–51 no general hospitals were built.[73] Much time was given to preparing plans for future development and to coping with the organisational problems consequent in the vesting in the Ministry of Health on 5 July 1948 of over 2,700 hospitals and 500,000 beds. The bulk of expenditure was on modernisation and extension schemes aimed at improving administrative efficiency.[74] Nursing accommodation was improved in an effort to recruit more nurses and ease the labour shortages which were keeping 60,000 beds out of use.[75] Efforts were also made to correct the imbalance between an excess of fever and tuberculosis (TB) beds and a shortage of maternity beds.[76] The increase in the size of the population placed a range of increased demands on the

---

[71] PRO CAB 134/442, IPC(51)1, Cabinet, Investment Programmes Committee, *Report on Capital Investment in 1951, 1952, and 1953*, 17 March 1951, para. 73.

[72] PRO CAB 134/441, IPC(50)2, Cabinet, Investment Programmes Committee, *Report on Capital Investment in 1951 and 1952*, 24 April 1950, para. 215.

[73] PRO CAB 134/439, IPC(48)8, Cabinet, Investment Programmes Committee, *Report on Capital Investment in 1949*, 16 July, 1948, para. 313. PRO CAB 134/982, IPC(53)1, *Report on Investment in 1953 and 1954*, 5 February 1953, p. 24. CAB 134/437, *Report*, p. 23, Appendix 7, paras. 1–2.

[74] PRO CAB 134/982, IPC(53)1, *Report on Investment in 1953 and 1954*, 5 February 1953, p. 24. PRO CAB 134/439, IPC(48)8, Cabinet, Investment Programmes Committee, *Report on Capital Investment in 1949*, 16 July 1948, para. 311.

[75] PRO CAB 134/439, IPC(48)8, Cabinet, Investment Programmes Committee, *Report on Capital Investment in 1949*, 16 July 1948, para. 312.

[76] PRO CAB 134/441, IPC(50)2, Cabinet, Investment Programmes Committee, *Report on Capital Investment in 1951 and 1952*, 24 April 1950, para. 216.

Table 2.4. *Gross domestic fixed capital formation in manufacturing industry, housing and social services, 1948–51* (per cent of total GDFCF)

	1948	1949	1950	1951
Total manufacturing	24.0	25.0	26.6	28.0
New housing	24.7	21.8	19.8	19.6
Education	1.7	2.4	3.0	3.1
Health services	0.9	1.0	1.0	0.8
Total, housing and social services	27.3	25.2	23.8	23.6

(*Source:* Central Statistical Office, *National Income and Expenditure, 1946–52*, London, HMSO, August 1953, Table 43)

health services, including the provisioning of mental hospitals. The incidence of mental disorder did not increase, but the increase in population size nevertheless required an additional 1,200 beds per year to be provided in mental hospitals, where 14,800 patients lacked adequate facilities and from which patients who would have been admitted before the war were now being turned away.[77]

While Table 2.4 reflects the static, if not decreasing, share of investment accounted for by health services, the increasing share of education is clear. The increase in the size of the population, the raising of the school-leaving age to fifteen, and the housing programme all increased the demand for school accommodation. The school-building programme often failed to keep pace with the house-building programme which preceded it, and by May 1949 the Official Cabinet Committee on Economic Development expressed its concern that, 'in virtually all areas where large housing projects are in progress, provision of schools is lagging behind the construction of houses'.[78] The building of houses in new towns and housing estates out of reach of existing schools, required the Ministry of Education to provide an additional 45,000 new places.[79] Government had a statutory duty to meet this demand for school places and nearly 60 per cent of the educational total building programme of the Attlee governments was concerned with the provision of new school places in primary and

[77] PRO CAB 134/439, IPC(48)8, Cabinet, Investment Programmes Committee, *Report on Capital Investment in 1949*, 16 July 1948, paras. 314–16. PRO CAB 134/442, IPC(51)1, Cabinet, Investment Programmes Committee, *Report on Capital Investment in 1951, 1952, and 1953*, 17 March 1951, para. 213.
[78] PRO CAB 134/192, ED(49)11, Cabinet, Official Committee on Economic Development, 'Educational Building Programme 1950 to 1952: Memorandum by the Ministry of Education', 19 May 1949, para. 2.
[79] PRO CAB 134/982, IPC(53)1, *Report on Investment in 1953 and 1954*, 5 February 1953, p. 25, para. 19.

secondary schools.[80] Simply providing buildings to meet demands created by raising the school leaving age and meeting the requirements for new housing estates accounted for three-quarters of projected expenditure in 1947 and over half in 1948. As the building programme struggled to keep up with demand, the Ministry and the local education authorities were encouraged to consider postponing the school-meals programme, making use of old pre-war schools, and devising a double shift system for classes.[81] Efforts were also made to reduce the specification and cost of new school buildings, but building costs continued to rise, despite Ministry threats to refuse to approve new building plans until reduced building costs estimates were accepted by Local Education Authorities.[82]

Given the Ministry of Education's struggle to meet its statutory obligation to provide buildings for schoolchildren and to ease the shortage of 66,000 places in schools on new housing estates which existed at the end of 1948, it is unsurprising that non-statutory demands received less attention. In lobbying for resources, the Ministry of Education had always made it clear that if its requests for resources were trimmed by the planners, then the effect of the cuts would fall on non-statutory parts of their programme. Particular threats included the postponement of teacher-training programmes, the delay in finishing school-meals buildings, and the cessation of all buildings for technical education. The Ministry estimated that it required a building ceiling of 20,000 in June 1948, an increase of one-third on its current activity, and a further increase to 30,000 by the end of 1948.[83] Part of this mix of requests and threats may have reflected game-playing within the planning system, but much of it reflected a genuine dilemma. With a large statutory obligation to provide additional school places, and with strong competition for building resources from the housing programme, non-school components of the educational programme were squeezed. This occurred despite the almost fervent espousal and advocacy of the benefits of further education by the IPC itself. In submitting their annual report to Cabinet in 1948, the Committee urged that the 'large expansion of technical education should be pushed ahead as fast as

[80] PRO CAB 134/440, IPC(49)3, Cabinet, Investment Programmes Committee, *Report on Capital Investment in 1950–1952*, 12 May 1949, para. 270.

[81] PRO CAB 134/437, IPC(46)9 Cabinet, Investment Programmes Committee, *Report on Capital Investment*, 8 October, 1947, Appendix 5, paras. 2, 5.

[82] PRO CAB 134/441, IPC(50)2, Cabinet, Investment Programmes Committee, *Report on Capital Investment in 1951 and 1952*, 24 April 1950, para. 226. The estimated costs for schools started in 1950 were £140 per place in primary schools, and £240 in secondary schools, as against £195 and £320 respectively in 1949.

[83] PRO CAB 134/437, IPC(46)9 Cabinet, Investment Programmes Committee, *Report on Capital Investment*, 8 October, 1947, Appendix 5, paras. 4–6.

possible. The small building programme for Universities should be increased because of its great importance and small cost.'[84] The Committee was explicit on the benefits of investing in technical education:

The Committee are of the opinion that this is a sector which will give a high return in a short time for a comparatively small expenditure, that a programme for the provision of adequate facilities for technical education should be pushed ahead with vigour and that the resources needed for this purpose should be made available, if necessary, at the expense of some other part of the social investment sector.[85]

The merits of technical education were strongly supported by the IPC, who promoted the adoption of the Percy Committee's recommendation that National Colleges for advanced technology and research be established, and that increased provision be made for technical training and research.[86] As the rhetoric of cuts gained sway, the IPC continued to urge that 'great importance should be attached to the provision for technical education which is vital to the industrial efficiency of the country'.[87] Working on the Percy Committee's estimates that in the postwar decade, technical colleges in England and Wales would need to produce at least 1,500 mechanical, electrical, and civil engineers a year to fill the vacancies in the engineering industry, negotiations were begun for an 'energetic' programme of expansion. By 1948, negotiations were well advanced for the establishment of such colleges for rubber, foundry work, scientific instrument-making, wool, and heating, ventilation, and refrigeration engineering. Meanwhile, the demand for technical education increased steadily. The number of full-time senior day students rose from 10,000 in 1936–7 to 45,000 in 1946–7, while part-time students advanced strikingly from 36,000 in 1936–7 to 200,000 in 1947–8.[88]

To accommodate this striking increase in demand, new buildings and facilities were required. In many places, overcrowding was serious. Where possible, use was made of primary- and secondary-school buildings but the scope for this was limited by the unsuitability of laboratories. Moreover, industry was becoming more interested in

[84] PRO CAB 134/439, IPC(48)8, Cabinet, Investment Programmes Committee, *Report on Capital Investment in 1949*, 16 July 1948, para. 52.
[85] PRO CAB 134/439, IPC(48)8, Cabinet, Investment Programmes Committee, *Report on Capital Investment in 1949*, 16 July 1948, para. 306.
[86] *Higher Technological Education* (Lord Eustace Percy), London, HMSO, 1945.
[87] PRO CAB 134/440, IPC(49)3, Cabinet, Investment Programmes Committee, *Report on Capital Investment in 1950–1952*, 12 May 1949, para. 283.
[88] PRO CAB 134/439, IPC(48)8, Cabinet, Investment Programmes Committee, *Report on Capital Investment in 1949*, 16 July 1948, paras. 304–5.

releasing workers during the day when the schools were occupied.[89] For lack of adequate facilities, students in many areas were turned away.[90] For example, during the session of 1947/8, one college in Birmingham, catering for 5,000 day and 6,000 evening students turned away 1,400 students.[91] To facilitate the building of the new accommodation, in 1949 the IPC recommended that the level of investment in technical education should be increased from less than £1 million in 1948 to £7 million in 1950 and £17 million in 1952.[92] On a more ambitious level, it was estimated that, while building for technical education in 1950 was expected to amount to £3.5 million, it would require investment of £50 million to provide the country with all the technical colleges needed if the industrial worker was to receive a proper training.[93]

Yet, as resources were directed towards the statutory requirements of school education, and as the housing programme was stabilised at 200,000 houses per annum, the resources left for technical education rapidly diminished. In 1949, cuts of £107 million were recommended in the 1950–2 educational building programme in England and Wales.[94] In 1951, the provision for Further Education was reduced, with further cuts planned for 1952 and 1953.[95] With reduced resources and statutory obligations to meet, the Ministry of Education warned that not only would 'many thousands of children of compulsory school age . . . be without school accommodation' but also 'that the programme for technical education, to which the Committee attach special importance, will be heavily cut and possibly even abandoned'.[96]

This last round of cuts in 1950 coincided with the demands of the Korean War rearmament programme, the associated rise in world prices, and a consequent 9 per cent shift in the terms of trade against the UK in 1951. Following an 8 per cent post-devaluation shift in 1950,

[89] PRO CAB 134/441, IPC(50)2, Cabinet, Investment Programmes Committee, *Report on Capital Investment in 1951 and 1952*, 24 April 1950, para. 228.
[90] PRO CAB 134/440, IPC(49)3, Cabinet, Investment Programmes Committee, *Report on Capital Investment in 1950–1952*, 12 May 1949, para. 274.
[91] PRO CAB 134/439, IPC(48)8, Cabinet, Investment Programmes Committee, *Report on Capital Investment in 1949*, 16 July 1948, para. 305.
[92] PRO CAB 134/440, IPC(49)3, Cabinet, Investment Programmes Committee, *Report on Capital Investment in 1950–1952*, 12 May 1949, para. 275.
[93] PRO CAB 134/441, IPC(50)2, Cabinet, Investment Programmes Committee, *Report on Capital Investment in 1951 and 1952*, 24 April 1950, para. 229.
[94] PRO CAB 134/192, ED(49)11, Cabinet, Official Committee on Economic Development, 'Educational Building Programme 1950 to 1952: Memorandum by the Ministry of Education', 19 May 1949, para. 1.
[95] PRO CAB 134/442, IPC(51)1, Cabinet, Investment Programmes Committee, *Report on Capital Investment in 1951, 1952, and 1953*, 17 March 1951, para. 231.
[96] PRO CAB 134/192, ED(49)11, Cabinet, Official Committee on Economic Development, 'Educational Building Programme 1950 to 1952: Memorandum by the Ministry of Education', 19 May 1949, para. 7

this not only contributed to an unexpectedly large balance-of-payments deficit but also constituted a shift in the terms of trade between 1949 and 1951, equivalent in Cairncross's view to a loss of over 3 per cent in real income, and was at least as great a burden as the additional cost of arms production and other defence expenditure.[97] Although the rearmament programme did not place as much strain as feared on the UK engineering industry, defence requirements barely doubling rather than quadrupling, it did none the less increase pressure on a metal-working machine-tool industry which was attempting to meet export targets which had been increased from 45–50 per cent in 1948, to 50–60 per cent.[98] With balance-of-payments considerations constraining imports, a defence effort taking one-eighth of total supplies of metal products in 1950, 1952, and 1953, compared with one-twelfth in 1949, absorbed about all the increase in supplies of metal goods during that period.[99] With the export drive continuing its emphasis on capital-equipment exports, investment was squeezed and industrial investment ground to a virtual standstill (see Table 2.2).

The prospect of what rearmament could cost brought a number of issues to a head. The Chancellor of the Exchequer, Hugh Gaitskell, warned of the increasing production demands which would fall on the metal and engineering industries.[100] Gaitskell's estimates proved to be mistaken, defence expenditure peaking in 1952 at some £500 million, or 30 per cent below the peak planned in January 1951. Wilson's defence expenditure estimates proved to be nearer the mark, and they were used by Bevan in arguments with Gaitskell which culminated in the resignation of Bevan, Wilson, and Freeman. Worried about rising expenditure, Gaitskell sought savings of £10 million in hospital-administration costs, and a contribution of £13 million from imposing charges on dentures and spectacles.[101] This was opposed by Bevan, although he had conceded the principle of prescription charges the previous year. Indeed, Bevan was as keen as anyone to stop 'the ceaseless cascades of medicine pouring down people's throats'.[102] In fact, this critical split in the rising generation of Labour politicians had little to do with the principle of prescription charges or with the saving of £13 million, which in the greater scheme of things was negligible. In

---

[97] Cairncross, *Years of Recovery*, p. 229.
[98] PRO CAB 134/437, IPC(46)9 Cabinet, Investment Programmes Committee, *Report on Capital Investment*, 8 October 1947, Appendix 16, para. 4.
[99] *Economic Survey for 1954*, Cmd 9108, March 1954, para. 126.
[100] PRO CAB 129/44, CP(51)20 'Economic Implications of the Defence Proposals', memorandum by the Chancellor of the Exchequer, 19 January 1951.
[101] PRO CAB 128/19, CM(51)22, 22 March 1951. Cairncross, *Years of Recovery*, ch. 8.
[102] R. Klein, *The Politics of the NHS*, 2nd edn, London, Longman, 1989, p. 34.

part, it was about the clash of two ambitious and very different personalities in the same peer group. It was also about the Treasury facing up to the minister who had demanded ever more resources for his health and housing programme.

These arguments were to persist into the 1950s, as too was the defence burden. Dalton had fought to halve defence expenditure between 1946 and 1948, but thereafter the defence bill had begun to rise again, and it was always above the £500 million per annum which some leading Conservative members of the wartime coalition government had regarded as imposing too heavy a burden on the national economy.[103] Verbal assurances from the USA that it would 'pick up the check' for the Korean rearmament programme were not realised. Forced to rearm at a time when it had been disposing of ammunition and surplus stores, the UK continued to devote an internationally large share of resources to defence. At 6 per cent of GNP in 1948, the UK devoted a higher share of national resources to defence than both the USA, at 5 per cent, and France, at 4 per cent. On the back of the Korean War it was to climb to 10 per cent of GNP in 1952.[104] With the demands of the rearmament programme added to those of an already stretched economy, it was perhaps unsurprising that the postwar annual increase in gross domestic fixed capital formation ground to a halt between 1950–2 (see Table 2.2). There was a strong sense in which Britain in 1950–2 was simply attempting to do too much. Yet, even as gross domestic fixed capital formation (GDFCF) marked time, in 1951 the share invested in manufacturing industry rose to an unprecedented proportion for the postwar period. Although in 1950–3 the GDFCF/GNP ratio was higher in West Germany, in the UK a larger share of the GDFCF was accounted for by manufacturing industry.[105] The West German share of investment in housing was higher, although at 6 per cent in 1952 the West German defence effort was a lower proportion of GNP. Nor was the intensity of pressure for exports to relieve balance-of-payments crises as great in either France or West Germany.[106] While it is undeniable that the UK GDFCF/GNP ratio was lower than in most

---

[103] PRO CAB 128/9, CM10(47) p. 69. In 1947, Dalton was struggling to reduce expenditure from £963 million to something in the region of £850 million.

[104] Organisation for European Economic Co-operation (OEEC), *Statistics of National Product and Expenditure, 1938, 1947 to 1952*. In 1955, ten years after the end of World War II, it still stood at 8.2%. R. Middleton, *Government versus the Market*, p. 615.

[105] United Nations, Secretariat of the Economic Commission for Europe, *Some Factors in Economic Growth in Europe during the 1950s*, Part 2, Geneva, 1964, pp. A12–13, A30–1.

[106] For continuing constraints of balance of payments, see C. Schenk, *Britain and the Sterling Area from Devaluation to Convertibility in the 1950s*, London, Routledge, 1994, and review by B. Eichengreen, *Journal of Economic History*, 55 (1995), pp. 940–2.

other countries, there is little evidence of this being due to the planners' deliberately neglecting the needs of investment. Indeed, the evidence is of planners continually seeking more resources for industrial investment, and in particular for investment in manufacturing industry. The low GDFCF/GNP ratio may be due to the intensity of demands made on all economic resources during this period, but it may also reflect something more fundamental about the demand for fixed capital investment within the UK. Even after the postwar shortages and planning had disappeared, GDFCF/GNP ratios in the UK continued to be relatively low.

3   Allocating resources

On the assumptions made in this report it is clear that total fixed investment over the next few years on the scale envisaged by Departments would not be possible without diverting resources away from exports and immediate home consumption to an extent which we could not afford. If the decision were left to ordinary market forces, there could be no assurance that such a diversion would not occur. In any event the economy could ill afford the inflationary struggle which would take place in deciding between the claims of consumption and investment by competitive bidding for the available resources. For this reason some measure of control over both the volume and direction of investment will continue to be necessary throughout the period with which we are concerned.

The need for some control does not rest solely on these grounds. In the past both private industry and the State have tended to over-expand investment at certain times and to do too little at others, thus accentuating the peaks and depressions of the trade cycle. It is Government policy to try to prevent such violent swings of investment in the future, and in particular to influence the scale and timing of public capital expenditure with this in view. A supplementary reason, therefore, for holding back some forms of investment now may well be to have them in reserve in order that investment may be increased readily as soon as any signs of a trade recession appear.

(Investment Programmes Committee, *Report on Capital Investment in 1950–1952*, 12 May 1949.)[1]

In addition to their concern with the general level of investment, planners were also acutely interested in the pattern and timing of investment activity. Influencing the pattern of investment was part-and-parcel of their wider efforts to ease supply bottlenecks in the domestic economy and to encourage exports and import-substitution as contributions to improving the balance of payments. Influencing the timing of investment activity was a wider ambition of the planners, largely arising from their wish to engage in counter-cyclical investment activity as a

[1] PRO CAB 134/440, IPC(49)3, Cabinet, Investment Programmes Committee, *Report on Capital Investment in 1950–1952*, 12 May 1949, paras. 71–2.

means of counteracting the onset of the next slump. As with economic planning in general, the ambition both to shape the pattern and to influence the timing of investment were adjusted in response to the crises of 1947. As with the National Investment Council (NIC), the concern shifted from preparing projects which could be initiated when the boom faltered, to worrying about how to rein in and reduce the investment demands being made by major industries. The fuel and convertibility crises also gave a clearer definition to the statements on the pattern of investment sought by planners. Whereas before the fuel crisis, the IWP in May 1946, had produced an unranked list of favoured projects, which included housing, exports, and rather vague references to capital expenditure, maintenance and renewal, relief of bottlenecks, factory building, and expansion of services in Development Areas, thereafter the order of priorities was shorter and sharper.[2] A Cabinet memorandum of 20 March 1947 gave clear 'precedence' to projects likely to increase supplies of coal, gas and electricity and to the movement of coal by rail.[3] To this was added, after the convertibility crisis, an emphasis on exports, as the IPC declared that 'the chief aim must be to regain national economic independence at the first possible moment'.[4]

A number of measures can be used to capture the pattern of resource distribution favoured by the planners. One obvious measure is the allocation of steel (see Table 3.1). While a necessarily imperfect measure, because of the varying importance of steel to each industry, the appeal of using data on steel allocations is that this was a measure which the planners took very seriously. Steel allocations were regarded as a key planning instrument, not least because more than half of the total supplies of steel went into investment.[5] Although the steel distribution scheme was subject to over-ordering and a small amount of black-market activity, in general the steel distribution scheme seems to

---

[2] PRO CAB 134/188, IWP(46)4(Revise), 'First Report by the Investment Working Party', 12 March 1946, para. 4.

[3] PRO CAB 129/17, 'Expansion of Fuel and Power Resources', Cabinet Memorandum, CP(47)92, 20 March 1947.

[4] PRO CAB 134/439, IPC(48)8, Cabinet, Investment Programmes Committee, *Report on Capital Investment in 1949*, 16 July 1948, para. 25.

[5] PRO CAB 134/440, IPC(49)3, Cabinet, Investment Programmes Committee, *Report on Capital Investment in 1950–1952*, 12 May 1949, para. 62. One instance of this imperfection is that the 1.8 per cent of steel allocated to electricity does not capture its subsequent purchase of steel engineering plant from Ministry of Supply-sponsored industries or provide an indication that the electricity industry accounted for 15% of GDFCF in plant and machinery. In general, there was not a significant variation between the pattern of allocation and deliveries.

Table 3.1. *Planned annual allocations of steel, 1946–9* (per cent)

Departments	1946	1947	1948	1949	1946–9
Home Office	0.05	0.03	0.04	0.09	0.05
Admiralty–Naval	1.9	0.7	0.6	0.8	1.0
–Mercantile	9.1	8.6	7.8	7.8	8.3
War Office	0.4	0.1	0.1	0.1	0.1
Ministry of Supply	31.5	36.1	39.8	37.0	36.3
Air ministries	0.6	0.1	0.1	0.1	0.2
Scottish departments	0.6	0.8	0.7	0.6	0.7
Board of Trade: home civil and					
indirect export	6.1	3.5	3.3	2.8	3.8
Direct export	14.6	9.0	8.4	9.7	10.4
Ministry of Health	2.0	2.0	1.6	1.6	1.8
Ministry of Agriculture and					
Fisheries	1.6	2.5	2.6	2.5	2.3
Ministry of Transport	6.7	8.7	7.4	6.7	7.3
Ministry of Food	2.9	3.2	2.9	2.8	2.9
Ministry of Works	9.1	7.9	8.0	8.9	8.5
Post Office	0.2	0.2	0.4	0.4	0.3
Ministry of Fuel and Power:					
Gas Division	0.8	1.1	1.3	1.3	1.1
Mines Division	6.3	7.6	5.5	5.4	6.1
Petroleum Division	3.4	5.5	4.4	6.0	4.8
Electricity Division	1.7	1.4	1.7	2.2	1.8
Northern Ireland	0.4	0.4	0.5	0.4	0.4
Iron and Steel	–	–	2.6	2.3	1.3
Ministry of Education	–	0.4	0.3	0.5	0.3

(*Source:* PRO CAB 134/475–485, Departmental Steel Allocations, 1946–1949)

have succeeded in delivering steel in accord with the pattern of allocations made by the planners.[6]

Steel allocations were made on a quarterly basis, and varied in specificity from those made to individual industries like electricity, gas, and iron and steel, to those made to sponsoring departments representing a range of industries and constituent firms. By far the largest intended recipient of allocated steel was the Ministry of Supply, followed by the Board of Trade. Within these aggregate allocative totals, Douglas Jay, Chairman of the Materials Allocation Committee, did attempt to make quarterly adjustments to the pattern of allocation in response to the current perception of needs and difficulties. In Period 4 of 1947 and Period 1 of 1948, Jay supervised heavy cuts in

[6] PRO CAB 134/89, CE(48)22, Cabinet, Controls and Efficiency Committee, 'Note on the Report of the Joint Committee on the Working of the Steel Distribution System', 8 November 1948, para. 8.

allocations to building programmes, while sharply increasing those to the Ministry of Supply export programmes. After the convertibility crisis, the Ministry of Supply had its allocation of total steel increased from 32.9 per cent in Period 2 1946, to 41.7 per cent in Period 1 1948 before declining slightly to 37.2 per cent in Period 1 1950.[7] Increased allocations were also made to the Board of Trade (mainly for use in bilateral negotiations) in Period II of 1948 and to shipbuilding.[8] In 1947, an added layer of priorities was built into the steel-allocation process, with a proportion of the allocations made to leading departments being designated as either 'priority' or 'non-priority' between Period 2, 1947 and Period 1 1948. Thus, in Period 3 1947, the Ministry of Supply received 19.8 per cent of its steel allocation on a 'priority' basis, the equivalent 'priority' shares for coal, petroleum and electricity being 96.6 per cent, 62.5 per cent, and 84.2 per cent respectively.[9]

The steel allocation data can be read alongside Table 3.2, which shows both the distribution of programmed investment approved by the IPC and their estimates of the subsequent actual pattern of investment. The immediate concern is with the pattern of investment sought by the Committee rather than the actual outcome, which will be considered later. Again the largest single designated area of investment was manufacturing industry, although here both the approved and the actual share of investment falls. This is in contrast with the data in the national income and expenditure accounts, where manufacturing industry's share of total investment rises continuously to an all-time high during the postwar period of 28.1 per cent in 1951.[10] This is largely explained by differing definitions of manufacturing industry, the national income and expenditure accounts including such industries as iron and steel and mineral oil-refining in their definition of manufacturing industries.

[7] PRO CAB 134/477, PRO CAB 134/482, PRO CAB 134/485 Ministry of Supply, Iron and Steel Control, Departmental Allocation Statistics, Total Steel.
[8] PRO CAB 134/637, PC(48)52, Cabinet, Production Committee, 'Steel Allocation Policy in Period IV, 1948', memorandum by the Economic Secretary to the Treasury, Douglas Jay, 21 April 1948, para. 3.
[9] PRO CAB 134/480 Ministry of Supply, Steel Allocation Data.
[10] Central Statistical Office, National Income and Expenditure, London, HMSO, August 1953, Table 43. This is based on the Blue Book definition of total manufacturing industry and excludes the separate entry for the building and contracting industry. Total GDFCF includes legal fees, stamp duties, etc. Cairncross calculates fixed investment (including the building and contracting industry) as 31% of total GDFCF, excluding legal fees, stamp duties, etc. None the less, his observation that manufacturing industry's share of total investment peaked in 1951 remains valid. Cairncross, Years of Recovery: British Economic Policy, 1948–51, London, Methuen, 1985, university paperback, 1987, p. 455.

Table 3.2. *Investment Programmes Committee: approved programmes and outcomes 1948–51*[11] (per cent)

	1948	1949		1950		1951	
	Outcome	Approved	Outcome	Approved	Outcome	Approved	Outcome
Coal mining	1.9	2.2	2.1	2.7	2.2	3.0	2.2
Electricity	6.2	7.8	7.3	7.7	7.8	7.4	8.9
Gas	2.1	2.3	1.9	2.4	2.6	1.9	2.7
Petroleum	0.6	1.4	1.1	1.6	2.2	2.5	2.4
Railways	5.6	6.0	4.4	5.8	4.1	4.8	4.4
Roads	2.8	3.2	3.2	3.0	3.4	2.8	3.5
Public-service vehicles	2.2	1.8	2.5	1.8	2.5	2.7	1.7
Commercial goods vehicles	3.9	2.2	4.5	2.7	4.5	4.9	4.5
Civil aviation	1.2	1.5	1.8	1.2	1.1	1.1	0.9
GPO	2.4	2.6	2.8	2.7	2.7	2.6	2.4
Shipping	5.0	3.8	4.2	3.7	5.0	3.1	5.3
Agriculture	5.4	5.5	5.0	5.1	5.2	4.5	4.9
Iron and steel	2.2	3.1	2.8	2.9	3.3	2.6	3.3
Manufacturing industry	26.2	26.5	25.1	26.2	23.8	23.7	22.1
New housing	21.1	15.6	17.7	15.4	17.6	16.3	17.2
Water and sewerage	1.1	1.6	1.4	1.6	1.5	1.6	1.8
Health and local services	1.4	1.7	1.1	1.7	1.9	1.3	1.9
Education	1.8	2.6	2.6	3.0	3.3	3.5	3.8
Administration and defence	3.8	4.4	4.5	4.7	5.3	5.4	11.3
Northern Ireland	2.0	2.5	2.4	2.3	2.7	2.1	2.8

(*Sources:* PRO CAB 134/440, IPC(49)3, Cabinet, Investment Programmes Committee, *Report on Capital Investment in 1950–52*, p .98, Table 87. PRO CAB 134/441, IPC(50)3, Cabinet, Investment Programmes Committee, *Capital Investment in 1951 and 1952*, note by the Joint Secretaries, F. R. P. Vinter and P. J. Moorhouse, 1 June 1950. PRO CAB 134/442, IPC(51)2, Cabinet, Investment Programmes Committee, *Capital Investment in 1951, 1952 and 1953*, note by the Secretariat, 5 September 1951, Table 61(Revise))

Table 3.2 reflects not only the pattern of investment sought by the IPC but also the shifts within that pattern. Concentrating on the pattern of approvals, we see that housing, education, coal mining, petroleum, commercial goods vehicles, and administration and defence all enjoyed a rising share of approved investment across the period, reflecting their persistent and increasing importance to the government. By contrast,

[11] Coal mining includes deep-mined coal (1.2% in 1949), open-cast coal (0.1% in 1949), and hard coke (0.3% in 1949). Electricity includes British Electricity Authority and North of Scotland Hydro-Electric Board. Education includes universities (0.2% in 1949). Administration and defence includes Admiralty (works at home) (0.4% in 1949), War Office (0.5% in 1949), Air Ministry (0.3% in 1949), Home Office (Civil Defence) (0.01% in 1949), Ministry of Supply (Direct) (0.9% in 1949) and government building (1.2% in 1949). Percentages do not total exactly because of rounding up.

many infrastructure and transport and communication programmes, including those of the post office, health and local services, and water and sewerage, were held at a static share of approved investment, while the share of investment approved for railways, roads, civil aviation, and shipping fell. Efforts were also made to reduce the share of investment taken by electricity, and to establish some better control over the erratic category of public service vehicles. This general pattern of allocation sought by the IPC is not surprising, reflecting the emphasis placed on production for export and the relief of bottlenecks, and the associated wish to maintain the infrastructure on a minimal basis. Quite why the share of total investment allotted to iron and steel should decline is not clear, although it is possible that the industry was generally receiving as much investment resources as it required, especially given the shortages of coal. Certainly, the declining share of approved investment did not prevent its share of actual investment from rising.

While the general pattern of approved investment is unsurprising for a production-maximising, balance-of-payments constrained economy, political priorities also influenced the allocative pattern. That across the period a rising share of investment should have been allocated to housing is perhaps the clearest example of political considerations overriding the better judgements of many planners. To a lesser extent, political influence also contributed to the rising share of investment allocated to coal mining. That coal mining was a priority industry was clear, particularly after the 1947 fuel crisis. It was also obvious that the industry enjoyed the political sympathies of the Labour government from Attlee downwards.[12] However, when the industry consistently undershot the planners' investment allocations, there was a move to reduce the share of resources allocated to the industry. Douglas Jay made some progress in reducing the industry's share of steel allocations, but similar efforts by the IPC were fiercely resisted by the industry, which exploited its position of political strength.[13] In the face of objections from planning committees, investment allocations continued to be made to the industry which it continued to under-use.

Doubts about the allocation of resources to coal mining were fuelled not only by the industry's apparent difficulties in achieving its annual investment programme, but also by more fundamental concerns about

[12] C. Attlee, *As It Happened*, London, Heinemann, 1954, p. 164: 'An order of priority was adopted. It was obvious, for instance, that the coal industry was more urgently in need of reconstruction than iron and steel . . . First things had to come first.'

[13] PRO CAB 134/439, IPC(48)8, Cabinet, Investment Programmes Committee, *Report on Capital Investment in 1949*, 16 July 1948, para. 75. PRO COAL 23/169, letter from C. A. Roberts (National Coal Board) to G. L. Watkinson (Ministry of Fuel and Power), 18 June 1949.

the contribution which investment was likely to make to the immediate need to increase the industry's output. The concern of Douglas Jay was that all the talk of 'mechanisation, output per head, and absenteeism' constituted little more than 'long-term red herrings' when set against the immediate contribution which increased labour recruitment could make to raising output. As Jay pointed out in 1946, with labour 'wastage' averaging more than 1,250 workers a week over the past year, and with a gross intake averaging only 1,600 workers a week in the January–March 1946 quarter, 850 of whom were ex-miners from the Armed Forces and therefore a non-recurrent item, the industry faced a general labour shortage as well as a specific shortage of skilled coal-face workers.[14]

Whatever the misgivings about the neglect of the issue of labour recruitment, the coal industry continued to lobby for increasing capital investment resources, not least in the form of mechanised coal-cutters, in the first instance, followed by haulage and winding plant.[15] That more immediate additions to output could be achieved by increased labour rather than capital input, did not negate the general argument of the industry that increased capital investment was the best source of long-term productivity improvements. Seeking to test this proposition, the IPC sought information on capital productivity from the National Coal Board (NCB). Extracting almost any information, let alone production function data, from the NCB proved difficult, as the Board preferred to wait upon the completion of Divisional and Area Surveys before producing detailed replies to enquiries.[16] In the meantime, the IPC was left to complain that its attempts at programme appraisal were bedevilled by 'the lack of any estimate of the results, in the shape either of increased output or reduced costs, which are expected from the investment proposed'.[17]

The Ministry of Fuel and Power enjoyed more success in extracting information from the industry. By 1951, the Statistics Branch of the Ministry of Fuel and Power was beginning to calculate output returns on NCB capital expenditure of some £100 million between 1946–9.[18]

[14] PRO CAB 124/706, note by Douglas Jay on the 'Coal Crisis', June 1946, para. 5.

[15] PRO CAB 134/441, IPC(50)2, Cabinet, Investment Programmes Committee, *Report on Capital Investment in 1951 and 1952*, 24 April 1950, paras. 83 and 89. PRO CAB 134/440, IPC(49)3, Cabinet, Investment Programmes Committee, *Report on Capital Investment in 1950–1952*, 12 May 1949, para. 88. PRO CAB 134/442, IPC(51)1, *Report on Capital Investment in 1951, 1952 and 1953*, 17 March 1951, para. 116.

[16] PRO CAB 134/439, IPC(48)8, Cabinet, Investment Programmes Committee, *Report on Capital Investment in 1949*, 16 July 1948, para. 67.

[17] PRO CAB 134/439, IPC(48)8, Cabinet, Investment Programmes Committee, *Report on Capital Investment in 1949*, 16 July 1948, para. 69.

[18] PRO POWE 37/99, Ministry of Fuel and Power, Statistics Branch, paper on 'Investment in the Coal Mining Industry', April 1951.

Area comparisons for the years 1946–9 showed a correlation coefficient of 0.39 between increases in capital and output per manshift, which if anything was somewhat lowered by the inclusion of investment in coal-preparation plants and other colliery assets which did not make a direct contribution to output. Areas with the largest increases in manshifts also had the largest output, with changes in capital employed and manshifts together accounting for over three-quarters of the total Area variation in increased output. In relation to output, exponents of 0.75 for labour and 0.25 for capital were calculated (with a constant of 1.13). These output elasticities, of 0.75 for labour and 0.25 for capital, were held to reflect deep-seated relationships in the industry and largely to agree with the results reported by Rhodes and Lomax, and also with the findings of Douglas, who studied such relationships in the pre-war US and Australian economies.[19]

These calculations of the labour and capital components of the production function were followed by financial estimates of the returns on additional capital and labour inputs. A 1 per cent (2 million tons) increase in output from a 1.33 per cent increase in labour employed would, at 1949 costs, correspond to an increase in labour costs of £4.16 million, with additional costs of £0.55 million for general stores and roof supports occasioned by the rise in output. The marginal cost of one ton of coal secured by increased manpower use only was put at almost 46s. Equivalent calculations of net capital costs, including interest, indicated a total cost per ton of 42s 6d per ton, 3s 6d per ton lower than that for labour alone. The policy conclusion drawn was that in a resource-constrained economy 'it may be all the more important to secure the needed increase in coal output by modernising the equipment of the mines rather than by increasing their labour force'. The Board intended to secure its planned increase in coal output to 240 million tons in 1965, an 18 per cent increase on the 1949 output of 203 million tons, with total capital expenditure at collieries of £520 million at 1949 prices, while its labour force fell to 618,000, a decrease of 14.5 per cent on 1949.[20] Given calculations that marginal increases in output could be obtained more economically by increased investment than by increased manpower, the Ministry of Fuel and Power supported the NCB's emphasis on investment as the way forward. This was not to

[19] E. C. Rhodes, 'Output, Labour and Machines in the Coal Mining Industry in Great Britain', *Economica*, n.s. 12 (1945), pp. 101–10. K. S. Lomax, 'The Demand for Coal in Great Britain', *Oxford Economic Papers*, 4, 1 (February 1952), pp. 50–67. PRO POWE 37/99, paper on 'Investment in the Coal Mining Industry', Ministry of Fuel and Power, Statistics Branch, April 1951, para. 18.

[20] PRO POWE 37/99, paper on 'Investment in the Coal Mining Industry', Ministry of Fuel and Power, Statistics Branch, April 1951, para. 15.

contradict Jay's initial attempts to get more labour into the mines as the quickest means of increasing output, but rather to accept that, particularly in a low-unemployment economy, the coal industry was likely to look to capital investment for increased output. Whether the predictions of persistent high demand for coal were safe, given that they were extrapolated from the demand curve for price-controlled coal, with little consideration given to the price elasticity of demand for close substitutes such as oil, was another matter.

While the comparative returns on capital and labour were calculated for the coal industry, in such a highly capital-intensive industry as electricity, which was working to the limits of its capacity, the main strategy pursued by the IPC was to attempt to persuade the industry to reduce its non-industrial peak-hour demand through the use of pricing mechanisms and load limiters.[21] It was peak-hour demand which determined capacity requirements,[22] and with the Economic Survey for 1948 estimating a peak-hour capacity deficit running at 1,420MW (megawatts) (14.9 per cent of available peak capacity) and unlikely to be cleared until 1950, the resource implications of the electricity investment programme looked formidable.[23] With the industry accounting for around 8 per cent of gross domestic fixed capital formation, the generating plant programme proposed by the industry to the IPC was likely to consume 279,000 tons of steel in 1948, rising to 332,000 tons in 1949, to which could be added the corresponding annual steel requirements for building of 125,000 tons and 165,000 tons respectively.[24] The programme submitted to the IPC by the BEA had a total cost in the five years 1948–52 of nearly £600 million, the cost of the proposals for 1952 being 75 per cent greater than the actual expenditure in 1948.[25] The proposed electricity programme would also divert heavy electrical equipment from the export drive, but without being able to guarantee any rapid additions to

[21] PRO CAB 134/442, IPC(51)1, Cabinet, Investment Programmes Committee, *Report on Capital Investment in 1951, 1952 and 1953*, 17 March 1951, para. 129. PRO CAB 134/440, IPC(49)3, Cabinet, Investment Programmes Committee, *Report on Capital Investment in 1950–1952*, 12 May 1949, para. 113.

[22] PRO POWE 14/110, Investment Programmes Committee, 'Power Stations Programme', 1948.

[23] PRO CAB 134/439, IPC(48)8, Cabinet, Investment Programmes Committee, *Report on Capital Investment in 1949*, 16 July 1948, para. 89.

[24] PRO CAB 134/437, IPC(47)9, Cabinet, Investment Programmes Committee, *Report on Capital Investment*, 8 October 1947, p. 34, para. 10. PRO POWE 14/110, 'Cuts in the Electricity Generating Plant Programme', notes of a meeting between the Minister of Fuel and Power and the British Electricity Authority, 7 November 1947, P. Chantler, 10 November 1947.

[25] PRO CAB 134/441, IPC(50)2, Cabinet, Investment Programmes Committee, *Report on Capital Investment in 1951 and 1952*, 24 April 1950, para. 95.

output, largely because the plant and building components of the industry's investment were badly out of step.[26] As is evident in Table 3.2, the IPC persistently and unsuccessfully attempted to contain and, if possible, reduce the share of resources absorbed by the electricity industry's capital-investment programme. The IPC seriously doubted whether 'in the country's present straitened circumstances it could afford to undertake investment on the scale involved by this programme in order to meet a peak load to which domestic consumption makes such a large contribution'.[27]

Aside from electricity and coal mining, other fuel industries struggled to attract resources. In putting the gas industry on a virtual standstill, patching basis, with the partial intention of reducing its competition with coke ovens for silica bricks and construction resources, the planners recognised the danger of continuing the industry's history of 'penny wise, pound foolish' investment policy.[28] Resources were allocated to prevent a breakdown in supplies, 90 per cent of sanctioned work consisting of the replacement of existing capacity.[29] Wartime depreciation had eroded the 25 per cent spare capacity enjoyed by the pre-war gas industry, gas demand was 20 per cent higher than in 1938, and in place of the pre-war usage of 180,000 tons of steel a year, allocations had run at an average rate of 50,000 tons a year.[30] Even so, in 1947, in line with a steel allocation of 100,000 tons a year to the industry, the IPC recommended a reduction in investment, including repair and maintenance, regarding it as one more risk that had to be run.[31]

The predominant investment strategy urged by the IPC for most industries was one of 'patch-and-mend' in which capital investment was concentrated on getting 'more output from existing plant rather than the creation of fresh capacity'. Keeping old and obsolete plant in use, the encouragement of overtime and double-shift working, and the better preparation and treatment of raw material inputs were all

---

[26] PRO CAB 134/982, *Investment in 1953 and 1954*, report by the Investment Programmes Committee, p. 17. PRO CAB 134/440, IPC(49)3, Cabinet, Investment Programmes Committee, *Report on Capital Investment in 1950–1952*, 12 May 1949, para. 105.

[27] PRO CAB 134/439, IPC(48)8, Cabinet, Investment Programmes Committee, *Report on Capital Investment in 1949*, 16 July 1948, para. 99.

[28] PRO CAB 134/439, IPC(48)8, Cabinet, Investment Programmes Committee, *Report on Capital Investment in 1949*, 16 July 1948, para. 106.

[29] PRO CAB 134/437, IPC(47)9, Cabinet, Investment Programmes Committee, *Report on Capital Investment*, 8 October 1947, p. 36, para. 16.

[30] PRO CAB 134/437, IPC(47)9, Cabinet, Investment Programmes Committee, *Report on Capital Investment*, 8 October 1947, p. 36, para. 16.

[31] PRO CAB 134/437, IPC(47)9, Cabinet, Investment Programmes Committee, *Report on Capital Investment*, 8 October 1947, p. 36, para. 17.

suggested as ways of maximising output 'with less capital expenditure than by more ambitious projects which in other circumstances might be pushed ahead'.[32] The emphasis was on maximising production rather than on long-term modernisation, infrastructure projects being put on a minimal, subsistence basis. In manufacturing industry resources were directed to projects likely to produce rapid cost savings, relieve bottlenecks, and provide direct replacements for imports. Highlighted bottlenecks in manufacturing industry included alkalis, cements, dyestuff intermediates, refractories, ball bearings, precision chain, and electric motors. Investment in increased production of oil-refinery equipment, x-ray equipment, giant tyres, and oil base was favoured as providing direct replacements for imports, while investment in agricultural machinery, synthetic detergents, and grass driers, which reduced the need for imported feeding stuffs, were favoured as import substitutes.

Although the overwhelming concern was to increase production from the existing industrial structure, where possible, efforts were made to develop new products likely to enjoy 'continuing demand in the more advantageous markets'. These included tunnel kilns for pottery, new synthetic fibres such as 'ardil' and 'terylene', plastics generally, and gas turbines.[33] Among the newer industries, a quarter of the approved projects of the largest sponsoring department, the Board of Trade, concerned the chemical industry, and in particular the production and development of dyestuffs, sulphuric acid, alkalis and solvents from oil.[34] The ICI dyestuffs expansion programme was worth £5.3 million, with similar projects from Board of Trade-sponsored firms being worth another £3 million. Alkalis, soda ash, and caustic soda were all in high demand, both for bilateral exports, and to meet the increasing requirements of the rayon, glass-making, oils and fats, textiles, paper and other industries. Other investment programmes included those to ease shortages of phosphoric acid, to reduce dollar imports of film base, and to reduce the costs of cracking acetane and alcohol from petroleum.[35] In motor vehicles, while setting export targets for cars, and noting growing congestion in several factories, especially those of Ford and

[32] PRO CAB 134/439, IPC(48)8, Cabinet, Investment Programmes Committee, *Report on Capital Investment in 1949*, 16 July 1948, para. 29.
[33] PRO CAB 134/439, IPC(48)8, Cabinet, Investment Programmes Committee, *Report on Capital Investment in 1949*, 16 July 1948, para. 247. PRO CAB 134/440, IPC(49)3, Cabinet, Investment Programmes Committee, *Report on Capital Investment in 1950–1952*, 12 May 1949, para. 364. Ardil was manufactured from the residues of groundnuts after the extraction of oil, while terylene was a petroleum derivative.
[34] PRO CAB 134/440, IPC(49)3, Cabinet, Investment Programmes Committee, *Report on Capital Investment in 1950–1952*, 12 May 1949, para. 365.
[35] PRO CAB 134/439, IPC(48)8, Cabinet, Investment Programmes Committee, *Report on Capital Investment in 1949*, 16 July 1948, paras. 254–5.

Vauxhall, large new investment programmes were not expected to make a significant immediate difference to the industry's capacity of half a million vehicles per annum. In 1946, £2.75 million of building work was authorised, with the hope that this would rise to £3 million in 1949 and £3.5 million in 1950.[36]

While many industries struggled against the constraints imposed by the IPC, in some cases there was evidence that the committee's willingness to sanction investment was greater than that of the industry itself to undertake such investment. One such case was the machine-tool industry, where manufacturers appeared to the IPC to be haunted by memories of the difficulties experienced after World War I and fearful of the revival of German competition. With production in 1948 above its 1938 level, but below that for 1942, the industry seemed happy to exploit its wartime additions to capacity and to confine its applications for investment resources to a number of small building and expansion schemes. During 1947, the amount of building work approved amounted to only £157,000, with a small increase to £210,000 in 1948. The IPC grew concerned at the perceived ageing of the stock of machine tools. While 50 per cent were less than ten years old in 1949, in two or three years this was expected to fall to about 30 per cent. Equally, there appeared to be some disappointment that very few new projects were submitted by textile firms, the largest single scheme being that of J & P Coats for complete reorganisation over a period of ten years involving an ultimate building expenditure of at least £3 million. Textile industry projects were predominantly for the small extensions, alterations, and adaptations required for the installation of new machinery or the replacing of existing machinery, and the provision of canteens and other amenity works designed to attract labour to these industries. There was more buoyancy in artificial fibres, where good export prospects, especially in viscose-rayon exports, and such import-saving possibilities as the development of artificial fibres for use in tyre fabrics and conveyer belting, drove projects intended to double the output of industrial yarn.[37]

That this 'patching' programme might neglect opportunities to modernise industries was well appreciated by the IPC. So too were the longer-term costs of restricting investment in infrastructure. Yet, whatever its longer-term importance, investment in infrastructure was

---

[36] PRO CAB 134/440, IPC(49)3, Cabinet, Investment Programmes Committee, *Report on Capital Investment in 1950–1952*, 12 May 1949, para. 372.

[37] PRO CAB 134/440, IPC(49)3, Cabinet, Investment Programmes Committee, *Report on Capital Investment in 1950–1952*, 12 May, 1949, p. 89. Appendix, paras. 361–4, 382–4. PRO CAB 134/439, IPC(48)8, Cabinet, Investment Programmes Committee, *Report on Capital Investment in 1949*, 16 July 1948, para. 251.

unlikely to make a rapid contribution to increasing production. Thus, the railways were kept on a care-and-maintenance basis, operating a system with twice the number of pre-war speed restrictions.[38] Such bursts of investment as did occur were designed to prevent breakdown in the movement of such essentials as coal. When essential maintenance work was carried out, concrete sleepers were laid in addition to scarce timber, with some 70 per cent of the replaced tracks being returned to the iron and steel industry as scrap.[39] When new projects were sanctioned it was often, as with the £17 million investment on the Shenfield electrification of the London and North Eastern Railway (LNER) (and the east–west extensions to the London Passenger Transport Board), because by 1947 the work was half to three-quarters complete.[40] Limited electrification work was approved, including £6.2 million of work on the coal-carrying Manchester–Sheffield line.

On trunk and classified roads, maintenance work was held at two-thirds of its pre-war volume per mile of road, while 80 per cent cuts were made in planned new roads. The Stevenage bypass (£1.6 million), the Newport bypass (£1.8 million), Severn Bridge (£9.0 million), the Dartford–Purfleet Tunnel (£6.0 million) and the reconstruction of the Elephant and Castle (£3.6 million) were among the postponed new projects.[41] The restrictions on road investment raised further questions about the timing of the New Town programme. Although originally designed as self-contained projects, the development of Stevenage and Harlow required £14 million and £10 million of work respectively, as well as increasing pressure on the north London railway termini. New Towns and the government's housing programme also made additional demands on water and sewerage facilities, their off-site water and sewerage works being estimated to cost £7.6 million in 1949 as well as competing for cast-iron supplies.[42] Growing demand for water and sewerage facilities from London, Manchester, and Liverpool, from new industrial developments in the Tees Valley, and from rural areas,

---

[38] PRO CAB 134/441, IPC(50)2, Cabinet, Investment Programmes Committee, *Report on Capital Investment in 1951 and 1952*, 24 April 1950, para. 120.

[39] PRO CAB 134/440, IPC(49)3, Cabinet, Investment Programmes Committee, *Report on Capital Investment in 1950–1952*, 12 May 1949, para. 138.

[40] PRO CAB 134/437, IPC(47)9, Cabinet, Investment Programmes Committee, *Report on Capital Investment*, 8 October 1947, Appendix 10, para. 5. PRO CAB 134/439, IPC(48)8, Cabinet, Investment Programmes Committee, *Report on Capital Investment in 1949*, 16 July 1948, para. 125. Some large resignalling works were approved, of which that on the London end of the Southern Region Brighton line was the largest.

[41] PRO CAB 134/437, IPC(47)9, Cabinet, Investment Programmes Committee, *Report on Capital Investment*, 8 October 1947, Appendix 10, para. 2.

[42] PRO CAB 134/439, IPC(48)8, Cabinet, Investment Programmes Committee, *Report on Capital Investment in 1949*, 16 July 1948, paras. 129, 179, 184.

especially for ley farming, were added to a backlog from wartime under-investment.[43]

Newer forms of communication also felt the impact of investment constraints. The Post Office investment programme was severely cut in 1947, hindering efforts to reduce arrears of £64 million engineering and £2.3m building work.[44] Nearly two-thirds of this maintenance and investment programme was directed at the rapidly increasing telephone service. As telephone-exchange equipment and cable could both be exported, the supply of such equipment to the Post Office programme was reduced to 91 per cent of its anticipated requirements in 1949, and to 84 per cent in 1950, 87.5 per cent in 1951, and 93 per cent in 1952.[45] While 833,000 new exchange lines were connected and 1.5 million telephones installed between 1945 and mid-1948 (i.e. 60 per cent more than in the corresponding peak pre-war period), the waiting list of applicants grew to 450,000, of whom 30 per cent were business and 70 per cent were residential applicants. There was a steady increase in the demand for telephones, although by international standards telephone density was not high: the 8.55 telephones per 100 of the population in the UK, compared with 22 in the USA, 15.5 in New Zealand, 19 in Sweden, and 14 in Denmark. As exchanges became overloaded and lobbying began for a switch from manual to automatic systems, the IPC encouraged the Post Office to test the price elasticity of demand by increasing rental charges.[46]

Among other newer forms of travel and communication, similar capacity problems were experienced at London's Heathrow airport as air traffic doubled between 1946 and 1947, and where peak-hour movements were expected to increase from twenty-four in 1947 to an estimated sixty-two in 1952 and to seventy-three in 1955.[47] Pressure

---

[43] PRO CAB 134/441, IPC(50)2, Cabinet, Investment Programmes Committee, *Report on Capital Investment in 1951 and 1952*, 24 April 1950, para. 212. PRO CAB 134/440, IPC(49)3, Cabinet, Investment Programmes Committee, *Report on Capital Investment in 1950–1952*, 12 May, 1949, paras. 252–6. The qualitative improvements of the 1944 Rural Water Supplies and Sewerage Act also had to be met. The new River Boards established under the River Boards Act 1948 pressed for the improvement of facilities for sewerage disposal so as to prevent river pollution.

[44] PRO CAB 134/439, IPC(48)8, Cabinet, Investment Programmes Committee, *Report on Capital Investment in 1949*, 16 July 1948, A12, para. 186.

[45] PRO CAB 134/440, IPC(49)3, Cabinet, Investment Programmes Committee, *Report on Capital Investment in 1950–1952*, 12 May 1949, para. 187.

[46] PRO CAB 134/439, IPC(48)8, Cabinet, Investment Programmes Committee, *Report on Capital Investment in 1949*, 16 July 1948, A12, paras. 188, 193.

[47] PRO CAB 134/437, IPC(47)9, Cabinet, Investment Programmes Committee, *Report on Capital Investment*, 8 October 1947, Appendix 4, para. 1. PRO CAB 134/439, IPC(48)8, Cabinet, Investment Programmes Committee, *Report on Capital Investment in 1949*, 16 July 1948, A12 para. 170.

from the Ministry of Civil Aviation to provide extra labour for maintenance and to build a further three runways by 1951 so as to complete the double runway system was resisted by the IPC. Although the resources requested were small, the committee feared that they would cause acute difficulties for the already overloaded building programme of the western side of London.[48]

To this general picture of industries being urged to maximise output from existing capacity, to seek rapid additions to output, and to 'patch-and-mend' existing plant, there was one conspicuous exception. An increasing share of investment resources was directed to the development of domestic oil-refining industry capacity, even though this investment was not likely to produce any returns until the 1950s at the earliest. In the meantime, the domestic oil-refining programme was to make significant claims on scarce investment resources, both in its own right and in its knock-on effects on related industries such as shipping. Shipping was already struggling to meet the demands of the export programme and to overcome imbalances in its dry cargo tonnage, being particularly deficient in specialised types of ship, such as cargo and passenger lines, and the smaller tramps. Although the UK-registered tanker fleet was 0.5 million gross tons above its 1938 tonnage, it had not kept pace with the increased world trade in oil.[49] While calculations of the dollar returns on steel allocations to shipbuilding were attractive, especially for tankers, tonnage would take time to build up, reaching perhaps 4.3 million gross tons by the end of 1952 (compared with 3.6 million gross tons in 1949). In the meantime, British oil companies expected to cover 60 per cent of their requirements from British tanker tonnage, competing in a world market which was short of T2-tankers for the remaining 40 per cent of tanker capacity.[50]

Why, then, was an increasing share of scarce investment resources allocated to domestic oil refining? That the prospects for oil and oil products were attractive was reasonably clear, but so too were the longer-term prospects for other industries such as motor vehicles and chemicals. Moreover, investment in domestic oil refining was by no means risk free. Crucial to the priority given to the oil-refining

---

[48] PRO CAB 134/437, IPC(47)9, Cabinet, Investment Programmes Committee, *Report on Capital Investment*, 8 October 1947, Appendix 4, para. 2. The committee also disputed the projections of peak-hour demand.

[49] PRO CAB 134/440, IPC(49)3, Cabinet, Investment Programmes Committee, *Report on Capital Investment in 1950–1952*, 12 May 1949, para. 195.

[50] PRO CAB 134/440, IPC(49)3, Cabinet, Investment Programmes Committee, *Report on Capital Investment in 1950–1952*, 12 May 1949, para. 196. PRO CAB 134/439, IPC(48)8, Cabinet, Investment Programmes Committee, *Report on Capital Investment in 1949*, 16 July 1948, A12, paras. 233, 241.

programme was the backing which the programme received from the Treasury, the Bank of England and the defence departments. The Treasury recognised that in a world in which the USA had moved from having a surplus of oil-product exports over imports of 18 million tons in 1938, to running a deficit of 2.5 million tons by 1948, the dollar-earning potential of refined oil was considerable.[51] Increased drilling activities by British companies in the Middle East meant that of a total of about 700 million tons of crude oil expected to be available to British companies by 1948–55, compared with 370 million in 1939–46, the share from the Middle East was likely to increase from 48 per cent in 1948 to 60.5 per cent in 1950 and 64 per cent in 1955.[52] British-owned company production was classified as sterling oil, and its increased production offered opportunities for importing sterling oil and selling refined oil products for dollars.

In the light of such a potential contribution to the balance of payments, Treasury officials began to argue before planning committees the case for allocating resources to the development of a domestic oil-refining capacity.[53] Both the Treasury and the Bank of England recognised that the development programme would itself involve dollar expenditure and that the long-term prospects for the trade were by no means certain.[54] However, the general view of the Treasury, the Bank of England, and Douglas Jay in the Materials Allocation Committee was that the programme 'in theory in the long run' was 'a great potential source of dollars'.[55] Given the importance of drilling activities in the Middle East, rising Arab nationalism, with its threat to appropriate oil-refining facilities, and increasing Arab hostility over the Palestine question only served to encourage governments and companies to

---

[51] PRO CAB 134/217, 'Oil Supply Situation', memorandum by Hugh Gaitskell, Economic Policy Committee, 6 January 1948. PRO T229/58 'Investment Programmes – petroleum', Paper by B. J. Ellis, 20 October 1947. BKEA EC5 1238, G. Leigh-Jones, speech to Parliamentary Scientific Committee, 28 June 1949. 'Britain's £125 million Oil Refinery Programme – Its Economic and Technological Significance', p. 7.

[52] PRO CAB 134/217, OOC(47)16, Cabinet, Official Oil Committee, 'Cost of British Oil Company's Expansion Programme. Memorandum by the Ministry of Fuel and Power', 9 October 1947, paras. 4–6.

[53] PRO CAB 124/797, Materials Committee meeting, minutes, 3 February 1948. On 3 February 1946 at a meeting of the Materials Committee, the Treasury gave as its opinion that the requirements of the petroleum programme were the most important of all the demands being made on steel.

[54] BKEA EC5/1238, G. Leigh-Jones, speech to Parliamentary Scientific Committee, 28 June 1949. 'Britain's £125 million Oil Refinery Programme – Its Economic and Technological Significance', p. 6. It was quite possible, as suggested by figures tabled before the Official Oil Committee, that by 1956 the USA might be able to source itself with oil, leaving only soft-currency markets to Britain.

[55] PRO T229/58, note from Douglas Jay to Chancellor of the Exchequer, 5 March 1948, para. 1.

locate as much of the value-added activities and plant away from drilling sites. Douglas Jay, G. Leigh-Jones of the Bank of England, and Hugh Gaitskell, Minister of Fuel and Power, all warned of the vulnerability of refineries to attack and appropriation, and counselled reducing reliance on Middle-East refining capacity, thus marking a break with the common practice up to 1938 whereby the greatest proportion of the world's needs was supplied from refineries situated at or near the main centres of oil production.[56] Such fears seemed confirmed by the activities of the Tudeh Party, and the seizure of Abadan.[57]

Once the programme was initiated, considerable efforts were made to reduce the dollar content of the oil trade and construction programme.[58] However, the scope for reducing the dollar content of expenditure on pipelines, refineries, specialised equipment reaction chambers, catalysts, specialised valves and instruments, design fees, and US construction consultants was limited by the fact 'that due to its longer experience, the US refinery plant industry has a monopoly of certain processes and equipment, and a very large share in the remainder'.[59] The actual trade in oil itself was a further cause of dollar drain, arising from imports from dollar sources, US-owned oil companies' remittance of profits in distribution, and purchases by US-owned refineries in the sterling area of crude oil from their US parent companies.[60] Efforts by the British government from January 1950 to reduce this dollar drain by introducing a substitution policy whereby any surplus low-dollar cost oil held by British-controlled companies could be used to displace oil imported into the sterling area by US-controlled companies at a high dollar cost, aroused opposition in the USA, where it was suspected of being a ruse to increase British companies' share of the trade. In response, US companies were offered 'incentives' to retain sales which would otherwise have been lost

[56] BKEA EC5/1238, G. Leigh-Jones, speech to Parliamentary Scientific Committee, 28 June 1949. 'Britain's £125 million Oil Refinery Programme – Its Economic and Technological Significance', p. 4. PRO T229/58, PC(48)34, Cabinet, Production Committee, 'The Oil Companies' Expansion Programme', memorandum by the Economic Secretary (Jay) to the Treasury, 10 March 1948, para. 10.

[57] US worries about developments in the Middle East, and most recently in Palestine, had led the USA to decide not to construct a Trans-Arabian pipeline.

[58] PRO CAB 134/438, IPC(WP)(48)87, Investment Programmes Committee, consideration of a note by the Ministry of Fuel and Power on capital investment in the petroleum industry for the period 1947–52. BKEA, EC5/255 'The Dollar Drain Due to American Companies' Operations in the Sterling Area', by M Rudd, 10 August 1949.

[59] PRO CAB 134/217, OOC(47)16, Cabinet, Official Oil Committee, 'Cost of British Oil Companies' expansion programme; Memorandum by the Ministry of Fuel and Power', 9 October 1947, para. 26.

[60] BKEA EC5/255, 'The Dollar Drain Due to American Companies' Operations in the Sterling Area', by M Rudd, 10 August 1949, para. 1.

through substitution, and after direct negotiations with US oil companies the controversy over substitution was ended. The US oil companies agreed to reduce the dollar content of their oil to the average gross dollar content in British-controlled companies' oil of about 30 per cent, in return for which the British government agreed to free them forthwith from all restrictions on their trade in the sterling area other than those imposed on all British companies. The Ministry of Fuel and Power was pleased with the outcome, not least because the increasing demand for oil, including stockpiling, had absorbed British companies' surpluses and thereby foreshortened the likely duration of a substitution policy.[61]

The dominant criteria in the allocation of resources made by planners were the need to expand output rapidly, so as to clear bottlenecks, to maintain coal and electricity supplies, and, increasingly, to promote exports and import substitution, so as to ease the balance-of-payments difficulties. The details of the planned allocations were at their most specific when made to nationalised industries and major government departmental investment programmes; they were vaguer when made to smaller manufacturing industries. Yet, although an anachronism, since the term was not in general use at the time, the government's 'industrial policy' was clear in the industries to which it gave priority. With the possible exception of domestic oil refining, there was little consideration of 'picking winners'. Resources were allocated on a production-minded, output-maximising basis in which projects which made no immediate visible contribution to increasing output were put on a care-and-maintenance basis. The concern was not so much with planning for some bright modern future, as with concentrating on getting through today's array of problems.

Whatever the criteria employed for the allocation of resources and the approval of investment programmes, ultimately what mattered was the ability of the planners to secure their desired outcomes. Table 3.3 provides one measure of the disparity between intentions and outcomes, showing as it does the deviation between the IPC's annual approved programmes and the actual outcome. Clearly, the gap between investment approvals and outcomes was of considerable interest to planners, both as a gauge of their ability to influence the pattern of investment and also because of the implications for any vestigial ambitions for the counter-cyclical use of capital investment. Although for total invest-

---

[61] BKEA EC5/258, Cabinet, GEN 295/98, Working Party on the Oil Expansion Programme, 1 August 1950, agreed minutes of Tripartite Meeting held on 7 June 1950, p. 5. BKEA EC5/258, GEN 295/112, 3 April 1951, Cabinet, Working Party on the Oil Expansion Programme, note by Treasury and Ministry of Fuel and Power, Economic Policy Committee, 'Oil and the Balance of Payments: Memorandum by the Chancellor of the Exchequer and the Minister of Fuel and Power', para. 9.

Table 3.3. *Investment Programmes Committee: deviation between actual/approved investment, 1949–52* (per cent deviation)

	1949	1950	1951	1952	1949–52
Deep-mined coal	13.3	−16.9	−32.9	16.9	−8.3
Electricity BEA	−12.8	9.4	11.1	−11.8	−1.7
Electricity NSHEB	15.0	−7.7	−9.9	−24.0	−6.8
Gas	−9.4	30.3	35.1	−9.8	8.9
Petroleum	−8.2	−22.6	−12.7	−22.7	−18.0
Railway Executive	−33.6	−17.1	−13.9	−35.7	−25.8
Roads	−18.0	14.9	11.1	−9.5	−1.2
Public-service vehicles	38.7	19.4	−43.4	3.5	−4.4
Commercial goods vehicles	105.1	35.6	23.5	12.0	37.7
Civil aviation	21.7	−12.5	−30.5	−3.9	−4.2
GPO	0.9	−1.7	−16.9	2.2	−5.5
Shipping	19.5	44.3	54.9	0.1	26.4
Agriculture, fisheries and forestry	−9.9	7.0	−3.0	1.3	−1.6
Iron and steel	−4.9	−13.4	17.8	−27.2	−8.4
New housing	11.4	0.0	−5.6	−1.0	1.1
Education, England and Wales	−10.6	1.0	−6.9	−8.2	−5.9
Education, Scotland	−15.8	−18.7	−32.3	−27.8	−24.4
Total: principal sectors	−1.9	5.6	−3.5	−6.3	−1.5
Grand total (including miscellaneous)	−1.0	−3.7	3.5	−0.8	−0.5

(*Sources:* PRO CAB 134/440–442 and CAB 134/982, Investment Programmes Committee, *Reports on Capital Investment 1950–1954*. Current prices were converted into 1948 prices using C. H. Feinstein, *National Income, Expenditure and Output of the United Kingdom, 1855–1965*, Cambridge, Cambridge University Press, 1972, Table 63; and PRO CAB 134/982, Investment Programmes Committee, *Report on Gross Fixed Investment for 1950–1952*, Appendix 2)

ment, approvals and outcomes were reasonably close, this accord shielded the tendency for variations above and below the approved investment for each industry to balance each other out. Within this aggregate accord there was particularist disharmony, as investment in individual industries could fluctuate either side of its approved levels from one year to another. In 1949, investment in deep-mined coal was 13.3 per cent above the approved level, but 16.9 per cent below the approved level in 1950. Other industries, notably shipping, public-service vehicles, and commercial goods vehicles, deviated considerably from the planners' intentions. In 1949, investment in commercial-goods vehicles was twice the approved level. Other industries, such as railways and petroleum, consistently failed to achieve their full programme of approved investment. To the exasperation of planners, there was often an inverse relationship between approvals and outcomes. Where increases were approved, so investment achieved fell short, and vice versa. In short, there was often a negative correlation between approved programmes and their outcomes. Electricity, deep-mined coal, roads, gas, and iron and steel all had negative correlations, while the positive correlations for shipping and public service vehicles were low.[62]

Programmes of future investment were always vulnerable to unforeseen changes, such as the Korean War rearmament programme, or as in 1949, the late approval of the housing programme for 1950.[63] Yet, apart from such unforeseen developments, there were some persistent factors which assailed the efforts of the IPC to narrow the gap between approved and actual investment. Three main problem areas can be identified: (1) the problems of obtaining accurate statistics on investment activity; (2) the problems caused by long and often unpredictable construction times; and (3) the limited control exercised by economic planners in general over important components of investment such as plant and machinery.

All planning was affected by the general difficulties of obtaining reliable statistical data on fixed capital investment activity. When preparing their annual report and recommendations to Cabinet for the forthcoming year, the IPC had to estimate the current rate of fixed capital formation. The difficulty of obtaining such reliable data was well known, not least as Stone and Meade had warned of the specific difficulties attending investment data during their wartime work on the development of national-income accounting.[64] Contributing to the

[62] For the period 1949–52, the correlation data for the main programmes are as follows: deep-mined coal (−0.67); BEA (−0.45); NSHEB (−0.03); gas (−0.31); petroleum (+0.98); total fuel and power (+0.83); railway executive (−0.17); roads (−0.17); public service vehicles (+0.28); commercial goods vehicles (−0.47); civil aviation (+0.85); GPO (+0.69); total transport & communication (+0.6); shipping (+0.22); agriculture, fisheries and forestry (+0.85); iron and steel (−0.37); new housing (+0.69); education England and Wales (+0.95), Scotland (+0.72); total principal sectors (−0.15); and grand total (+0.94). Correlation estimates can mislead. For example, while the correlation for the Railway Executive was quite high at +0.63, the industry consistently failed to meet the level of investment approved by the planners.

[63] PRO CAB 134/441, IPC(50)2, Cabinet, Investment Programmes Committee, *Report on Capital Investment in 1951 and 1952*, 24 April 1950, para. 12(i).

[64] Cyclical fluctuations in employment could be reduced by stimulating capital investment in slack times, particularly in the public sector, and contracting it in boom times. Morrison recalled this in 1949 as part of the review of the powers of government to control the socialised industries, this review having been initiated by Morrison in April 1949. See Sir Norman Chester, *The Nationalisation of British Industry*, London, HMSO, 1975, p. 981. Cmd 6438. 'An Analysis of the Sources of War Finance and an Estimate of the National Income and Expenditure in 1938, 1940, 1941 and 1942'. PRO CAB 124/242, R(43)4, War Cabinet, Reconstruction Committee: 'Capital Expenditure After the War: Report by the Central Statistical Office', 2 December 1943. PRO 124/242, 'Report by the Central Statistical Office on "Capital Expenditure after the War", R(43)4', paper by James Meade, Economic Section, 15 December 1943.

difficulties of collecting and presenting reliable estimates were the constraints of time and personnel. Data gathering was often a rushed business undertaken by a small staff. With no more than twenty members, the CEPS were given nine months to do the long-term work for the Economic Surveys, which, as Austin Robinson recalled, was 'not very long if one has in mind that virtually none of the background data and none of the material that goes into an input-output table was in existence'.[65] The problems were no less in preparing the IPC reports, and the committee was well aware that such 'investment planning' by central government was a 'novel task' in a 'field where exact and comprehensive statistics are lacking'.[66] E. F. Muir of the Ministry of Works regarded the data in the IPC *Report* of 1949 as having 'a wholly factitious air of exactness. In fact, there are, and must be, quite wide margins of error both in the totals and in the shares laid down for particular types of investment'.[67] Even in the subsequently much-lauded French First Plan, the leading French planner Jean Monnet's view was that 'the individual figures in the plan were all inaccurate and meant nothing'.[68]

Misgivings about the reliability and presentation of data were to dog most aspects of economic planning, including the preparation of the annual Economic Surveys, of which Keynes was a leading critic. Meade suspected that, following Stone's departure from the Central Statistical Office, Keynes did not think that the necessary 'work would be well done'.[69] Doubts about statistical reliability and errors in the recording of inventories and work in progress caused Keynes to object strongly to the inclusion of the national income and expenditure table C in the draft Economic Survey of January 1946.[70] One of Keynes' main concerns was that if the forecasts of likely investment proved to be exaggerated, then an immediate disinflationary bias would be introduced into the survey. Keynes worried that planners could find themselves pruning departmental programmes so as to accommodate inflated investment forecasts such that 'one actually caused deflation

---

[65] E. A. G. Robinson, *Economic Planning in the United Kingdom: Some Lessons*, Cambridge, Cambridge University Press, p. 4.

[66] PRO CAB 134/440, IPC(49)3, Cabinet, Investment Programmes Committee, *Report on Capital Investment in 1950–52*, 12 May 1949, para. 6.

[67] PRO T229/237, 'Note from Mr E. F. Muir to the Committee on the Control of Investment', Committee on Control of Investment, working papers, 29 July 1949.

[68] PRO BT 11/3357, Anglo–French discussions in Paris, January 1947. Quoted in F. Lynch, 'The Monnet Plan', *Economic History Review*, Second Series, 37, 2 (May 1984), pp. 229–43.

[69] BLPES, Meade papers, 1/6, 27 April 1946.

[70] PRO T247/78, 'Economic Survey of 1946', note from Keynes to Meade, 15 January 1946. Letter from Meade to Keynes, 18 January 1946.

and unemployment in a period of acute shortage'.[71] Keynes was also concerned lest the presentation of this information in terms of income and expenditure obscure the main lessons of the survey, since 'those not expert in these matters will, I fear, receive very confused counsel if they begin to bother their heads about this table. The answer is perhaps that they will not try to understand it. Nevertheless, that does not excuse one from trying to give them something which *prima facie* makes sense.'[72] While Meade disagreed with Keynes' view that 'this sort of work should not really be continued at all in its present form', he was much more sympathetic to Keynes' 'very strong feeling that this [survey] should not be published'. Meade and Keynes continued to argue about the Economic Survey right up until Keynes' death, Meade recalling from their last meeting that 'it was a painful and distressing interview, in which I had to meet the whole battery of Keynes' wit, petulance, rudeness and quick unscrupulousness in argument. I was actually reduced to tears. And then Maynard died.'[73]

Steadily, efforts were made to improve the quality of investment data, especially that on private industrial investment. The 'chief moral' drawn by Peter Vinter from his dispute with the FBI and *The Times* over industrial investment, was the 'pressing need' to improve on the 'shockingly inadequate' information on industrial investment.[74] Central Statistical Office and IPC estimates of gross fixed investment were inevitably subject to constant revision, but information on 'miscellaneous building', 'unprogrammed investment (a host of small miscellaneous work) and industrial investment in plant and machinery was extremely uncertain.[75] Much of the data on industrial investment in plant and machinery were 'in effect a residual heading cross-checked by some rather crude ratios linking industrial building, about which a good deal more is known, with plant and machinery'.

In an effort to improve the flow and quality of investment data, Peter Vinter sought to persuade the FBI to implement the National Produc-

[71] BLPES Meade Papers, Box 1/6, diary 6 April 1946 and 27 April 1946.
[72] PRO T247/78, 'Economic Survey of 1946', note from Keynes to Meade, 15 January 1946. Comments on table C of the revised Economic Survey for 1946/7.
[73] BLPES Meade Papers, Box 1/6, diary, 27 April 1946.
[74] PRO T229/464, 'Industrial Investment', paper by Peter Vinter, 2 November 1948.
[75] PRO CAB 134/442, IPC(51)1, *Report on Capital Investment in 1951, 1952 and 1953*, 17 March 1951, para. 4. A year ago we estimated the out-turn of investment in 1950 at £2,251 million at 1949 prices. Further statistical information has become available since then, e.g., from the sample survey of capital expenditure in manufacturing industry in 1948 and 1949. Moreover, in several sectors the basis of calculating investment has been altered to obtain greater consistency in the definition of investment in different sectors. On this revised basis our earlier estimate of investment in 1950 would have been £2,200 million. The present estimate of the actual out-turn is £2,238 million.

tivity Advisory Council for Industry's recommendation that a questionnaire of a sample of private industries be conducted. This would seek to imitate the 'encouraging results' of similar exercises organised by the Canadian government and US Department of Commerce in 1945. The IWP did not think that the task would be as difficult as some imagined. Although the 1935 Census of Production covered 53,000 firms, more than half of the total net output was produced by 2,000 firms employing 500 or more workers each.[76] However, when Norman Kipping, the President of the FBI, was asked by Sir Edwin Plowden for his co-operation, he flatly refused. Since Kipping was at the same time complaining of the neglect of the needs of private industrial investment, there was, as Sir James Helmore of the Board of Trade observed, 'the most obvious inconsistency between Kipping's attitude about the collection of figures and his attitude on industrial investment generally'.[77] The Board of Trade was left to press for a questionnaire of a suitable sample of business, and Vinter left to conclude 'that a vital part of investment programme work is bound to be seriously hampered until a proper enquiry of industrial investment is put in hand'.[78]

Once gathered, the estimates of previous and current fixed capital investment formation provided some basis from which the IPC could make investment recommendations for the forthcoming year. In capital investment, this planning on an annual basis was always recognised to be an unusually awkward exercise, since the completion time for capital-investment projects varied from the twelve months taken to complete houses and locomotives to the thirty to thirty-six months required for power stations. Similarly, long production cycles in such industries as shipbuilding and motor vehicles made rapid changes difficult.[79] In 1949, the IPC extended its planning period from one to three years, acknowledging that since 'in the short run the pattern of investment is largely governed by the work already in progress', then 'the pattern cannot be radically changed at short notice without dislocation and loss. If, therefore, investment is to be influenced, it is necessary to look ahead and formulate policies before commitments have been undertaken.'[80]

[76] PRO T229/464, 'Industrial Investment; Paper by Peter Vinter', 2 November 1948. PRO CAB 134/188, IWP/46/1, 'Investment Working Party; Memorandum by the Treasury', 6 February 1946, para. 9.
[77] PRO T229/464, letter to Sir Edwin Plowden from James Helmore (Board of Trade), 11 November 1948.
[78] PRO T229/464 'Industrial Investment; Paper by Peter Vinter', 2 November 1948.
[79] PRO CAB 134/439, IPC(48)8, Cabinet, Investment Programmes Committee, *Report on Capital Investment in 1949*, 16 July 1948, paras. 7(ii), 232.
[80] PRO CAB 134/440, IPC(49)3, Cabinet, Investment Programmes Committee, *Report on Capital Investment in 1950–1952*, 12 May 1949, p. 6, para. 2.

The rate at which fixed capital investment formation occurred was closely related to the speed of construction. The uncertain, but usually long, construction times in this period simply compounded the difficulties for both planners and managers of estimating future rates and costs of fixed capital investment.[81] It was in part the problem of getting investment projects completed which had prompted the establishment of the IPC and its cutting of new work so as to allow work-in-progress to be completed.[82] Political embarrassment at the slow rate of house construction led the government to establish, first, the Girdwood Committee to report on house construction, and then the Philips Committee to examine the wider problems of the construction industry.[83] These committees, and the Anglo-American Building Industry Productivity Team, which visited the USA in July and August 1949, all estimated the productivity of the building industry in 1949 as only three-quarters of its 1938 level, and unlikely to improve.[84] This was dismally prescient, the poor productivity performance of the industry between 1937 and 1951 being characterised in 1982 by Matthews, Feinstein and Odling-Smee as 'unique', while the absence of any net rise in productivity in construction between 1937 and the late 1960s was without parallel in any other sector.[85] In a period of high growth and technical advances in construction machinery, materials, and methods, the fact that the absolute level of productivity in construction prevailing before World War II was not regained until near the end of the 1960s was striking.[86]

That construction times in a resource-constrained, excess-demand

[81] Anglo–American Council on Productivity, Productivity Team Report, *Building; Report of a Visit to the USA in 1949 of a Productivity Team representing the Building Industry*, London, May 1950, p. 14.

[82] PRO CAB 134/439, IPC(48)8, Cabinet, Investment Programmes Committee, *Report on Capital Investment in 1949*, 16 July 1948, Appendix B5, para. 245.

[83] PRO T229/219, LP(50)6, Cabinet, Lord President's Committee: Building Industry Working Party Report-Memorandum by Minister of Works. Report of Philips Committee, 20 March 1950. The establishment of what was to become the Philips Committee was initiated at a meeting of the Lord President's Committee on July 25 1947 (LP(47)23 meeting). The Working Party began its work in July 1948 and presented its report in January 1950.

[84] PRO T229/219 Memorandum on the 'Report of the Working Party on Building', p. 81.

[85] R. C. O. Matthews, C. H. Feinstein, and J. C. Odling-Smee, *British Economic Growth, 1956–1973*, Oxford, Clarendon Press, 1982, p. 236, Appendix H, p. 587. Later studies confirmed the contemporary estimate of postwar labour productivity being three-quarters that of 1938 in the house-building industry and 70% in other buildings and works, which contributed to labour costs and total costs being 2.5 times those of 1938, exceeding the 180% increase in GDP.

[86] M. Bowley, *The British Building Industry*, Cambridge, Cambridge University Press 1966; M. Bowley, *Innovation in British Building Materials*, London, Duckworth, 1967; F. Zweig, *Productivity and Trade Unions*, Oxford, Blackwell, 1951; C. F. Carter, 'The

economy should be longer than those in pre-war Britain was unsurprising. Not only did shortages of plant, materials, and labour abound, but their scarcity placed great weight on managers' ability to co-ordinate and sequence construction operations. The high interdependence of construction operations meant that specific delays had widespread effects.[87] One of the main themes of the British Institute of Management's investigation into how the Esso refinery at Fawley had been built in less than two-and-a-half years, and two months ahead of schedule, was the importance of the role of US foremen in forward-planning the sourcing and co-ordination of materials and labour.[88] It was partly to improve the co-ordinating and sequencing of construction operations that a joint ICI–government panel was established on 15 August 1945 to discuss the company's forward-ordering of controlled resources. Similar arrangements were made for the oil-refinery and electricity power station programmes.[89] This greater attention to the management of electricity construction operations was precipitated by the cruel exposure of the costs of imbalance in construction stages, as in 1948, when 300,000–400,000 kilowatts (kW) of generating plant, worth £2–3 million, had to be stored for a year because the buildings to house it had not been finished. Built to individual specifications, the turbo-alternators were unsuitable for export.[90]

The demand for construction resources derived both from the government's own housing programme, and from the unprecedented size and technical specification of industrial construction projects. The electricity industry's commissioning rate was four times that of the inter-war period, ICI's £25 million of investment at Wilton across the Tees from Billingham, was 'of a kind formerly unknown in Britain', and the construction of oil-refining capacity at Fawley, near Southampton, at Shell Haven, and at Grangemouth in Scotland involved impressive feats of industrial construction, including the supply of Grangemouth

Building Industry', in D. L. Burn (ed.), *The Structure of British Industry*, vol. I, Cambridge, Cambridge University Press, 1958.

[87] British Productivity Council, Review No. 16, *A Review of Productivity in the Building Industry*, para. 1.

[88] A. P. Gray and Mark Abrams, *Construction of Esso Refinery, Fawley. A Study in Organisation*, London, British Institute of Management, Occasional Papers, No. 6, 1954, p. 7.

[89] ICI Archive; Technical Reports, 22 November 1945. ICI Archive; Wilton File, letter from C. Bruce-Gardner (Board of Trade) to Sir Frederick Bain (ICI), 22 January 1945. W. Reader, *Imperial Chemical Industries*, Oxford, Oxford University Press, 1975, vol. II, p. 392. PRO T229/58, 'Investment Programmes – Petroleum', memorandum by B. J. Ellis, 30 October 1947.

[90] PRO CAB 134/439, IPC(48)8, Cabinet, Investment Programmes Committee, *Report on Capital Investment in 1949*, 16 July 1948, paras. 36, 93.

with crude oil through a 57-mile pipeline link.[91] At all levels, there was a scramble for construction plant, as the export drive took 48.8 per cent of all earth-moving machinery, 48.3 per cent of all excavators, and 33.1 per cent of all metal-working machine tools between 1948 and 1955.[92] Despite an increase in UK production of construction machinery, machinery was not always available for lower-priority, non-dollar-funded projects. Foundations were dug by spade-wielding men, a sight which while normal before the war had become a costly anachronism and source of delay.[93] While relief was gradually afforded by the importing of earth-moving equipment from the USA and Canada, transatlantic observers continued to be struck by the comparative shortage in Britain of modern plant such as excavators and cranes, as well as more modern material developments such as transit or ready-mixed concrete, which were much more common in USA.[94]

Apart from the difficulties with obtaining reliable statistics over the whole range of investment activity and the uncertainties surrounding the length of construction times, the third factor identified as affecting the planners' ability to secure their desired pattern of investment was their limited control over the plant, machinery, and vehicles components of total gross domestic fixed capital formation. In 1949, investment in plant and machinery accounted for 36.8 per cent, vehicles, ships, and aircraft for 18.0 per cent, and new buildings and works for 45.2 per cent of total gross domestic fixed capital formation. Of gross domestic fixed capital formation in manufacturing industry alone, on Blue Book definitions, plant and machinery accounted for 67.4 per cent, vehicles for 7.6 per cent, and new buildings and works for 25.1 per cent.[95] While the mix of building licences and direct controls

[91] The Federation of Civil Engineering Contractors, *The British Civil Engineering Contracting Industry: Illustrated History*, London, 1956, pp. 85–91. Gray and Abrams, *Fawley*, p. 5. PRO POWE 14/111 'Electricity Station Generating Programme'. PRO POWE 14/365, note to Mr Murphy from M. P. Murray, 5 July 1948. PRO POWE 14/115, Note by Mr F. W. Smith, 2 September 1948. W. Reader, *Imperial Chemical Industries*, vol. II, p. 391.

[92] *Monthly Digest of Statistics* (June 1952), No. 78, tables 65, 66, and 70 for the 1948–51 data and *Monthly Digest of Statistics* (August 1957), No. 140, tables 66, 67, and 71 for the 1952–5 data. *Annual Abstract of Statistics* (1954), No. 91, table 211.

[93] D. L. Burn, *The Steel Industry 1939–1959*, Cambridge, Cambridge University Press, 1961, p. 267, footnote 3.

[94] Anglo–American Council on Productivity, *Building*, paras. 24–6.

[95] The term 'Blue Books' is the common shorthand for the annual tables of *National Income and Expenditure* published by the Central Statistical office. In this case, see Central Statistical Office, *National Income and Expenditure 1946–1952*, London, HMSO, August 1953, Tables 43 and 44. Deviation estimates for manufacturing investment are deliberately excluded from Table 3.3 because the Investment Programmes Committee's own misgivings about its data on the plant and machinery component makes the calculation of dubious worth.

provided planners with some control over the new buildings and works component of gross domestic fixed capital formation, in comparison the control of plant and machinery was looser. Control over investment in plant and machinery had always been weak and it compounded the weakness of control over private industry, since, on IPC estimates, private firms and individuals accounted for 75 per cent of investment in plant and machinery in 1949, as well as 50 per cent of investment in building and civil engineering, and 61 per cent of total investment.[96] Although building controls had been retained, even if subsequently overloaded, after World War II, the wartime controls on plant and machinery which had covered about half the engineering industry had been greatly relaxed. While the absence of detailed control over plant and machinery was regarded as only a 'short-lived embarrassment' and preferable to detailed bureaucratic arrangements, it did make the control of investment in plant and machinery by private industry a highly unpredictable component in the IPC estimates.[97]

By 1953, of the 37.8 per cent of total investment designated by the IPC as 'uncontrolled', 99.4 per cent was accounted for by vehicles, plant, and machinery.[98] In Table 3.3, the most glaring deviation from the level of investment approved by the IPC is the level of actual investment in commercial goods vehicles, and, to a lesser extent, public-service vehicles. Here was a specific instance of the planning system struggling to contain fundamental market demand. In 1948, 9,000, rather than the approved 6,000, public-service vehicles, and 75,000 commercial vehicles, rather than the expected 50,000, went to the domestic market.[99] The high demand for public-service vehicles arose from a largely employed economy, the development of suburbs with longer distances between home and work, public commitments to improving services in rural areas, and the free transport provisions of the Education Act. In 1947, London Transport carried 11 per cent more passengers on trams, trolley vehicles, and buses than in 1938. Bristol Tramways and Carriage Company carried 27 per cent more. In

[96] PRO CAB 134/441, IPC(50)2, Cabinet, Investment Programmes Committee, *Report on Capital Investment in 1951 and 1952*, 24 April 1950, p. 12, Table 7.
[97] PRO CAB 134/188, IWP(46)4 (Revise), 'First Report by the Investment Working Party', 12 March 1946, para. 8.
[98] PRO CAB 134/982, IPC(53)2, Cabinet, Investment Programmes Committee, *Investment in 1953 and 1954*, note by the Joint Secretaries, Annex, 9 April 1953.
[99] PRO CAB 134/439, IPC(48)8, Cabinet, Investment Programmes Committee, *Report on Capital Investment in 1949*, 16 July 1948, para. 6. PRO CAB 134/442, IPC(51)1, Cabinet, Investment Programmes Committee, *Report on Capital Investment in 1951, 1952 and 1953*, 17 March 1951, p. 45, para. 165. In 1950, partly in response to the introduction of purchase tax, domestic demand fell with 15,000 fewer vehicles being purchased than in 1949.

both cities, the increase in passenger miles was even greater, being 31 per cent in London and 60 per cent in Bristol. By March 1948, the number of public-service passenger vehicles had been increased by 20 per cent to 63,000, compared with the pre-war figure of approximately 52,000. In London, there were regularly daily shortages of 300–400 vehicles, and the average life of vehicles lengthened from the pre-war average of 8 years to some 13 years for a quarter of the fleet, thus necessitating greater repairs and maintenance.[100] Similarly, in conditions of high demand, the demise of 50,000 commercial, licensed goods vehicles left the remaining stock of 450,000 struggling to meet demand. Although their number had risen to 800,000 by the end of 1949, these included worn-down ex-service vehicles and many others which would normally have been scrapped.[101]

The limited influence over the distribution of plant and machinery, and vehicles reflected the limited extent of the economic controls operated during the Attlee governments. The extent of controls was limited by considerations of bureaucracy and, more importantly, of civil liberties. Nowhere was this truer than in the planners' inability to influence the distribution of labour. While the planners effectively had little control over the movement of labour, one of the main purposes of their efforts to influence the level and pattern of investment was to affect the level and pattern of output, and in so doing to shift labour between industries. Yet, in a full-employment economy, there was very little certainty about where labour so released would go. This increasingly frustrated the Economic Survey Working Party, which in 1946, in attempting to switch labour between the Group I (investment and exports) to the Group III (consumer goods) industries, worried that even if other industries shed labour 'what means have we of securing that this labour would in fact go to those Group III industries where it is needed and not, for example, into distribution?'[102] By December 1946, the Economic Survey Working Party was arguing that 'the main obstacle to economic planning is the lack of adequate means for affecting the distribution of the labour force'.[103] During 1946 there was a widening recognition that achieving such labour switches formed 'perhaps the

[100] PRO CAB 134/439, IPC(48)8, Cabinet, Investment Programmes Committee, *Report on Capital Investment in 1949*, 16 July 1948, para. 143.
[101] PRO CAB 134/441, IPC(50)2, Cabinet, Investment Programmes Committee, *Report on Capital Investment in 1951 and 1952*, 24 April 1950, para. 137.
[102] PRO CAB 134/503, MEP(46)7, Cabinet, Ministerial Committee on Economic Planning, 'Economic Survey for 1946/7: Note by the Chairman of the Official Steering Committee on Economic Survey', 11 July 1946, para. 14.
[103] PRO CAB 134/503, MEP(46)15, Cabinet, Ministerial Committee on Economic Planning, 'Economic Survey for 1947: Report by the Economic Survey Working Party', 21 December 1946, p. 11, para. 35.

biggest single issue for economic planning in the next few years', and that as Thomas Balogh had observed, the sheer 'difficulty of transferring labour from one place to another, or from one type of work to another' had been 'vastly underestimated'.[104] One deflationary approach to the problem associated with Paish and Balogh was to consider engineering an increase in unemployment. However, quite apart from the political problems attending this strategy, opinion varied on how much unemployment was required. Balogh was alleged to favour unemployment of 1.5–2 million, while Meade was reported to consider an increase of 200,000 sufficient to encourage the desired labour mobility.[105] However, increased mobility would not necessarily solve problems of skill mismatch. Arguing against Meade's wish to present the Economic Survey in terms of national income and expenditure rather than manpower, Richard Clarke thought that not only was this more difficult for ministers to understand but that it also reflected an economist's unrealistic but 'implicit assumption that all types of resources are thoroughly mobile, both industrially and locationally and marketwise'.[106] Put more bluntly by Bevan, such assumptions that somehow 'a building worker in Liverpool became a cowman in Kent' would be seen as mere 'whistle blowing'.[107]

Fundamental issues of civil liberties ruled out direct controls over labour, although there were moments when planners toyed with introducing some such specific controls. The market approach of making significant adjustments to the relative wage structure was eschewed, for fear of precipitating an inflationary wage spiral and industrial unrest. By 1948, the inappropriate wage structure was effectively frozen by the wage-restraint agreement.[108] Denied the full use of market mechanisms, thinking did begin to drift towards more forcible means of alleviating specific labour shortages. In July 1946, the Ministerial Committee on Economic Planning considered directing a proportion of the labour employed in non-essential occupations into industries of national importance and stopping unemployment benefit

[104] PRO CAB 134/503, MEP(46)7, Cabinet, Ministerial Committee on Economic Planning, 'Economic Survey for 1946/7; Note by the Chairman of the Official Steering Committee on Economic Survey', 11 July 1946, para. 16.
[105] UGA McCance Papers, 24 Private Nuffield Conference, 'The Present Position of Controls', 27 June 1948. Balogh was later adviser to the Wilson governments and author of the *Irrelevance of Conventional Economics*, London, Weidenfeld & Nicolson, 1982.
[106] R. Clarke, *Anglo-American Economic Collaboration in War and Peace, 1942–1949*, Oxford, Clarendon Press, 1982, p. 77.
[107] M. Foot, *Aneurin Bevan*, vol. II, pbk, London, Granada, 1979, p. 93.
[108] Cmd 7321, Prime Minister, *Statement on Personal Incomes, Costs and Prices*, London, HMSO, 1948.

when jobs offered by the Ministry of Labour were persistently refused.[109] Towards the end of 1946, among tough measures submitted by the Economic Steering Committee for ministerial consideration was one for the conscription of young women into national service, so that they could be directed into industries such as textiles. Although agreed by the Ministerial Planning Committee, this idea was rejected in Cabinet.[110] In coal mining, Douglas Jay argued that 'all unemployed men in coal-mining districts [particularly in Development Areas] should be personally interviewed by the Ministry of Labour and urged pointedly to go into the Coal Industry'.[111] Looking across the Channel, economic advisers urged a greater imitation of the French use of foreign labour, despite the implications for housing.[112] The Cabinet was more hesitant, fearing that the use of prisoner-of-war labour might provoke strikes in the collieries. The National Union of Mineworkers, although seemingly prepared to accept Italian prisoners-of-war in mines, objected to the employment of Poles, who were employed more successfully in agriculture.[113] Meade, Chantler, Jay, Nicolson, and Tress all tried to make the introduction of the five-day week in coal mining conditional on the greater use of foreign labour, a link which was supported by Morrison, 'xenophobe though he is', but which did not prevail with Shinwell, who, in Meade's view, seemed to have 'got away with approval of the five-day week without any precise condition about the introduction of foreign labour'.[114] Perhaps resistance to new conditions was less

[109] PRO CAB 134/503, MEP(46)8, Cabinet, Ministerial Committee on Economic Planning, 'Diversion of Labour to Industries of National Importance', 17 July 1946, and LP(46)25 Meeting, Minutes of meeting, 12 July 1946.

[110] R. Clarke, *Anglo–American Economic Collaboration*, p. 78.

[111] PRO CAB 124/706, 'Coal crisis', paper by Douglas Jay, sent to J. A. R. Pimlott (Office of the Lord President), 19 June 1946, p. 2, para. 3. PRO CAB 134/503, MEP(46)7, Cabinet, Ministerial Committee on Economic Planning, 'Economic Survey for 1946/47: Note by the Chairman of the Official Steering Committee on Economic Survey', 11 July 1946, para. 18. The Working Party thought that 'the coal situation illustrates an important limitation on the possibilities of economic planning as an instrument of Government viz. the difficulty of making quick adjustments to remedy deep-seated industrial problems when they have been foreseen'.

[112] PRO CAB 124/706, LP(46)53, 'Statistical Report (Coal) for January 1946', memo from Nita Watts to Lord President, 7 March 1946. PRO CAB 134/503, MEP(46)15, Cabinet, Ministerial Committee on Economic Planning, 'Economic Survey for 1947: Report by the Economic Survey Working Party', 21 December 1946, para. 62.

[113] PRO CAB 124/707, 'Recruitment to the Coal Mining Industry: Memorandum by the Parliamentary Secretary to the Ministry of Fuel and Power', LP(46)173, Memo by R. Tress to Lord President, 10 July 1946.

[114] PRO CAB 124/706, CP(46)232, 'Output, Recruitment and Conditions of Employment in the Coal-Mining Industry', Note from J. E. Meade to Lord President, 19 June 1946, para. 2. Meade, *The Collected Papers of James Meade: Vol. IV, The Cabinet Office, 1944–46*, ed. S. Howson and D. Moggridge, London, Unwin Hyman, 1990, pp. 286–7, 30 June 1946.

in defeated countries; it certainly appeared easier to get labour to work longer and alongside foreign labour in such countries, the Economic Section noting approvingly in 1947 that 'Monnet has obtained appreciation of need for 48-hour week and for foreign labour. This sort of thing badly needed here.' However, Monnet was not considered to have made any more progress than the British planners in 'getting Jean and Jacques to go to this occupation rather than that'.[115]

The limited control of plant and machinery and the effective absence of control over the distribution of labour pointed up the limitations of what planners were able and attempting to achieve. Their main ambition was to use such controls as they had to target controlled resources towards the high-priority industries, among which the nationalised industries, highly concentrated private industries, and large government departmental investment programmes were the most amenable to such planning. Yet, even here the planners' influence was variable and unlikely to encourage notions of any ability to engage in 'fine-tuning'. These problems were as little, however, when set against their very limited ability to influence private industrial investment. Although planners might be able to stop projects, their instruments for influencing the pattern of investment undertaken by private industry were blunt, of which the planners in the CEPS and the IPC were well aware. As reconversion progressed and controls disappeared, the planners' powers to influence investment would inevitably weaken and give way to the no more certain instruments of fiscal and depreciation manipulation. Even so, what the central planning system from 1947 did provide was an ability within government to force politicians to address issues, to attempt to balance supply and demand, and to set priorities. Even when on its last legs in 1953, this was a discipline which the remaining planners were reluctant to lose, and which arguably had a purpose surviving beyond the passing of controls.

[115] PRO T230/24, Economic Section papers on the Monnet Plan, various.

4   Nationalisation

Of all the Attlee governments' economic policies, it is the nationalisation programme with which they are most immediately identified. Between 1945 and 1951, gas, electricity, coal, railways, inland waterways, road transport, airlines, and iron and steel were all nationalised and established anew as public corporations.[1] By 1951, public corporations accounted for 19.5 per cent of gross fixed capital formation.[2] Certain characteristics were common to many of these industries: their operation was often attended by externalities and spillovers, where the social value of output exceeded its private value; many of them were important areas of fixed capital investment, often containing a natural monopoly component, where the minimum efficient scale was large relative to the size of the market, and unusually subject to decreasing costs; their output was widely used by an electorate which had a persistent interest in its availability and price.

These characteristics had prompted central and local government involvement in many of these industries which considerably pre-dated nationalisation. Since the nineteenth century, municipal government had been interested in the safety of utility supply and the external benefits of the wider supply of mains water, gas, and electricity. This concern with externalities coincided and blended with an emerging public concern to extend availability of output.[3] This interest was sufficiently great for the number of publicly owned water undertakings to treble from 250 to 786 in the period from 1871 to 1915, with approximately 80 per cent of authorised water undertakings being in

---

[1] Other nationalisations included the Bank of England. See J. Fforde, *The Bank of England and Public Policy, 1941–1958*, Cambridge, Cambridge University Press, 1992, ch. 1.

[2] Central Statistical Office, *National Income and Expenditure, 1946–1952*, London, HMSO, August 1953, Table 39.

[3] M. Falkus, 'The Development of Municipal Trading in the Nineteenth Century', *Business History*, 19, 2 (July 1977), pp. 134–61. J. Hassan, 'The Growth and Impact of the British Water Industry in the Nineteenth Century', *Economic History Review*, 38, 4 (November 1985), pp. 531–47. D. Matthews, 'Laissez-faire and the London Gas Industry in the Nineteenth Century: Another Look', *Economic History Review*, 39, 2 (1986), pp. 244–63.

municipal hands by 1912–15.[4] On the eve of World War I there were 300 publicly owned gas enterprises, accounting for nearly 40 per cent of the total of authorised undertakings.[5]

After World War I, central government extended its involvement in the regulation, organisation, and ownership of transport and energy utilities.[6] In the railways, there was growing support for amalgamations, Churchill's 1909 view that 'there is no real economic future for British railways apart from amalgamation of one kind or another' reflecting a growing opinion among independent, informed observers.[7] After World War I, the railways narrowly avoided being nationalised, being subject instead to an enforced amalgamation into four main-line railways in the Railways Act of 1921.[8] Government intervention to improve the efficiency of network industries became a common theme of inter-war central and local government involvement in network industries. In the early twentieth century, central government was increasingly lobbied by industrial groups to resolve a fundamental problem in electricity generation arising from the historical development of the industry. Technological progress facilitated the generation of electricity in ever-larger sets, in which economies of scale caused unit costs to fall. However, the character of the development of the electricity generating industry in Britain resulted in electricity coming to be generated by a myriad of small local monopolies whose markets were too small, as well as free of competition, to provide any incentive to purchase the larger and more efficient plant. By the 1920s, London could have been supplied by four of the most modern power stations instead of the seventy undertakings which were operating. Pressure from industrial users pushed the Conservative Baldwin government into appointing the Weir Committee in 1925, whose main recommendation was the establishment of a Central Electricity Board (CEB), in 1926, which would supervise the construction of a national grid network.[9] This would provide 'selected' generators with access to a

[4] R. Millward, 'Privatisation in Historical Perspective: the UK Water Industry', in David Cobham, Richard Harrington, and George Zis (eds.), *Money, Trade and Payments*, Manchester, Manchester University Press, 1989, pp. 205–6.

[5] R. Millward, 'Emergence of Gas and Water Monopolies in Nineteenth Century Britain: Contested Markets and Public Control', in J. Foreman-Peck (ed.), *New Perspectives on the Late Victorian Economy*, Cambridge, Cambridge University Press, 1991, p. 117.

[6] R. Millward and J. Singleton (eds.), *The Political Economy of Nationalisation in Britain, 1920–50*, Cambridge, Cambridge University Press, 1995. M. Chick, 'Nationalisation and the Background to Recent Regulatory Issues', in R. Sugden (ed.), *Industrial Economic Regulation*, London, Routledge, 1993, pp. 63–84.

[7] C. D. Foster, *Privatisation, Public Ownership and the Regulation of Natural Monopoly*, Oxford, Clarendon Press, 1992, p. 56.

[8] Foster, *Privatisation*, p. 59.

[9] L. Hannah, 'A Pioneer of Public Enterprise: The Central Electricity Board and the

larger national market, as well as introducing competition between generators. Crucially, it circumvented the issue of transferring ownership, since the ownership of generating stations was left untouched.

The CEB was very successful, initiating a series of productivity improvements whereby, from generating 443 units of electricity per ton of coal in 1914, and 631 units in 1920, output rose to 1,566 units per ton by 1939. Rising efficiency was reflected in falling prices, the cost of electricity 'at the busbars' (the point at which electricity entered the transmission or distribution system) falling from 1.098d per unit in 1923, to an average of 0.34d per unit in 1936 and 0.39d per unit in 1940.[10] By the late 1930s, the gap which had existed in the 1920s between the thermal efficiency of British and US power stations had virtually been closed.[11] The main sources of productivity improvement were the improved generation of electricity by stations selected by the CEB, the introduction of the merit-order system, a rescheduling of the base load, and a reduced use of higher marginal cost stations for peak load and back-up. In general, productivity benefits derived from increasing the average scale of operations, rather than increasing the rate of technical progress.[12] Somewhat paradoxically, the Conservative government facilitated greater market competition by constructing a natural monopoly.

The neatness of an explanation centring on networks, externalities, and the price and availability of output is spoilt by some notable exceptions. A utility, such as water, which possessed all of these characteristics was not nationalised, although it might well have been had the Attlee government been re-elected in October 1951.[13] Equally, coal mining, which was nationalised in 1947, possessed neither a natural monopoly network nor, in those less environmentally concerned days, particularly large externalities in its operation. Neither did iron and steel, which was nationalised in 1951 and 'privatised' from 1953. Not sharing many of the characteristics common to the nationalised utilities, it is perhaps significant that the nationalisations of coal mining and iron and steel were respectively the most politically significant and contentious of the nationalisations effected by the Attlee governments.

National Grid, 1927–1940', in B. Supple (ed.), *Essays in British Business History*, Oxford, Clarendon Press, 1977, pp. 207–26.

[10] Hannah, 'Pioneer of Public Enterprise', p. 223.

[11] J. Foreman-Peck and R. Millward, *Public and Private Ownership of British Industry 1820–1990*, Oxford, Clarendon Press, 1994, p. 281.

[12] J. Foreman-Peck and C. Hammond, 'Closing the Productivity Gap: the Achievements of Central Planning in the British Electricity Supply Industry during the 1930s', unpublished discussion paper.

[13] J. A. Hassan, 'The Water Industry 1900–51: a Failure of Public Policy', in Millward and Singleton (eds.), *Political Economy*, pp. 189–211.

More than any other nationalisation, that of coal mining centred on the inadequacies and failings of private ownership, whereas that of iron and steel raised similarly serious questions as to what advantages were to be gained by transferring the industry from private to public ownership. What coal mining and iron and steel did have in common with many of the other nationalised industries was that they too had experienced government involvement in their industries during the inter-war period. In the Coal Mines Act of 1930, job-saving state-sponsored cartels were established in each of the coal fields, with the accompanying Liberal-inspired provision that owners would work with the newly created Coal Mines Reorganisation Commission to restructure the industry into larger and, it was assumed, more efficient, competitive productive units.[14] The assumption made was that a reorganisation of each industry into larger units would provide a greater opportunity to exploit economies of scale, increase productivity, and thereby improve international competitiveness. In 1932, the iron and steel industry had gained additional tariff protection, again in return for assurances of working with the Import Duties Advisory Committee to effect a productivity-improving restructuring of their industry. Such public intervention for this purpose was not new. It characterised the 1921 Railway Reorganisation Act and the establishment of the CEB in 1926. The absence of networks in coal and iron and steel meant that reorganisation would have to be effected by the existing private owners. In coal mining, all the major reports on the industry's condition, whether by Sankey in 1919, Samuel in 1925 or Reid in 1945 were interpreted as pointing to a route to improved productivity and international competitiveness through changes to the structure of the industry.[15] The statistics of the industry's conditions were frequently recited, not least in internal Labour Party documents on coal. In the mid-1920s, of a total of 2,481 pits, one-third employed fewer than 50 men, produced less than 1 per cent of total output, and employed just over 1 per cent of total workers. Another third had 50–500 workers, and produced one-sixth of total output. The 2,481 pits were owned by over 1,400 separate undertakings, of which 685 employed fewer than 100 workers each, and some 780 produced under 5,000 tons a year each.

[14] J. Foreman-Peck and R. Millward, *Public and Private Ownership*, p. 287. B. Supple, 'Ideology or Pragmatism? The Nationalisation of Coal, 1916–46', in N. McKendrick and R. B. Outhwaite (eds.), *Business Life and Public Policy*, Cambridge, Cambridge University Press, 1986, pp. 236–40.

[15] M. W. Kirby, 'The Control of Competition in the Coal Mining Industry in the Thirties', *Economic History Review*, 26 (1973), pp. 273–84. N. K. Buxton, 'Entrepreneurial Efficiency in the British Coal Industry between the Wars', *Economic History Review*, 23 (1970), pp. 476–97.

The mines were old and worn out – 4 of every 100 medium- and large-size pits were over 100 years old, 13 over 70 years old, and another third over 50 years old.[16] While from the mid-1920s to the cyclical maximum of 1936, output per manshift (OMS) rose by 118 per cent in the Netherlands, 81 per cent in the Ruhr, and 54 per cent in Poland, in Britain it rose by only 14 per cent. By 1936, OMS averaged 35.94 cwt (hundred weight) in the Netherlands and 33.66 cwt in the Ruhr, compared with only 23.54 cwt in Britain.[17] That a relative productivity problem existed seemed clear, but both owners then and some researchers since have doubted whether there was ever such a simple, strong, positive relationship between mine size and productivity as tended to be claimed by advocates of nationalisation.[18]

That coal owners were not successful in making this case at the time reflected in part the increasingly political, rather than purely economic, perspective from which the industry's problems were discussed. Important in this development was the fate of the Coal Mines Reorganisation Commission. While the owners enjoyed the cartel arrangements, they also used their parliamentary influence to neuter the Commission. An ineffective Commission and the operation of quotas characterised a period in which the structure of the industry was effectively frozen, with inadequate use being made of the most efficient pits in the Midlands. By 1938, only 12.6 per cent of British coal came from high-productivity pits in north Derbyshire and Nottinghamshire, a figure not much above the 11.2 per cent share in 1929.[19] The sight of owners taking public protection while obstructing the work of the Commission and stifling productivity improvement in the industry was politically unappealing. Not only was it unattractive, but it seemed to confirm wider change in attitudes towards businessmen as a breed. This was noted by Keynes at the start of the 1930s:

In short, the average businessman is no longer envisaged as the feverishly active and alert figure of the classical economists, who never missed a chance of making a penny if it was humanly possible, and was always in a state of stimulus up to the limit of his capacity. The new view of him seems to be that he is a

[16] LPA RD8, paper on 'Coal', November 1945, p. 2.
[17] Ministry of Fuel and Power, *Coal Mining: Report of the Technical Advisory Committee*, Cmd. 6610 (Reid Report), 1945, p. 29. W. Ashworth, *The History of the British Coal Industry, vol. V, 1946–1982: the Nationalised Industry*, Oxford, Clarendon Press, 1986. B. Supple, *The History of the British Coal Industry*, vol. IV, Oxford, Clarendon Press, 1987, p. 285.
[18] D. Greasley, 'The Coal Industry: Images and Realities on the Road to Nationalisation', in R. Millward and J. Singleton (eds.), *Political Economy*, p. 44. M. Kirby, 'The Control of Competition', *Economic History Review*, 26 (1973), p. 281.
[19] Greasley, 'The Coal Industry', in Millward and Singleton (eds.), *Political Economy*, p. 42.

fellow who is easy-going and content with a given income and does not bestir himself unduly to increase it to what would be for him the maximum attainable.[20]

Clearly, this was a broad generalisation, but it was supported by particularly acidic contemporary criticism of the owners in the older coal-mining, iron and steel, and textile industries. Famously, there was Lord Birkenhead's remark that 'it would be possible to say without exaggeration that the miners' leaders were the stupidest men in England if we had not had frequent occasion to meet the owners'.[21] Keynes himself was withering about the 'bone-headedness' of many textile owners, those 'old jossers who want to live the rest of their lives in peace'.[22] To this scorn, was added increasingly concerned references to the powers of vested interests. In April 1935, Sir Ernest Gowers, the oft-frustrated Chairman of the Coal Mines Reorganisation Commission, reported to government that 'public opinion is now . . . sick of the obstructiveness of the old school of employers in coal, cotton and iron and steel'.[23] In iron and steel, aspirant reformers such as William Firth of Richard Thomas wrote to *The Times* in 1934 complaining 'of the futility of hoping that individuals will subordinate their private interests to national interests'.[24] While Keynes in the concluding paragraph of *The General Theory of Employment, Interest and Money*, published in 1936, was 'sure that the power of vested interests is vastly exaggerated compared with the gradual encroachment of ideas', he none the less tacitly recognised the contemporary concern with vested interests.[25] Within the Labour Party, with Clause IV in its constitution since January 1918, there was growing concern with vested interests, ownership structures, and the extent of interlocking directorates within industries like iron and steel.[26] Internal research papers pointed to an

[20] J. M. Keynes, 'The Question of High Wages', *The Political Quarterly* (January–March 1930), pp. 5–6, in D. Moggridge (ed.), *The Collected Writings of John Maynard Keynes*, vol. XX, *Activities 1929–31*, Macmillan and Cambridge University Press, 1981.

[21] B. Fine, *The Coal Question: Political Economy and Industrial Change from the Nineteenth Century to the Present Day*, London, Routledge, 1990, p. 19. Quoted in D. Greasley, 'The Coal Industry', in Millward and Singleton, *Political Economy*, p. 50.

[22] M. Dupree, *Lancashire and Whitehall*, Manchester, Manchester University Press, 1987, p. 181. BLPES, Dalton papers, D1/30, p. 26, 31 January 1944. Quoted in J. Singleton, *Lancashire on the Scrapheap: The Cotton Industry 1945–1970*, Oxford, Oxford University Press, p. 28.

[23] Gowers was Chairman of both the Coal Mines Reorganisation Commission from 1930 and of its successor, the Coal Commission, from 1938. Supple, *British Coal*, vol. IV, p. 347.

[24] LPA RD 140, 'British Steel at Britain's Service', August 1948. William Firth, letter to *The Times*, 22 February 1934.

[25] J. M. Keynes, *The General Theory of Employment, Interest and Money*, London, Macmillan, 1936; pbk edn 1974, pp. 383–4.

[26] Since January 1918, Clause IV of the Labour Party's constitution had stated the party's

iron and steel industry in which the directors of the 'Big Six' companies controlled about 100 subsidiaries and held about 600 seats on the boards of other companies. Leading examples cited included the Earl of Dudley with twenty-one directorships, Lord Greenwood seventeen, Menzies-Wilson with twenty-one, A. G. Steward with nineteen, S. R. Beale with twenty, and Sir James Craig with twenty-one.[27]

Frustration with private owners, vested interests, and missed productivity improvements was not necessarily sufficient to legitimise the expropriation of property from private owners. What provided much of the professed legitimacy and context for the move to nationalisation were developments in government thinking and public opinion during World War II. An immediate effect of war and of wartime economic planning was to bring temporary civil servants such as John Fulton and Harold Wilson into much closer day-to-day contact with an industry such as coal mining. His ringside seat, enabling him to view at first hand the problems of this industry, in which wartime output fell year by year, while absenteeism rose, led Harold Wilson in 1945 to write a scathing book, *New Deal for Coal*, among whose criticisms industrial relations were characterised as akin to 'guerrilla warfare'. When the 1945 Reid Report of senior mining engineers reaffirmed the superior productivity of the Ruhr, the Netherlands, and Poland as well as the technical case for the reorganisation, if not the nationalisation, of the industry, many commentators had difficulty thinking of other options other than nationalisation which would enable reorganisation to be effected.[28] Even had the Conservatives been elected in 1945, it seems probable that coal mining would have been nationalised.[29] Suggestions from the owners in the Foot Plan that they might supervise the reorganisation of the industry were dismissed by Wilson as 'Bourbon self-government'. As the Labour Party's internal research paper, 'Coal', asked:

Can this huge recasting of the industry's structure, demanded by the Reid Committee, the Scottish Coalfields Committee and others, ever be realised by the mine owners? The whole history of the industry since 1930 makes the idea laughable . . . Nor will a revived, strengthened Coal Commission fit our needs. For if such bodies at last become effective, the coal-owners become useless

commitment 'to secure for the producers by hand and brain the full fruits of their industry, and the most equitable distribution thereof that may be possible, upon the basis of the common ownership of the means of production and the best obtainable system of popular administration and control of each industry or service'.

[27] LPA RD 140, 'British Steel at Britain's Service', August 1948.

[28] Cmd 6610, *Report of the Coalmining Technical Advisory Committee*, 1944–5. Greasley, in Millward and Singleton (eds.), *Political Economy*, p. 50. Foreman-Peck and Millward, *Public and Private Ownership*, pp. 287–8.

[29] M. Kirby, *The British Coal Mining Industry, 1870–1946*, London, Macmillan, 1977, p. 197.

appendages, playing no useful part in the industry but retaining some of their power to hamper and harass the controlling authorities.[30]

The wartime experience seemed to many to demonstrate that nationalisation was the only remaining hope of reorganising an industry which was in effect in long-term, historical decline. Its compatriot in twentieth-century decline, the railway industry, also emerged from World War II with the case for a nationally organised railway industry strengthened.[31] In both industries, but especially in coal, there were long-established links between the unions and the Labour Party. By contrast, other industries which were also nationalised, notably electricity, shared few of these characteristics. The electricity industry was capital, not labour, intensive, and it was very much in the historic ascendant. In electricity, there was no immediately apparent reason for nationalising the entire industry. The very success of the grid indicated how a mix of private generators and public networks could operate very successfully. Indeed, in recommending the establishment of the CEB, the Weir Committee had explicitly proposed not a 'change in ownership, but the partial subordination of vested interests in generation to that of a new authority for the benefit of all . . . in a manner which will preserve the value of the incentive of private enterprise'.[32]

The decision to nationalise the entire electricity industry reflected the increased importance of political and social-welfare arguments for nationalisation which had developed during the war. One such argument was the desirability of extending electricity supply to rural areas and sections of urban conurbations, which the market was less willing to supply. Calls for increasing the availability of electricity had grown during the 1930s, and were supported not only by the rural communities but also by the one-fifth of urban areas which were without distributing mains in 1934.[33] Herbert Morrison, as Minister of Transport in the minority Labour government of 1929–31, had been keen to extend supply and to reorganise all the existing undertakings under regional, publicly owned distribution boards supplying large areas in which alleged improvements in load factor could be achieved.[34] Extension of supply drew strong support from the 1936 McGowan Committee, which was concerned with the efficiency of the distribution

[30] LPA RD 8, 'Coal', November 1945.
[31] G. Crompton, 'The Railway Companies and the Nationalisation Issue 1920–50', in Millward and Singleton (eds.), *Political Economy*, pp. 116–43.
[32] Hannah, 'Pioneer of Public Enterprise', p. 210.
[33] PRO CAB 27/617, Report of the Committee on Electricity Distribution, May 1936, paras. 104–5, 359–60.
[34] L. Hannah, *Electricity before Nationalisation*, London, Macmillan, 1979, p. 239.

side of the industry.[35] While across the country as a whole the average cost of generation had fallen, from 0.9675d per unit sold in 1924–5 to 0.5231d in 1933–4, representing a reduction of 46 per cent in what may be termed the wholesale cost, by contrast the average cost of electrical energy attributable to local distribution had risen from 0.7573d per unit sold in 1924–5 to 0.8278d in 1931–2. Of the 635 separate undertakings in existence at the end of 1933–4, some 400 were selling under 10 million units per annum, less than 10 per cent of the sales of all 635 undertakings. The initial aim of the McGowan Committee, to reduce the existing total of some 640 undertakings to about 250 by allowing the larger and more efficient undertakings to absorb their smaller brethren in a gradual process taking some fifty years, ran into the parliamentary sand, which seemed to confirm suspicions of the obstructionist activities of vested interests.[36]

One domestic effect of the experience of total war was to raise expectations and reduce tolerance of inaction. Having initially used the disturbance of war to suspend discussion of the industry's future, by 1942 the subject was back on the agenda and being discussed in a markedly changed manner. Notable was the report by Sir William Jowitt, the Paymaster General, who was asked to take charge of reconstruction questions in March 1942 and, by August of the same year, had completed his report on the electricity industry. Jowitt's report marked a shift away from the 'evolutionary' scheme of the McGowan Committee. Jowitt regarded the case for reorganisation as being so self-evident as to require no further 'commission or fact-finding enquiry to take place'. Equally, as Jowitt emphasised, 'it is quite obvious that it is useless to rely on any voluntary system of reorganisation'. Arguing that the McGowan Report was 'obsolete', Jowitt recommended a solution rejected by the McGowan Committee, 'namely a complete reorganisation on a regional basis under public control by the setting up of regional boards which would buy out all existing undertakings. It is very possible, indeed, that if the McGowan Commission were sitting after three years of war they would have come to the same conclusion.' Jowitt's reading of the 'political situation' in 1942 led him to 'think that we should not hesitate to embark on bold measures of reconstruction which will appeal to the imagination of the public. There surely comes a time in the history of a nation when he who tinkers is lost.'[37]

---

[35] M. Chick, 'The Political Economy of Nationalisation: the Electricity Industry', in Millward and Singleton (eds.), *Political Economy*, pp. 257–74.

[36] PRO CAB 27/617, CP(64)37, Cabinet, Committee on Electricity Distribution, Second Report, 17 February 1937, paras. 4, 5, 420.

[37] PRO CAB 87/4, RP(42)37, War Cabinet, Committee on Reconstruction Problems,

Part of this shift in and heightening of opinion stemmed from a change in public expectations during total war. One such conviction was that electricity was not a luxury for higher-income and urban groups, but a basic necessity. In Jowitt's view, 'The Public have increasingly come to regard electricity as a necessity and not a mere luxury: and it should be regarded from the same point of view as sewerage or water.'[38] Public ownership could improve availability, not only by laying mains but also by cross-subsidising prices, so that high-cost consumers were not paying the full costs of supplying them. The proposal by the 1943 Sub-Committee on the Future of the Electricity Industry for the replacement of the 580 distribution undertakings by 14 Regional Distribution Boards attracted Morrison, as it seemed likely to facilitate his strong preference for uniformity of charges and ultimately 'postalisation' of prices.[39] These pricing ambitions would be assisted by the transfer of the generating side of the industry into public ownership. For Morrison, low uniform prices, efficiency and availability were all linked, since for him 'the fundamental purpose of nationalisation was . . . to secure greater efficiency in the industry . . . to reduce costs and provide surplus funds which could be used to extend the benefits of cheap electricity to rural areas where . . . electricity was either not available or unreasonably expensive'.[40] This growth of considerations of redistribution and social welfare was an important influence in the selection of industries for the first programme of nationalisation. In Labour Party headquarters, there were long lists of industries which could be considered for nationalisation. The much shorter list of industries which actually were nationalised contained a high proportion of those industries whose output in its price and availability fed directly into the household budget. At its crudest, it could be argued that anything supplied to the household kitchen was of interest to a nationalising government. Gas, electricity, coal, and even sugar were items of daily household consumption. Conversely, although there may

---

'Report on the Electricity Industry by the Paymaster General', 7 August 1942, paras. 9, 14, 24.
[38] PRO CAB 87/4, RP(42)37, War Cabinet, Committee on Reconstruction Problems, 'Report on the Electricity Industry by the Paymaster General', 7 August 1942, para. 20.
[39] PRO CAB 87/4, RP(ES)(43)36/46 (Final), War Cabinet, Reconstruction Committee, Report of the Sub-Committee on the Future of the Electricity Industry, 30 December 1943, para. 17. PRO CAB 27/617, CP288(36), Cabinet, Committee on Electricity Distribution, Second Report, 17 February 1937, para. 13. LPA Policy No. 56, H. Morrison, 'Reorganisation of Electricity', June 1932. PRO CAB 21/2208, Lord President's Office, Extract of Minutes of SI(M)(46)9 meeting, 22 May 1946.
[40] PRO CAB 21/2208, Lord President's Office, Extract of Minutes of SI(M)(46)9 meeting, 22 May 1946.

be other reasons for nationalising industries such as steel and shipbuilding, these did not carry the same 'kitchen' imperative.

While a complex of motives can be discerned for the transfer of ownership which constituted nationalisation, what also requires explanation is why industries were transferred into public ownership as national monopolies. Although common bed-fellows, there was no compelling reason why nationalisation and monopoly should have been so frequently coupled. As has been seen, there was no economic reason why the generating section of the electricity industry needed to be included in the nationalised electricity monopoly. If nationalisation was required to reorganise industrial structure, then why not sell all or part of the reorganised industries back into private ownership? Alternatively, the state might choose, for example, to compete within an industry against incumbent private producers. As it was, on vesting day, many industries were compressed into a monopoly. The 3,766 independent management units in the road-haulage industry became one single unit, as did the 1,000 in gas, the 560 in electricity, and the 800 in coal.[41] Competition within each industry, whether actual or potential, ceased. Whereas before the war, the largest unified organisations had been the General Post Office, and the London, Midland and Scottish Railway, with 231,877 and 222,220 employees respectively in 1935, after nationalisation, the National Coal Board acquired a labour force reaching 704,000 in 1955, and the nationalised transport services under the British Transport Commission employed 801,199 people.[42] Initially, it does look strange that a government which was initiating such anti-monopoly legislation as the 1948 Monopoly and Restrictive Practices Act should supervise the establishment of national monopolies in the utility and basic sector industries.[43] As has been seen, one of the immediate political attractions of forming the generating, network, and distribution sections of the electricity industry into a monopoly was the enhanced opportunity this provided for increasing the availability of and influencing the price of output. The fact that this monopoly industry was in public ownership was thought likely to prevent it from abusing its monopoly position. A fundamental assumption made was that with ownership came enhanced control, and that this control was greater

---

[41] A. Cairncross, *Years of Recovery: British Economic Policy 1945–51*, London, Methuen, 1985; university pbk 1987, p. 476.

[42] D. Jeremy, 'The Hundred Largest Employers in the United Kingdom in Manufacturing and Non-Manufacturing Industries in 1907, 1935 and 1955', *Business History*, 33, 1 (January 1991), pp. 93–111. In 1955, the General Post Office had 337,465 employees and the BEA 190,022.

[43] H. Mercer, *Constructing a Competitive Order: the Hidden History of British Anti-Trust Policies*, Cambridge, Cambridge University Press, 1995, ch. 5.

than that available through regulation, as pre-World War II evidence seemed to confirm.

That public ownership should have been regarded as providing improved control over monopolies was important, since Labour Party research documents frequently referred to 'significant and persistent features' of the twentieth-century British economy as being the 'growth of monopoly and the decline of competition'.[44] The increasing capital intensity of production was held to provide increasing incentives for producers to form price and output agreements. Labour Party documents advocating the nationalisation of the steel industry emphasised that it was 'important to recognise that monopoly is inevitable in the steel industry'. Given the capital intensity of production-scale economies and the high fixed costs of plant 'it would be idle to expect competition; the steel firms stand to lose too much'.[45] Some defence of competition could be provided by anti-trust legislation,[46] yet where monopolies were regarded as being virtually inevitable, then public ownership was held to be a more effective check against the abuse of their monopoly position. As the 1946 Labour Party document on the 'Criteria for Nationalisation' stated: 'Monopolies are objectionable and should, other things being equal, be transferred to public ownership.'[47]

Once transferred into public ownership, the very monopoly structure of the nationalised industries could be seen as offering scope for improved 'planning' and 'co-ordination'. Central control of industries such as steel were seen as offering better opportunities for enabling 'investment and production' to be 'closely balanced with demand', something which could 'only be done if both are centrally controlled. Under capitalism, or socialism, central control is required.'[48] Monopoly, by removing competition and supply-side uncertainty, could also be expected to lead to higher-quality fixed capital investment decisions, in which 'long-term' considerations would play a greater role.[49] As significant areas of capital investment, ownership, and, therefore, presumed control of their investment activity was also expected to play a useful role in the macro-economic, counter-cyclical management of effective demand.[50] Quite what role would be assigned to such market

[44] LPA RD 44, 'The Public Control of Monopoly', February 1947.
[45] LPA RD 140, 'British Steel at Britain's Service', August 1948.
[46] LPA RD 44, 'The Public Control of Monopoly', February 1947.
[47] LPA RD 33, 'Criteria for Nationalisation', November, 1946.
[48] LPA RD 140, 'British Steel at Britain's Service', August 1948.
[49] G. B. Richardson, *Information and Investment*, Oxford, Clarendon Press, 1960.
[50] 'The Socialisation of Industries: Memorandum by the Economic Section of the Cabinet Secretariat', in S. Howson (ed.), *The Collected Papers of James Meade*, vol. II, London, Allen & Unwin, 1988, p. 75.

mechanisms as price signals in the central balancing of investment and demand was not made clear, in part because such market mechanisms were held in a certain disrepute. Accompanying the pessimistic view of the potential for competition in an increasingly capital-intensive economy was an absence of faith in the ability of 'free markets' both to operate and to produce the outcomes credited to them by their supporters. There was particular scepticism for those who 'advocate free enterprise' and 'rest their case upon the theory of competition'. The argument that competition 'exerts a continuous downward pressure upon prices, so that only the most efficient and up-to-date firms can survive' was disputed. Even leaving aside the collusion which was held to exist in many industries, competition itself was regarded as being very slow and imperfect. That the range of costs in an industry could be 'staggeringly large' and yet without the inefficient being 'ruthlessly driven out' was held to arise to a great extent from 'the lack of standardisation which enables each firm to establish a limited monopoly in a brand of a particular commodity'. Monopoly arising from product differences was strengthened by advertising, which emphasised differences between brands.[51]

Having decided to legislate for the establishment of nationalised monopolies, the immediate task was to decide on what guiding principles on such issues as organisation and pricing should be written into the nationalising legislation. The arguments over pricing are discussed in the following chapter. Arguments over organisational structure generally divided people into those in favour of either centralised or decentralised arrangements, with the wider implications of this choice being drawn out by Peter Drucker, extracts of whose recently published book, *Big Business*, were circulated by Morrison to members of the Committee on the Socialisation of Industries:

The importance of the question whether decentralisation is absolutely more efficient than centralisation does not lie, primarily, in its application to business management. It is actually the question whether a socialist economy can be as efficient economically as a free-enterprise economy . . . The difference between the free-enterprise system and state socialism or state capitalism is the dependence of the former on the market as the determinant of prices, profitability and production. The chief argument in favour of the greater economic efficiency of the free-enterprise system has always been the effect of the competitive market check. The main counter-argument has always been that the market check can be replaced by cost accounting and by 'socialist competition', that is by cost efficiency alone . . . On the whole a centralised organisation, even if its cost accounting is anchored in a genuine market, is

[51] LPA RD1, 'A Labour Policy for Privately Owned Industry', September 1945.

inferior in productive efficiency to a decentralised organisation with its immediate double check of cost accounting and the market.[52]

Morrison's preference was for 'socialist competition', with competition being achieved through the publication of 'regional statistics' and the circulation of 'ideas coming from the regions, so as to stimulate initiative and emulation'.[53]

In Drucker's view, based on his examination of large enterprises in the USA in general, and of General Motors in particular, central headquarters should take responsibility for financial and legal matters, the supervision and management of a uniform accounting system, the handling of most union contracts and all labour negotiations.[54] The responsibility for residual functions should then be decentralised down to the divisions. The alleged advantages were improved managerial initiative, the development of powers of leadership, faster decision-making, and a clear identification of responsibility for decision-making.[55] In short, as Morrison quoted from Drucker, while central management had the task of 'thinking ahead for the whole Corporation', it then refrained 'as much as possible from telling a division how to do its job; it only lays down what to do'.[56] This was consistent with the structure for the coal industry, which allied a divisional organisation with a greater allocation of functions and importance to a centralised national board. The nine Divisions in the main coalfields each controlled a number of Areas, the Areas being the main operational units of the industry, each in turn running many pits.[57] Similarly, in the gas industry, in November 1945 the Heyworth Committee had recommended the establishment of ten regional boards, each dealing with production and distribution. Gaitskell, as Minister of Fuel and

[52] PRO CAB 134/688, SI(M)(47)50, Cabinet, Committee on the Socialisation of Industries, 'Decentralised Administration in an American Business', note by the Lord President of the Council, 15 December 1947. Morrison on Drucker, pp. 122–3.

[53] PRO CAB 21/2208, SI(M)(46) Cabinet, Committee on Socialisation of Industries, 'Organisation of Electricity Supply', memorandum by the Lord President of the Council, 4 June 1946, para. 17.

[54] Peter Drucker, *Big Business*, London, Heinemann, 1947, p. 11. As the largest industrial corporation in the USA, General Motors was to become a common comparator for the nationalised industries. In pre-war years, General Motors employed about 250,000 people and twice that number during the peak of World War II. Leonard Tivey, *Nationalisation in British Industry*, London, Jonathan Cape, first published 1966; revised edn, 1973, p. 98. PRO CAB 134/688, SI(M)(47)50, Cabinet, Committee on the Socialisation of Industries, 'Decentralised Administration in an American Business', note by the Lord President of the Council, 15 December 1947.

[55] PRO CAB 124/947, SI(M)(48)32, 'Some Current Problems in Socialised Industries', 12 April 1948, para. 10.

[56] Drucker, *Big Business*, pp. 52, 58–9.

[57] Tivey, *Nationalisation in British Industry*, p. 109.

Power, made it clear that he 'would deprecate more than the minimum of centralisation in the socialisation of the gas industry'.[58] Heyworth's recommendation for regional public boards was taken up in the 1948 Act which established twelve Area boards producing and selling gas, and reporting separately to Parliament.

With the gas industry lacking an effective national grid, there were practical reasons why the gas industry should lend itself to a more decentralised structure. It was where a national grid did exist in as economically and socially important an industry as electricity that arguments arose. The issue of the organisation of the electricity industry provoked clashes during the middle of 1946 between Shinwell, as Minister of Fuel and Power, and Morrison, as Lord President. Morrison's proposals for a centralised organisation were opposed by the more decentralist Shinwell and civil servants at the Ministry of Fuel and Power, who, citing the work of the wartime reconstruction committee, envisaged only limited co-ordination between autonomous regional distribution boards.[59] Within the Ministry there was a clear preference for 'the creation of a National Electricity Board to which the whole of the assets of the industry both for generation and distribution would be transferred', below which a series of Regional Boards would enjoy 'a certain amount of autonomy somewhat analogous to that given by a Parent Company to subsidising companies'.[60] The Regional Boards would be responsible to the National Electricity Board for servicing the capital represented by those assets and the Regional Boards would in turn set up area and district organisations. Responding to subsequent criticism of inadequate 'co-ordination', Shinwell modified the proposals to accommodate a more elaborate 'co-ordinating machinery', including a central supervisory board, central financing, and the pooling of revenues between regional boards.[61]

---

[58] PRO CAB 134/687, SI(M)(46)2, 18/1/46, Cabinet, Socialisation of Industries Committee, 'Nationalisation of Gas and Electricity Industries', memo by the Minister of Fuel and Power, para. 5. PRO CAB 134/688, SI(M)(47)9 meeting, 17 October 1947, Cabinet, Committee on Socialisation of Industries, Minutes of a meeting, 17 October 1947.

[59] PRO CAB 134/693, SI(O)(46)16, Cabinet, Official Committee on the Socialisation of Industries, 'Socialisation of the Electricity Supply Industry: National or Regional Boards, Notes by the Electricity Commission', 27 February 1946, para. 17. PRO CAB 21/2208, 'Organisation of the Electricity Supply Industry' (SI(M)(46) 21 and 22), Memo to Lord President by Philip Chantler, 24 June 1946.

[60] PRO CAB 21/2008, SI(M)(46)24, Cabinet, Committee on Socialisation of Industries: Organisation of Electricity Supply: memorandum by the Ministry of Fuel and Power, 4 July 1946. Also see annex, 'Proposed Scheme for Nationalised Electricity Supply Industry'.

[61] PRO CAB 21/2208 SI(M)(46)20, and see Committee's discussion of Shinwell's revised proposals, SI(M)(46)9 meeting, Item 1.

Morrison objected to both Shinwell's original and revised proposals. Citing the 'real test' of the efficiency of the electricity industry as being 'whether in fact the electricity supply industry is run cheaply and efficiently', Morrison sought a more centralised structure which would facilitate supply at low prices to a wider geographic and income range of consumers.[62] Cross-subsidisation attracted Morrison and was at the heart of his opposition to regional autonomy for 'even if the regions are made very large, it will be impossible to secure areas with a fair balance between urban and rural consumers in certain parts of the country. This is true of the west of England, East Anglia, and even south-east England.'[63] By contrast, under a National Board, it would not be necessary to frame bulk supply charges to be made by the Central Generating Board to Regional Distribution Boards, or between Regional Distribution Boards. Thus 'it should be easier and quicker to forge ahead with a reduction of charges in the rural and sparsely populated areas. And that is vital to agricultural well-being and to the support of the middle classes for socialisation.'[64] In a rather unconvincing denial that he was pursuing cross-subsidisation, Morrison explained that the rural consumer was to benefit not 'by raising prices to consumers in other areas in order to subsidise him, as by ensuring that ... [he] ... was the first to benefit from the considerable economies which would flow from the nationalisation of the industry'.[65] In the Economic Section, Philip Chantler fully recognised how a more autonomous, regionally weighted organisation would make such cross-subsidisation more difficult, since it would require specific statutory arrangements between boards concerning the amount and direction of levies and subsidies between areas. Indeed, the extent of cross-subsidisation might then be 'ascertainable by the public'.[66] The Ministry of Fuel and Power even questioned the legality of Morrison's

[62] PRO CAB 21/2208, SI(M)(46) 4 June 1946, Cabinet, Committee on Socialisation of Industries, 'Organisation of Electricity Supply', memorandum by the Lord President of the Council, para. 18

[63] PRO CAB 21/2208, SI(M)(46) 4 June 1946, Cabinet, Committee on Socialisation of Industries, 'Organisation of Electricity Supply', memorandum by the Lord President of the Council, para. 14.

[64] PRO CAB 21/2208, SI(M)(46) 4 June 1946, Cabinet, Committee on Socialisation of Industries, 'Organisation of Electricity Supply', memorandum by the Lord President of the Council, para. 23.

[65] PRO CAB 134/687, SI(M)(46) 1 meeting, Cabinet, Committee on the Socialisation of Industries, minutes of meeting, 24 January 1946.

[66] PRO CAB 21/2008, Philip Chantler, 'Organisation of the Electricity Supply Industry', 24 June 1946, p. 2. PRO CAB 134/693, SI(O)(46)15, Official Committee on Socialisation of Industries, 'Socialisation of the Electricity Supply Industry: National or Regional Boards', note by Ministry of Fuel and Power, 27 February 1946.

moves towards uniformity of pricing, which were attached to the coat-tails of cross-subsidisation, since this raised

a very important issue of national policy, which has not been decided or even considered by Ministers. There are few services in this country which are conducted on the basis of uniform charges to everyone wherever he lives. Postal services are generally quoted in this connection, but there the cost of transmitting a letter is a minor element and the cost of handling at each end the major element.

While it was undeniable that centralisation would make it 'easier for the urban population to carry on its back the rural population, the question to be settled is whether the advantages of this uniformity are so great that it is worthwhile foregoing the flexibility and keenness that arises from a local organisation as opposed to a Central Organisation with local offices guided in policy from the Centre'.[67]

Even Morrison's personal friends, such as George Wansbrough, wrote to warn him of 'the dangers of centralisation'.[68] Wansbrough thought Morrison underrated the dangers of centralisation because of his own unusual capacity for delegating within centralised organisations. What was more usual, as Wansbrough warned, was that 'in nine out of ten cases, people who get to the head of affairs love making decisions, and find it awfully difficult to pass the responsibility on. I know from what old friends of mine, who worked with you at County Hall and elsewhere, tell me, that you are one of the 10 per cent minority.'[69] Even in his own business, Wansbrough found that although 'the Board passionately believes in decentralisation, yet the tendency to centralisation of responsibility gains all the time'.[70]   Similar warnings were sounded by Andrew Duncan and Ronald Edwards.[71] Duncan drawing on his wartime observation of Royal Ordnance Factories, considered it 'the most difficult thing in the world . . . to secure a responsible,

---

[67] PRO CAB 134/693, SI(O)(46)15, Cabinet, Official Committee on Socialisation of Industries, 'Socialisation of the Electricity Supply Industry: National or Regional Boards', note by Ministry of Fuel and Power, 27 February 1946, paras. 5 and 7.

[68] Wansbrough was chairman of Morphy-Richards Ltd, 1945–54.

[69] PRO CAB 21/2008, letter to Herbert Morrison from George Wansbrough, 21 June 1946.

[70] PRO CAB 21/2008, memorandum, 'Electric Supply Reorganisation; One Big Organisation or Several?', by George Wansbrough, 21 June 1946.

[71] Before the war, Ronald Edwards had run a seminar with Hugh Gaitskell at the London School of Economics (LSE) on pricing in public utilities. In May 1940, Edwards joined the Ministry of Aircraft Production, later assisting within central government in the management of the manpower allocated by Cabinet to the Ministry of Aircraft Production. In 1946 he returned to the LSE and was appointed Sir Edward Cassell Reader in Commerce, becoming Professor of Economics in 1949. M. Ackrill, 'Sir Ronald Edwards', in D. J. Jeremy (ed.) *Dictionary of Business Biography*, London, Butterworth, 1984, pp. 237–44.

creative and flexible management in the units when the real responsibility lies at the centre'.[72] Edwards warned specifically against being seduced by the 'obvious and tempting' economies of scale:

The technical specialist is likely to see these as a desirable end and to seek to achieve them through ever larger and larger organisational units, unmindful of the diseconomies imposed by the growing complexities of administration and co-ordination. The costs of large-scale organisation are often under-estimated . . . The fact – and I think it is an extremely important fact – is that economies in the use of specialised factors of production are normally measurable, while on the other hand, diseconomies that spring from the need for more co-ordination as undertakings grow in size and from the loss of flexibility that ensues, are normally difficult to measure. The odds are, therefore, that the economies will exercise more influence than the diseconomies on the inexperienced planner . . . [I wish] to underline the point which may be a commonplace to senior civil servants, but is not a commonplace to the man in the street, that efficient large scale organisation is one of the most difficult things to achieve. In planning our national industries, we should take this to heart and make it a general rule to centralise control less than would appear to be justified by the paper gains.[73]

In addition to the allocative and organisational issues thrown up in these postwar discussions, there was also the crucial issue of how government could secure adequate accountability from their monopoly creations. Public ownership made government fully accountable in Parliament for the performance of these industries, and some balance had to be struck between securing accountability and allowing managers room to manage. In his early ponderings on the future structure of government–nationalised industry relations, Morrison considered the possibility of simply subsuming industries like electricity within government and running them 'on Post Office lines'.[74] Another option considered was to establish intermediary supervisory bodies to stand between government and the industries concerned. However, inter-war experience of statutory supervisory bodies such as the Milk Commission, the Air Commission, and the Agricultural Commission was not encouraging. All three had been aborted by Parliament in the Machinery of Government Committee, the common view being that such bodies would cause the 'channels for the exercise of Government direction' to become 'choked and perhaps distorted'.[75] As Morrison recalled in 1954, it was specifically to avoid such choking that

---

[72] PRO CAB 21/2008, Duncan quoted in memorandum 'Electricity Supply Reorganisation: One Big Organisation or several?' by George Wansbrough, 21 June 1946.

[73] PRO CAB 124/944, R. S. Edwards, 'The Efficiency of Nationalised Industries'.

[74] PRO CAB 21/2208, SI(M)(46), Cabinet, Committee on Socialisation of Industries, 'Organisation of Electricity Supply, Memorandum by the Lord President of the Council', 4 June 1946, para. 8.

[75] PRO CAB 21/2208, SI(M)(46)21, Cabinet, Committee on Socialisation of Industries,

'Parliament . . . deliberately took the line that this was a different outfit from a State Department and that we were giving this greater degree of managerial autonomy in order that we could get a higher degree of business efficiency and less red tape and bureaucracy.'[76]

While these options were considered it was always likely that the Morrisonian 'public corporation' as outlined in *Socialisation and Transport* would be the adopted model. For Morrison, the public corporation was the administrative embodiment of the public spirit, with clear distinctive advantages over the private corporation. The public corporation was 'no mere capitalist business, the be-all and end-all of which is profits and dividends', but rather a corporation with 'a different atmosphere at its board table from that of a shareholders' meeting' and whose 'board and its officers must regard themselves as the high custodians of the public interest'.[77] As experts and 'high custodians of the public interest', boards would be at an arm's length from government and be free from interference in the day-to-day management of their industries. As Gaitskell confirmed in May 1949, it was not for government 'to say which mines should be developed and which should be closed, what form of generating station ought to be constructed, nor what system of gas distribution would be appropriate in a particular area'.[78] Although Ministers did have the power to issue General Directions, Gaitskell made it clear to the BEA in April 1948 that he had 'not the slightest intention or desire to start giving directions', regarding such directions as 'powers which you may find it convenient to make me exercise occasionally'.[79] That managers should be given their head was held to be important if scarce managerial talent was to be recruited.[80] Although railway companies, the CEB, and supply companies such as Edmundsons, had some experience of large-scale organisation, in coal mining such experience and managerial resources was limited. For Gaitskell, this inexperience in managing a

'Organisation of Electricity Supply: Memorandum by the Lord President of the Council', 4 June 1946, para. 10.

[76] Morrison, 523, HC Deb, 5s, cols. 849–50, 8 February 1954. Quoted in Robson, *Nationalised Industry and Public Ownership*, 2nd edn, London, George Allen & Unwin, 1962, p. 69.

[77] H. Morrison, *Socialisation and Transport*, London, Constable, 1933, pp. 156–7.

[78] PRO CAB 134/690, Committee on Socialisation of Industries, SI(M)(49)33, 'Government Control over Socialised Industry', memorandum by the Minister of Fuel and Power, Hugh Gaitskell, 30 May 1949.

[79] PRO CAB 124/1202, J. H. Smith and T. E. Chester, 'The Distribution of Power in Nationalised Industry: an Introductory Analysis', p. 5. Hugh Gaitskell, speech at a conference of the BEA, 9 April 1948.

[80] PRO CAB 134/693, SI(O)(46)15, Cabinet, Official Committee on the Socialisation of Industries, 'Socialisation of the Electricity Supply Industry: National and Regional Boards', note by the Ministry of Fuel and Power, 27 February 1946, para. 14.

vast nation-wide organisation was the 'biggest difficulty' facing the NCB. Even in electricity, Morrison cited the difficulty of finding talented managers for the independent Regional Boards as one of his objections to decentralisation, evoking the sharp response from Shinwell that this problem was 'hardly solved by setting up a Central Board', which would have to devolve tasks to able men in the regions lest it be 'seriously crippled by over-centralisation'.[81]

Shinwell and Morrison were to clash again on the issue of salaries. While the recruitment of talented management was held to be the crucial factor in determining the success or failure of these 'experiments' in nationalisation, Shinwell's proposals in February 1946 to pay the NCB Chairman £10,000, the Deputy Chairman £7,500–8,000, and Board members £6,000 per annum were branded by Morrison as 'socially objectionable'.[82] These salaries were hardly extravagant, often being lower than those offered to managers in other industries, and lower even than those received by some managers in the inter-war coal industry.[83] As Shinwell noted, in pushing for approval of his proposed salary levels, decent salaries were required, since 'no doubt there are plenty of people of second-rate quality who are looking for jobs, [but] these are not the men for the National Coal Board'.[84]

The potential dangers of a centralised monopoly industry with a Board of experts becoming overly independent of government control was recognised to some extent by Morrison. If nationalised industries were to be at arm's length from government, asymmetries of information would inevitably exist between government and nationalised industries, since, as Morrison acknowledged in the case of electricity, 'with so many experts employed by the Authority and the Boards, there

[81] PRO CAB 134/687, SI(M)(46), 1 meeting, Cabinet, Committee on Socialisation of Industries, minutes of a meeting, 24 January 1946. PRO CAB 134/693, SI(O)(46)15, 27/2/46, Cabinet, Official Committee on the Socialisation of Industries, 'Socialisation of the Electricity Supply Industry: National and Regional Boards', note by the Ministry of Fuel and Power, para. 13.

[82] LPA RD 254, 'Administration of Nationalised Industries', comment by Mr Gaitskell on Draft Report of Sub-Committee, circulated to Labour Party Sub-Committee for Information, January 1949. PRO CAB 134/687, SI(M)(46), 2 meeting, 15 February 1946. PRO CAB 134/687, SI(M)(46)3, 8 February 1946, Cabinet, Socialisation of Industries Committee, 'Salaries of the National Coal Board', memorandum by the Minister of Fuel and Power.

[83] PRO POWE 37/16, letter from Hugh Gaitskell to Hugh Dalton, 24 January 1950.

[84] Emanuel Shinwell, *Conflict Without Malice*, London, Odhams Press, 1955. PRO CAB 134/687, SI(M)(46)3, 8 February 1946, Cabinet, Socialisation of Industries Committee, 'Salaries of the National Coal Board', memorandum by the Minister of Fuel and Power. LPA RD 253, 'Administration of Nationalised Industries', January 1949. For the continuing debate on salaries, see Robson, *Nationalised Industry and Public Ownership*, pp. xv, xvi. C. A. R. Crosland, *The Future of Socialism*, London, Jonathan Cape, pp. 487–90.

would be little scope for the Minister to employ officers with technical experience to advise him on disputes within the hierarchy'. None the less, as Morrison made clear in objecting to Shinwell's proposed scheme for the organisation of the electricity industry, he would 'rather face the risks of a powerful National Generating and Distribution Board than the ineffective squabbling among Boards and Authorities, with a rather worried and possibly powerless Minister on top, which the scheme suggests to my mind'.[85]

Ironically, it was in relations between the government and the electricity industry where the problems of a government's being accountable for the actions of a public corporation over which it had no direct control were most explicitly revealed. Concerned at the resources both actually and potentially being absorbed by the electricity industry's power-station construction programme, Hugh Gaitskell, as Minister of Fuel and Power, sought to persuade the industry to take action to reduce peak-hour demand, the main determinant of electricity-generating-capacity requirements.[86] This rational exploration of the greater use of the pricing mechanism within the electricity industry appealed to Gaitskell. It held much less appeal for the electricity industry, whose chairman, Walter Citrine, preferred to pursue a sales-maximisation strategy, not least in competition with the gas industry for a larger share of Bevan's new housing market.

That the British Electricity Authority (BEA) should have resisted Gaitskell's attempts to introduce meters and time-of-day tariffs was, perhaps, unsurprising. What was more surprising, and certainly revealing of the dynamics of the emerging balance of power between ministers and the nationalised industries, was that their resistance should have proved successful. The success arose from the skilful exploitation of various asymmetries of information between the minister and the board, and of some unresolved issues concerning the working of the public-corporation model. Unwilling (and possibly legally unable) to issue a general direction to the industry, and respecting the public-corporation basis of their relationship, Gaitskell sought to win acceptance for his arguments through consultation. In February 1948, he established a committee under the chairmanship of Sir Alexander Clow,

[85] PRO CAB 21/2208, SI(M)(46) 4 June 1946, Cabinet, Committee on Socialisation of Industries, 'Organisation of Electricity Supply', memorandum by the Lord President of the Council, para. 9.

[86] M. Chick, 'Marginal Cost Pricing and the Peak-hour Demand for Electricity, 1945–51', in M. Chick (ed.), *Governments, Industries and Markets; Aspects of Government–Industry Relations in the UK, Japan, West Germany and the USA since 1945*, Aldershot, Edward Elgar, 1990, pp. 110–26. H. S. Houthakker, 'Electricity Tariffs in Theory and Practice', *Economic Journal*, 61, 241 (March 1951), pp. 1–25.

which was charged with examining and reporting on the scope for reducing peak-hour demand by using a mixture of meters, limiters, and alterations in the tariff for domestic and non-industrial consumers.[87] In the proper way of things, representatives from the industry, the ministry, as well as some independent experts, were appointed to the committee.

Gaitskell's intention in establishing the Clow Committee was to force the industry's opposition into the open, to expose its arguments to close scrutiny, and to push the industry towards addressing the peak-load problem. However, 'consultation' implies a degree of willingness on the part of all participants to co-operate for the greater good, and not work for the protection of a sectional interest. After all, one of the main aims of nationalisation had been to break the power of vested interests, not to replace them with fresh groups. One of the leading features of the public corporation, as defined by Morrison, was that while 'it is responsible to the nation, . . . it cannot be the instrument of this or that private or sectional interest'.[88] Clearly, it was not intended to become a sectional interest itself, yet any breadth of vision which Morrison might have anticipated as characterising the boards of public corporations was not in evidence during Clow's dealings with the BEA.

Clow found the BEA representatives stubborn, of 'too little elasticity of mind', and reflective of an industry whose 'technical leaders' were 'inspired by few ideas except the value of expansion'.[89] The BEA's representatives persistently obstructed the work of the committee. Exploiting their position as monopoly agents in the principal–agent relationship between the minister and the industry, they refused to release any information concerning the price elasticity of demand which might damage their case. Research on the system diversity of different appliances, which had been undertaken for some years by the Electricity Research Association, was taken over by the BEA in 1948 but, in contrast to pre-nationalisation practice, no results were published.[90] Nor were the Clow and later the Ridley Committee given access to the findings.[91] The BEA representatives also strove to slow down the rate of progress of the committee by means of a mixture of filibuster and obstruction. Days were consumed in repetitive restatements of the industry's opposition to tariff reform and their technical objections to

---

[87] *Report of the (Clow) Committee to Study the Peak Load Problem in Relation to Non-Industrial Consumers*, Cmd 7464, July 1948.

[88] Herbert Morrison, *Socialisation and Transport*, 1933, p. 149.

[89] PRO POWE 14/365, 'Sir Alexander Clow's Confidential Memorandum on the Clow Report'.

[90] Roughly speaking, system diversity is the inverse of the probability of the appliance's adding to peak demand.

[91] I. M. D. Little, *The Price of Fuel*, Oxford, Clarendon Press, 1953, p. 68.

schemes for metering. Only two of the twenty-three meetings were fully attended, and even in its final days the committee's discussions were slow and rancorous. Clow despaired of 'unfruitful' meetings and of the 'continuous struggle by individuals to modify the draft in such a way that its descriptive method leads to conclusions which they themselves favour'.[92] The final report was, on Clow's own admission, 'a mixture [but not always a blend] of different outlooks . . . [which] does not embark adequately on various issues of tariff policy'.[93] To a seasoned civil servant, not only did the report 'pull its punches', but illustrated 'the truth of the maxim "Blessed are they who expect nothing, for they shall not be disappointed"'.[94]

The final recommendations of the report simply did not address the issue of peak-hour pricing, confining its recommendations to the introduction of a seasonal differential between the winter quarter and the three (summer) quarters of the year. This seasonal differential was almost the very least that the committee could recommend without being silent. Even the size of the differential was contested by the electricity industry. While Gaitskell sought a 'substantial' differential, with winter unit charges being increased from 0.75d to 1.25d per kilowatt hour, and summer unit charges being reduced to 0.5d, the industry pushed for a winter–summer differential of 1.0d to 0.7d. The final outcome, after stormy meetings between the minister and the Area Board chairmen and private talks between Gaitskell and Citrine, was a compromise differential of 1.1d in winter and 0.65d in summer. Subsequently, any impact of the Clow differential was reduced by the industry's failure to publicise it sufficiently to the bulk of its customers who paid their bills after consumption.[95] This exploitation of asymmetries of access to consumers meant that apart from those with coin-operated meters, most consumers only became aware of the differential when the bills arrived for the 'winter' electricity which they had already used. Convinced that he had been right in principle, but beaten in practice, Gaitskell announced in the House of Commons on 11 July 1949 that the Clow differential would not be continued in the forthcoming winter.

The industry's ability to block Gaitskell's attempts to secure a more effective use of pricing mechanisms was of considerable political

---

[92] PRO POWE 14/362, GE 615/48, note by Clow, 24 April 1948.
[93] PRO POWE 14/365, 'Sir Alexander Clow's Confidential Memorandum on the Clow Report'.
[94] PRO POWE 14/365, note by W. G. Nott-Bower, 3 June 1948.
[95] Philip M. Williams, *The Diary of Hugh Gaitskell, 1945–56*, London, Jonathan Cape, 5 August 1948, p. 79. Little, *Price*, p. 108.

significance. The clash between the Minister and the industry was fundamentally a clash of two strongly differing views of what constituted the 'national interest'. That the industry's view prevailed had potentially wide implications, both for resource allocation within the economy and for the subsequent development of the relationship between nationalised industries and government. The clear implication for resource allocation was that if the electricity industry was able to continue with a promotional pricing policy then it might go on to consume a disproportionately large and rising proportion of national capital investment resources. Rather than private industrial investment being 'crowded out' by a nationalised sector enjoying lower borrowing costs, a danger was perceived that it might in fact be crowded out by an over-stimulation of under-priced demand for nationalised-industry output.[96] Facing high demand, pressure to supply, and asymmetries of information and expertise in its dealings with the industry, government might find it difficult to prevent this expansion. This was, in part, what Tom Wilson warned against in his debate with Meade and others in the *Economic Journal* over the pricing policy of the socialised industries. One of Wilson's objections to Meade's tolerance of loss-making by the socialised industries was that government could well find it difficult to rein in the expansionist mentality of the more technically based, and especially increasing-returns, socialised industries. Wilson envisaged a situation in which

the managers of the socialist undertakings, entranced with some new technical project or anxious to increase their own importance by 'empire-building' would come to the planning committee and declare that consumers would gladly pay for the new type of equipment proposed if they had to . . . Of course, the planning staff might argue, but would find difficulty in proving the managers wrong, and the allocation of resources would in fact be largely determined by crude political bargaining.[97]

Inevitably, resource allocation did involve a significant element of crude political bargaining.[98] In this respect, nationalised and private industries behaved no differently from one another. Contrary to Morrison's aspirations for the public corporations, nationalised industries, such as electricity, were behaving as sectional interests in a manner

---

[96] Little, *Price*, pp. 154–7. W. Shepherd, *Economic Performance under Public Ownership*, New Haven, CT, and London, Yale University Press, 1965, ch. 4.

[97] T. Wilson, 'Price and Outlay Policy of State Enterprise', *Economic Journal*, 55 (December 1945), pp. 454–61.

[98] P. Howlett, 'New Light through Old Windows: a New Perspective on the British Economy in the Second World War', *Journal of Contemporary History*, 28, 2 (April 1993), pp. 361–79.

which, being largely unanticipated, surprised observers. As Robert Hall noted, in February 1949, 'the present trend of the socialized industries is all towards independence; it makes nonsense of the reasons for socialising'.[99] In a government-read academic paper reflecting on the first five years of nationalisation, J. H. Smith and T. E. Chester concluded that 'the most striking feature of the past five years has been the emergence of the Boards as separate entities, with a life and purpose of their own, although projections of the State'.[100] Significantly, Smith and Chester also emphasised that 'in the days when nationalisation was a theoretical objective, no-one envisaged the degree of concentration of power which the particular form of nationalisation by public corporation has in fact entailed'.[101]

Emerging difficulties in the relationships between ministers such as Gaitskell and leading nationalised industries such as electricity began to prompt a serious reconsideration within government of the terms and structure of that relationship. Early signs of such a process of re-evaluation were evident in Gaitskell's reflections following his clash with the BEA over the Clow differential. Having promised to go away and consider the differential, Citrine appeared to have done little about it, until Gaitskell happened to hear by chance that 'the BEA are proposing to announce their decision tomorrow'. As a furious Gaitskell recorded in his diary,

this they will do without having consulted me or having been in contact with me since the row. Partly, no doubt, this kind of behaviour is due to C's personality. But it also illustrates the extraordinary difficulties of the relationship between the Minister and these Boards . . . It is really very unsatisfactory having to deal with the Boards as though they were independent authorities with no special obligations to the Government. Yet if they choose, that is the line they can take, and without a major and public row there is very little the Minister can do about it.[102]

In discussion with Donald Fergusson, the Permanent Secretary at the Ministry of Fuel and Power, on how to increase the minister's contact with and power over the boards, consideration was given to making the minister Chairman of the Board so that it would be 'quite separate from the ordinary Civil Service department but nevertheless quite publicly

---

[99] A. Cairncross (ed.), *The Robert Hall Diaries*, London, Unwin Hyman, 1989, p. 53, entry for 15 February 1949.

[100] J. H. Smith was Assistant Lecturer in the Department of Social Administration, LSE, and formerly of the Acton Society Trust.

[101] PRO CAB 124/1202, J. H. Smith and T. E. Chester, 'The Distribution of Power in Nationalised Industry: an Introductory Analysis', pp. 3–5.

[102] P. M. Williams, *Diary of Hugh Gaitskell*, 12 August 1948, p. 80.

and openly under his control. He would then, of course, have to take full responsibility for everything that happened'.[103]

Morrison's faith in the 'public spirit' of the board of the public corporation suddenly looked suspect and fragile. Similarly, the common assumption that public ownership would enhance public control also began to appear to be rather more complex than had previously been envisaged. Ownership did not bring control to anything like the extent assumed by advocates of nationalisation. Indeed, the act of nationalisation may have weakened the government's control over industries by exchanging the threat for the fact of nationalisation. In its relations with the privately owned ICI, the banks, and the pre-nationalised iron and steel industry, an important weapon in per-suading each respectively to comply with the atomic programme, to establish the Industrial and Commercial Finance Corporation and the Finance Corporation for Industry and to undertake 'planned rationali-sation' was the threat that in the absence of a satisfactory response, the government would consider moving towards the nationalisation of the recalcitrant industry.[104] For the nationalised industries, such threats were irrelevant. Indeed, if anything, nationalisation strengthened the industry's position in its relationship with the government, by allowing the industry to exploit the government's increased political responsi-bility for the performance of the now-nationalised industry. Just as there existed a principal–agent relationship between government and the nationalised industry, so too there existed a principal–agent relationship between the electorate and the government, in which the electorate sought and monitored the provision of certain goods from government. Unlike the government–nationalised industry relationship, the principal–agent relationship between government and the electorate was short term and not automatically renewable. One of the criteria used by the electorate in monitoring the government was the perfor-mance of the nationalised industries. The perceived performance of the nationalised industries was of particular political relevance for the Attlee government, since the nationalisation programme formed one of its major political achievements.

---

[103] P. M. Williams, *Diary of Hugh Gaitskell*, 12 August 1948, p. 80. Sir Donald Fergusson (1891–1963) was Permanent Secretary at the Ministry of Fuel and Power, 1945–52.

[104] M. Gowing, *Independence and Deterrence, Britain and Atomic Energy, 1945–52: vol. II, Policy Execution*, London, Macmillan, 1974, p. 159. W. B. Reddaway, 'The Chemical Industry', in D. L. Burn (ed.), *The Structure of British Industry*, vol. I, 1964, Cambridge, Cambridge University Press, p. 235. P. D. Henderson, 'Government and Industry', in G. D. N. Worswick and P. H. Ady (eds.), *The British Economy in the Nineteen-Fifties*, Oxford, Oxford University Press, 1962, p. 371. J. Kinross, *Fifty Years in the City*, London, John Murray, 1982.

The electorate's criteria for assessing performance was wide, and went beyond, sometimes contrarily so, issues of technical, productive, and allocative efficiency. Two popular criteria were price of output and reliability of supply. Fully understanding this, the BEA was able to exploit the government's sensitivity on issues of price and output. Had Gaitskell succeeded in raising prices, it is very likely that the BEA and Citrine would have lost little time in attributing responsibility for a politically and electorally unpopular decision to a minister who had acted against the best advice of the industry, which enjoyed strong asymmetries of information and expertise. Certainly, the industry was relentless in attributing responsibility for any interruptions in supply to central government's limiting of resources. A foretaste of this was provided by the CEB three months before the nationalisation of the electricity industry.

In January 1948, confronted with the government White Paper *Capital Investment in 1948*, which imposed limitations on the industry's plant-extension programmes for 1950 and 1951 as well as having consequences for the 1952 programme, the CEB pressed the minister to honour a previous assurance made to the CEB Chairman and Citrine on 7 November 1947, that 'if the Board did not regard the statement which was shortly to be published in the White Paper as satisfactory he would address a letter to them exonerating the Board from responsibility'.[105] As the CEB argued, such a statement was necessary for 'fear that the Board's attitude might be misunderstood by the public at large', and that the CEB 'desired it to be made clear that the decision had been reached by the Government on their own responsibility against the advice of the Board'.[106] Gaitskell, as Minister of Fuel and Power, duly agreed to 'exonerate both the Authority and the Board from blame for any failure to carry out those statutory duties insofar as such failure can be attributed to the cuts in question'.[107] The threat to appeal to public opinion carried its greatest potential as important

---

[105] Treasury, *Capital Investment in 1948*, London, HMSO, Cmd 7268, 1947. PRO POWE 14/110, letter from O. A. Sherrard, Secretary of the CEB, to the Secretary of the Ministry of Fuel and Power, 2 January 1948.

[106] PRO POWE 14/110, letter from O. A. Sherrard, Secretary of the CEB to the Secretary of the Ministry of Fuel and Power, 2 January 1948.

[107] PRO POWE 14/110, letter from Gaitskell to Citrine, 7 January 1948. CEB minutes 9 January 1948, letter from Secretary of Ministry of Fuel and Power to Secretary of the Central Electricity Board, 8 January 1948. This arrangement whereby the Board had the right to ask for a letter which it could publish in a case of disagreement became a standard practice in relations between government and the nationalised industries. See D. L. Munby in G. D. N. Worswick and P. H. Ady (eds.), *The British Economy in the 1950s*. Oxford, Clarendon Press, 1962, p. 423. Sir Ian Horobin, Parliamentary Secretary to the Ministry of Power, House of Commons, 14 July 1958, cols. 843–4.

elections approached. Thus, in 1951 the government was not only forced to abandon its attempts to reduce its investment allocation to the electricity industry, but actually obliged to increase the allocation of resources for supplying industry and the new housing estates.[108]

This unanticipated but evident development of nationalised industries provoked a shift in attitudes towards nationalised industries and the public corporation model for ministerial–board relations. Steadily, but perceptibly, over the course of the Attlee governments, discussion moved away from the early optimistic concern with realising economies of scale to a more pessimistic concern with preventing the abuse of monopoly power by these industries. Increasingly, there were calls for increased monitoring of the performance of the nationalised industries. Although proposals for a select committee on nationalised industries were rejected by the Attlee governments, by 1956 such a committee was in place. For that personification of the early independence of the inter-war public corporations, Lord Reith, such a select committee was 'almost a negation of what Parliament did in setting up these public corporations'.[109] Within the Labour Party, there were increasing efforts to force the Party to draw a sharper distinction between the issues of ownership and monopoly. Throughout, the aim was to sharpen thinking on the dangers of monopoly and not to be so sanguine on the ability of Ministers to control nationalised monopoly industries. In an internal Labour Party research paper in September 1948, Douglas Jay produced a sharp reminder of the civil-liberty issues involved in acts of nationalisation:

To pass an Act of Parliament ordaining that nobody other than the Government may produce a certain commodity and that the assets of all who hitherto did shall be compulsorily purchased is, even when justifiable, a serious step and a real limitation of individual freedom. The limitation is potentially the most unpopular side of Socialist policy, and the one against which our opponents can most easily work up feeling.[110]

In this paper and another in May 1952 Jay argued that in future the Party should be bolder in its thinking and 'move in the direction of establishing efficient public enterprises competing, if necessary, with private enterprise, rather than the old pattern – to which we have

---

[108] L. Hannah, *Engineers, Managers and Politicians*, London, Macmillan, 1982, p. 47.
[109] Lord Reith, 'Public Corporations', *The Times*, 3 July 1956. PRO CAB 124/1202, letter to Lord Salisbury from Lord Reith, 2 December 1953. Reith began by reflecting that 'if I had to say what had been the major pre-occupations of my life, I suppose they would be broadcasting . . . and the operation of the public corporation system. As to the first, all I did has gone for nothing, but that is neither here nor there; it is the other matter – public corporations – that I should like to write to you about.'
[110] LPA RD 161, Douglas Jay, 'Future Nationalisation Policy', September 1948, para. 3.

perhaps given a rather dogmatic adherence – of 100 per cent compulsory purchase by legislation, together with a ban on all outside competition with the public monopoly thus set up'.[111] While in Jay's view, there was no defence for private monopoly and that the case for public ownership was 'unassailable' when confronted with 'large-scale units already constituting a monopoly or quasi-monopoly', the government should take considerable care when establishing a new monopoly itself.[112] As Jay argued, 'it may be true, but it is not obvious, that a public monopoly is better for the public than competition. Public monopolies will not restrict production out of a desire for profits; but they may fail to increase production – in the absence of competition – out of inertia and complacency.' This was not to reject the idea of public ownership, but rather to question why public ownership was so frequently accompanied by the establishment of a national monopoly. Intervention could still occur: government would not only consider using old-style nationalisation in the case of largely self-contained 'homogeneous' industries such as shipbuilding, where government might even out the demand cycles, but it might also move against particular firms like ICI, Unilever, Tate & Lyle, and Ranks, which were regarded as being monopoly suppliers of vital commodities. This would be to nationalise the firm, but not the industry.[113]

While Jay argued for a more critical examination of the case for establishing nationalised industries as monopolies, he also proposed a more sophisticated form of government intervention. While keen to escape from the 'artificial and indeed ridiculous dilemma – thanks to the 100 per cent dogma – of not feeling able to start a direct Government enterprise in a line of production where it may be badly needed, until we have "nationalised" the whole "industry"', he saw no reason why the wartime practice by which a few modern efficient units were established to produce drop forgings, rifles, explosives or whatever was necessary, might not be applied to industries such as cotton spinning. The government would enter the industry as a competitor to the existing firms, building large-scale modern efficient new mills in areas such as Merseyside, where labour was available.[114] The hope was that the demonstration effect provided by efficient state-operated mills would boost efficiency within the industry as a whole. This consideration of the scope for what Jay dubbed as 'competitive socialism' in such

[111] LPA RD 161, Douglas Jay, 'Future Nationalisation Policy', September 1948, para. 2.
[112] LPA RD 161, Douglas Jay, 'Future Nationalisation Policy', September 1948, para. 3.
[113] LPA RD 161, Douglas Jay, 'Future Nationalisation Policy', September 1948, paras. 3–5.
[114] LPA RD 161, Douglas Jay, 'Future Nationalisation Policy', September 1948, para. 3.

industries as machine tools characterised the thinking of the rising generation of Wilson, Gaitskell, and Jay.[115] It surfaced in discussions on a memorandum, 'The State and Private Industry', written by Wilson to fill a perceived 'vacuum in Socialist thought' on relations between government and private industry.[116] Allied to the questioning of traditional monopoly forms of ownership was a wish by Wilson and Christopher Mayhew to present the government as the defender of consumer interests against private industries, rather than as the representatives of big nationalised producer groups.[117] It was these strands of thought from the rising generation of Labour politicians, characterised as they were by a concern with the problems of monopoly and the benefits of competition, which were to feed into Crosland's *The Future of Socialism* in 1956.[118]

By 1952, Jay's emphasis on the encouragement of competition and the avoidance of monopoly when possible had increased, while by 1953 the Labour Party, in *Challenge to Britain*, had assimilated Jay's proposals for establishing competitive public enterprises within certain industries, such as machine tools.[119] These developments in thinking on monopoly and competition also impacted on specific organisational issues. Gaitskell, arguing in the Fabian Tract *Socialisation and Nationalisation*, written in 1953 but not published until 1956, said that 'it is much easier to get the right atmosphere, and therefore greater efficiency in large-scale undertakings, if the element of competition or rivalry is somehow retained'.[120] Coincidentally, the Herbert Report in 1956 on the organisation of the electricity industry came down firmly in favour of the further decentralisation of powers away from the Central Authority to the Area Boards, the Committee's main findings being subsequently incorporated into the 1957 Electricity Act.[121] By the time of Crosland's *The Future of Socialism*, the arguments concerning the respective merits of monopoly and competition had become very explicit, Crosland considering that, in contrast to immediate post-war thinking, 'the

---

[115] PRO CAB 124/200, Meeting to discuss the memorandum, 'The State and Private Industry', by Harold Wilson, President of the Board of Trade. Comments by Douglas Jay, Financial Secretary, Treasury. 17 May 1950.

[116] PRO CAB 124/1200, 'Personal Covering Note to Memorandum on "The State and Private Industry" (revised)' by Harold Wilson.

[117] PRO CAB 124/1200, 'Personal Covering Note to Memorandum on "The State and Private Industry" (revised)' by Harold Wilson.

[118] C. A. R. Crosland, *Future of Socialism*, pp. 469–70.

[119] LPA R 117, D. Jay, 'Future Policy for Social Ownership', May 1952.

[120] H. Gaitskell, *Socialisation and Nationalisation*, London, Fabian Tract No. 300, 1956, pp. 26–7.

[121] *Report of the Committee of Inquiry into the Electricity Supply Industry*, HMSO, Cmd 9672, 1956.

balance of advantage' between monopoly and competition 'now looks rather different'.[122] In short, Crosland concluded, 'public-monopoly nationalisation, despite considerable achievements in certain exceptionally difficult industries, no longer seems the panacea that it used to'.[123]

[122] Crosland, *Future of Socialism*, pp. 469–70.
[123] Crosland, *Future of Socialism*, pp. 470.

5 Monopoly pricing

You ask me what I feel about the general position over the pricing policy of socialised industries. The answer, in short, is that I feel that it is dreadful, and it is no credit whatever to the Government or to the Civil Service. It is part, though a very important part, of a wider problem, i.e. that nobody has laid down any principles about the manner in which socialised industries should be conducted.[1]

(R. F. Kahn to A. Johnston, Office of the Lord President, 24 July 1948)

The use of the pricing mechanism is central to any discussion of economic planning. Contrary to what was sometimes suggested in the 1940s economic planning did not mark the supplanting of the pricing mechanism, but rather a movement to a different set of prices. As Ely Devons informed the Nuffield conference on controls in June 1948, 'the suggestion that when you operate through controls you are not operating though the price mechanism [is] . . . a great fallacy. The idea that controls allocate in terms of real resources is quite wrong. The people who control are in fact paying attention to prices. No one could operate a control system unless there were prices. But they are having regard to the entirely wrong set of prices.'[2]

Discussions of pricing share some common ground with our previous concern with centralisation and decentralisation, many critics of socialist planning, notably von Mises in the 1920s and Hayek in the 1930s, accusing central planners of underestimating the ability of a decentralised structure of market prices to produce accurate and complex flows of information. Not only were planners held to be deluding themselves in thinking that they could administratively imitate such a system, but also of neglecting the right of individuals to autonomy.[3]

[1] PRO CAB 124/950, letter, R. F. Kahn to A. Johnston, Office of the Lord President, 24 July 1948.
[2] UGA McCance papers, Devons on 27 June 1948 at the 24th Nuffield private conference on 'The Government's Controls of Industry and Trade'.
[3] L. von Mises, 'Economic Calculation in the Socialist Commonwealth' (1920), in F. Hayek (ed.), *Collectivist Economic Planning*, London, Routledge, 1935, pp. 87–130. F. Hayek, *The Road to Serfdom*, Chicago, IL, University of Chicago Press, 1944.

Socialist economists answered that decentralised mechanisms could operate, either mimicking the market system while being free of its deficiencies, or using different modes of information gathering.[4] Arguments concerning the use of pricing mechanisms and the possibility of establishing decentralised planning procedures were to continue throughout the 1940s and 1950s, and erupt again during the 1960s in discussions of planning in eastern and western Europe.[5] Within these general arguments on the virtues of planning, there were varied sub-sets of arguments, one of which concerned the appropriate procedures for the pricing of public goods.[6]

During the lifetime of the Attlee governments, it was the pricing of the output of nationalised industries which provided the occasion for the fullest and most explicit discussion of the pricing mechanism. The early discussions, in 1945 and 1946, of the appropriate cost basis for pricing public monopoly output gave way to discussions of the scope for pricing to decrease peak-hour demand, lower capacity requirements, and provide a basis for establishing the relative prices of largely substitute outputs.[7] The pricing issue was particularly relevant in the fuel and power industries, which, as they supplied mainly producer goods, were less dependent than consumer goods on the correct pricing of other outputs for their own resource allocation, and, as producer goods, were at the head of a chain of information concerning prices and resource values which sent information down and throughout the economy.[8] As close substitutes, there were also strong reasons for wanting to get their relative prices right. Getting these prices wrong meant sending some potentially misleading signals to subsequent users.

The developing interest in the applied economics of pricing coincided with the emergence of what was to become known familiarly as 'welfare economics'.[9] Where theory and application coincided during the Attlee

[4] F. M. Taylor, 'The Guidance of Production in a Socialist State', *American Economic Review*, 19 (March 1929), pp. 1–8.

[5] K. Arrow and L. Hurwicz, 'Decentralisation and Computation in Resource Allocation', in R. Pfouts (ed.), *Essays in Economics and Econometrics in Honour of Harold Hotelling*, Chapel Hill, University of North Carolina Press, 1960, pp. 34–104. J. Kornai, 1967, *Mathematical Planning of Structural Decisions*, Amsterdam, North-Holland. E. Malinvaud, 'Decentralised Procedures for Planning', in E. Malinvaud and M. Bacharach (eds.), *Activity Analysis in the Theory of Growth and Planning*, London, Macmillan, 1967, pp. 170–208.

[6] E. Malinvaud, 'A Planning Approach to the Public Good Problem', *Swedish Journal of Economics*, 11 (1971), pp. 96–112.

[7] I. M. D. Little, *The Price of Fuel*, Oxford, Clarendon Press, 1953. J. Meade, *Planning and the Price Mechanism*, London, Allen & Unwin, 1948.

[8] I. Little, *Price of Fuel*, p. xi.

[9] I. Little, *A Critique of Welfare Economics*, Oxford, Clarendon Press, 1950.

governments was in the discussions on the appropriate pricing policy for the nationalised monopoly industries. Later characterised as a 'crabbed and esoteric debate', numerous economists, among whom James Meade, Ronald Coase, Arthur Lewis, Marcus Fleming, and Tom Wilson were notable, devoted considerable time to discussing the respective merits of average cost pricing and marginal cost pricing.[10] While agreement was not reached, the main arguments were outlined, even if later economists were to point to a series of requirements which were sufficiently unlikely to exist as to allow only 'second-best' solutions to be practicable. Nevertheless, the arguments over cost-based pricing should not be dismissed as mere exercises in theoretical economics by ivory-towered economists. The issues which they raised were to recur in the 1961 and 1967 White Papers on the nationalised industries, and that the recommendations of economists were also then largely dismissed did not, of course, invalidate the recommendations.[11] Indeed, the general question of how governments, and the Attlee governments in particular, used the economic advice which they received is one of the main concerns of this chapter. Often it was not the intricacies of the average versus marginal cost pricing arguments which were ignored by the Attlee governments, but rather the more widely supported argument that the government should in general make greater use of pricing mechanisms.

In the immediate postwar years, there was a widespread opinion that the nationalised industries, as monopolies, should be subject to some form of price regulation. There was a political impulse to keep prices low, Emanuel Shinwell, as Minister of Fuel and Power, noting on 31 October 1945 that the government could not 'ignore the widespread feeling that the present price of coal in this country ought to be reduced as much and as quickly as possible'.[12] There was little appetite for letting nationalised industries' prices float freely to market-equilibrium levels, both because of the presumed inflationary effects and because of political sensitivity regarding profit-making in nationalised monopolies. If the nationalised monopolies were not to allow prices to find their own level, then an alternative basis for pricing had to be devised. The eventual statutory requirement that the nationalised industries should cover costs, taking one year with another, reflected the view of the

[10] William G. Shepherd, *Economic Performance under Public Ownership*, New Haven, CT, and London, Yale University Press, 1965, p. 42.
[11] *Financial and Economic Obligations of the Nationalised Industries*, London, HMSO, Cmnd 1336, 1961. *Nationalised Industries: A Review of Economic and Financial Objectives*, London, HMSO, Cmnd 3437, 1967.
[12] PRO CAB 134/693, GEN 98/1 meeting, note of a meeting of ministers, 9 November 1945, including a memo by Shinwell, GEN 98/3, 31 October 1945, para. 23.

majority of the Official Committee on the Socialisation of Industries in May 1946 that there should be 'a general rule that each industry should cover its costs, including the service of capital, over an average of good and bad years, without making an unduly high profit over and above such costs'.[13] While such cost-based pricing was regarded by many as providing an important check against 'monopoly profits', it was not a basis for pricing acceptable to all economists.[14] In particular, it was opposed by the government's own economic advisers in the Economic Section. James Meade, Director of the Economic Section and a member of the Official Committee on the Socialisation of Industries, consistently raised the issue of what constituted appropriate costs for such cost-based pricing policies. An early suggestion from the Committee that these costs should include the costs of compensation was immediately opposed by Meade on the grounds that there should be greater flexibility in pricing, and that future trading conditions might well require a socialised industry to 'even permanently earn more or less than the annual cost of its compensating stock'. Moreover, in time, the real cost of servicing the compensation stock would decline in relevance and in difficult trading conditions 'it would be economically unjustifiable to attempt, by restricting output and raising prices, to cover the previous level of capital charges so long as the lower level of demand persisted'.[15]

In such views Meade was 'left with a minority view of one' and he remained as the sole dissenting voice when the Second Report of the Official Committee on the Socialisation of Industries was circulated by Morrison on 10 May 1946.[16] However, outside the committee, Meade's concern over cost-based pricing was more widely shared by economists. Where Meade and some fellow economists parted company was over Meade's advocacy of marginal cost pricing, rather than average cost pricing, as the basis for nationalised industry pricing. Meade, Fleming, and like-minded economists in the Economic Section promoted marginal cost pricing as providing more precise and decentralised cost-

---

[13] PRO CAB 124/950, SI(M)(46)18, Cabinet, Official Committee on the Socialisation of Industries, circulated by Herbert Morrison, 10 May 1946, para. 2. The Economic Section prepared a note of dissent on price policy for the draft report in February 1946. See PRO CAB 134/693, SI(O)(46)8, Note by the Economic Section, circulated by M. T. Flett, 12 February 1946.

[14] PRO CAB 124/950, GEN 245/2 meeting, Cabinet, Working Party on Price Policy of Socialised Industries, 29 September 1948.

[15] PRO CAB 124/950, SI(M)(46)18, Cabinet, Official Committee on the Socialisation of Industries, circulated by Morrison, 10 May 1946, paras. 8, 17.

[16] BLPES, Meade Papers, 1/6, 27 April 1946. PRO CAB 124/950, SI(M)(46)18, Cabinet, Official Committee on the Socialisation of Industries, circulated by Morrison, 10 May 1946.

based information for the allocation of resources than either average cost pricing or anything emerging from a more administrative system of resource allocation. This blend of improving the efficiency of resource allocation and providing checks against administrative over-centralisation appealed to the fundamentally liberal Meade. Meade was attracted by the allocative benefits of marginal cost pricing, since 'if the prices of finished products are set in this way, the price paid by consumers may be taken as a measure of the value to them of the last additional units of each commodity or service. Similarly, the prices of the factors of production will measure the relative scarcity to the community of the various factors of production.'[17]

As importantly, perhaps, the defence which pricing afforded against overly bureaucratic, over-centralised administrative planning was also recognised. If demands were not to be 'automatically screened by the charging of a price' then 'some more arbitrary system of allocation' would have to be used. The implications were clearly spelled out by the Economic Section:

If the alternative uses of human and material resources are not reflected in the money costs of production some central body will be responsible for the impossible task of trying to envisage all the alternative uses of resources in all the different industries and of choosing the most productive combination. In the absence of a properly functioning price system to serve as a guide, the managers of plants in socialised industries would lack criteria for the economic conduct of their enterprises and it would become necessary to transfer to the centre the responsibility for many types of decisions which could otherwise, with advantage, have been taken locally.[18]

The objections raised by some economists to Meade's preference for marginal cost pricing were more to its financial than to its allocative consequences, in particular in industries enjoying increasing, rather than diminishing, returns. The economics of marginal cost pricing in a classic diminishing-returns industry with rising costs were clear, textbook material. However, in an industry such as electricity, increasing returns could leave marginal costs below average costs, with a marginal cost pricing policy therefore failing to cover the total costs of the industry. What divided the economists who entered the debate on the

[17] PRO CAB 134/693, SI(O)(45)3, Cabinet, Official Committee on the Socialisation of Industries, 'The Problems of Socialisation', Economic Section's response to Lord President's questions on price policy, wage rates, the planning and timing of new investment, and the conduct of the import and export trade in socialised industries, para. 5. Circulated by M. T. Flett, 4 December 1945.

[18] PRO CAB 134/693, SI(O)(45)3, Cabinet, Official Committee on the Socialisation of Industries, 'The Problems of Socialisation', memorandum by Economic Section, circulated by M. T. Flett, 4 December 1945, para. 8.

pricing policy of nationalised industries were their attitudes towards loss-making by these state enterprises. Meade, Fleming, and Lerner were prepared to tolerate such losses, and, if necessary, to offset these losses against profits made by other socialised industries, so as to bring the total financial account of the socialised industries into balance.[19] Just as it was willing to tolerate losses, so too was the Economic Section happy for profits to be earned as a result of charging prices designed to keep demand in balance with the capacity of an industry until that capacity could be increased.[20]

One of Meade's reasons for not wanting to compensate former owners with fixed-interest national debt was to leave 'public utility free to make such profit or loss as is in the public interest'.[21] This was in fact closer to the line that would be taken by the government from 1961, in which profits were required to be earned.[22] The main opposition to Meade's position came from Tom Wilson, in particular, and from Ronald Coase, both of whom engaged Meade and Fleming in a debate on state-enterprise pricing in the *Economic Journal* during 1944 and 1945. Wilson argued strongly that if loss-making was tolerated then an important discipline and incentive would be removed from mangers in a monopoly industry.[23] Against this, however, it could be argued that the instruction to maximise profits where possible might provide a better managerial incentive to efficiency than simply requiring costs to be covered (especially where it was all too easy to cover them). Moreover, as Little was to remark in 1950, if an industry could make profits without distorting output, 'then it seems manifestly wrong that it should throw the whole burden of finding the savings required for its own investment on to the government or the rest of the economy'.[24]

Wilson acknowledged the pricing problems of industries such as the

---

[19] T. Wilson 'Price and Outlay Policy of State Enterprise', *Economic Journal*, 55 (December 1945), pp. 454–61. J. Meade and J. Fleming, 'Price and Output Policy of State Enterprise', *Economic Journal*, 54 (December 1944), pp. 321ff. R. H. Coase, 'Price and Output Policy of State Enterprise: a Comment', *Economic Journal*, 55 (April 1945), pp. 112–13. J. Meade and J. Fleming, 'Price and Output Policy of State Enterprise', *Economic Journal*, 54 (1944), pp. 321–39.

[20] PRO CAB 124/950, SI(M)(46)18, Official Committee on the Socialisation of Industries, Second Report, circulated by Morrison, 10 May 1946.

[21] S. Howson (ed.), *The Collected Papers of James Meade, vol. IV: The Cabinet Office Diary, 1944–47*, London, Unwin Hyman, 1990, p. 18, 16 December 1944.

[22] *The Financial and Economic Obligations of the Nationalised Industries*, 1961, Cmd 1337. S. R. Dennison, 'Investment in the Nationalised Industries', *Transactions of the Manchester Statistical Society* (paper read on 11 February 1959) (1958–9), pp. 1–25. A Beacham, 'Price Policy of the Coal Industry', *Journal of Industrial Economics*, 2 (1953), pp. 140–54. D. N. Chester, 'Notes on the Price Policy Indicated by the Nationalisation Acts', *Oxford Economic Papers*, 2 (1950), pp. 69–74.

[23] Little, *Critique*, p. 193.   [24] Little, *Critique*, p. 215.

railways which were in historic decline, but his preference was for the state either to provide the industry with a fixed subsidy or to write down the capital of the industry and then require the reduced total costs to be covered. At least then, 'the manager would still have a definite obligation instead of a blank cheque'.[25] As for decreasing-cost industries such as electricity, Coase suggested that marginal cost pricing might be possible if a two-part tariff were introduced, in preference to financing losses out of general taxation.[26] However, where two-part tariffs could not be used, Coase was inclined to charge a price equal to average cost. Although the relation between costs and receipts at the margin would be faulty, he regarded this as being preferable to a correct marginal relationship which subsidised consumers of the product, and produced an incorrect relationship between total costs and total receipts.

The debate among economists was precipitated by a review article by Meade of Abba Lerner's *Economics of Control* which appeared in the *Economic Journal* in April 1945.[27] These early developments in welfare economics built on Lerner's earlier work and roughly coincided with seminal articles such as that by Hotelling in 1938, which discussed the use of marginal cost pricing in public utilities in mixed economies. In his *Economics of Control* Lerner considered the application of welfare economics in a mixed economy, in which he assumed that pure, or nearly pure, competition prevailed in the private sector.[28] To Meade, Lerner, whom he characterised in his diary as 'a real Liberal-Socialist-Welfare-Marginalist economist', represented 'a breath of fresh air . . . after the dreadful arbitrary and authoritarian quantitative planning of a Balogh on the one hand and the extreme *laissez-faire* attitude of a Hayek on the other'.[29]

The arguments between Meade and Wilson on pricing policy continued within the Economic Section, of which both were members. Despite Wilson, according to Meade, continuing to 'lay down the golden rule that prices should cover average cost', it was eventually

[25] Wilson, 'Price and Outlay Policy', *Economic Journal*, p. 460.
[26] C. L. Paine, 'Some Aspects of Discrimination by Public Utilities', *Economica*, n.s. 4, 16, (November 1937), pp. 425–39.
[27] Abba P. Lerner, *The Economics of Control: Principles of Welfare Economics*, New York, Macmillan, 1944. J. Meade, 'Mr Lerner on *The Economics of Control*', *Economic Journal*, 55 (April 1945), pp. 47–69, reprinted in S. Howson (ed.), *The Collected Papers of James Meade, vol. II, Value, Distribution and Growth*, London, Allen & Unwin, 1988, ch. 4.
[28] A. P. Lerner, 'Statics and Dynamics in Socialist Economics', *Economic Journal*, 47 (June 1937), pp. 253–70. H. Hotelling, 'The General Welfare in Relation to Problems of Taxation and of Railway and Utility Rates', *Econometrica*, 6 (July 1938), pp. 242–69. Little, *Critique*, ch. 11.
[29] James Meade, *Diary*, pp. 37–8, 28 January 1945. On Meade's surprise at the controversy sparked by his and Marcus Fleming's symposium in the *Economic Journal*, see his diary entry for 7 January 1947, p. 27.

decided by the Economic Section, after 'much discussion', that it would be better 'to start straight off with the principle that prices should cover marginal costs'.[30] Not that the arguments over average and marginal cost pricing were ever over. The difficulties of applying marginal cost pricing continued to be pointed out during the 1950s and 1960s.[31] The continued concern with the difficulties of defining and measuring marginal costs, worries over the use of short- or long-run marginal cost, persistent objections to the possible generation of financial deficits in increasing return industries, the alleged misrepresentation of the costs of externalities, and a growing objection that the application of marginal cost pricing in conditions in which perfect competition and ideal allocation did not exist elsewhere in the economy would actually further distort resource allocation within the economy, all combined to give rise to 'the problem of second-best'.[32] The problem then became that of discovering the best 'second-best' solution.

Given the persistence of the arguments over average and marginal cost pricing, it is perhaps not surprising that fundamental differences of view between the likes of Meade and Wilson were not resolved quickly. Their arguments were important not only for the future development of welfare economics, but also because crucial decisions were being made during 1945 to 1947 on what principles should form the statutory basis for the subsequent pricing behaviour of large publicly owned sections of the economy. It seems unlikely that many ministers and civil servants understood the details of the arguments among economists; but it seems clear that they knew that economists were disagreeing among themselves. In mid-1948, in response to a plea for help from Alec Johnston, the Chairman of the Working Party on the Price Policy of Socialised Industries, Richard Kahn, summarised the debate over average and marginal cost pricing as one in which there was 'by no means any clear agreement among economists as to the principles which should apply'.[33]

[30] Meade, *Diary*, 3 November 1945, 18 November 1945, pp. 158, 168.

[31] N. Ruggles, 'The Welfare Basis of the Marginal Cost Pricing Principle', *Review of Economic Studies*, 16–17 (1949–50), pp. 29–46, and 'Recent Developments in the Theory of Marginal Cost Pricing', *Review of Economic Studies*, 16–17 (1949–50), pp. 107–26.

[32] R. G. Lipsey and K. Lancaster, 'The General Theory of Second Best', *Review of Economic Studies*, 23–4 (1956–7), pp. 11–32. Some of the difficulties were recognised by the Section: 'These criteria of pricing are by no means easy to apply, and nothing but a very rough approximation to the economic price can be expected. No matter how full the cost-accounting data supplied to the price-fixing authority, the latter, judging from a distance, can do little more than make a guess at the additional cost of producing the last units of output.' PRO CAB 124/950, GEN 98/8, memorandum by Economic Section on 'Socialisation of Industries', circulated by Morrison, 15 December 1945.

[33] PRO CAB 124/950, R. F. Kahn to A. Johnston, 24 July 1948.

While pointing up the nature of the arguments over average and marginal cost pricing, Kahn also emphasised 'that there are certain principles on which general agreement would be secured'.[34] Preeminent among these was the widespread opinion that considerably greater use could be made of the pricing mechanism in general, ignoring the particular disputes about cost-based pricing. Indeed, the arguments about marginal cost pricing were irrelevant until supply and demand were back in some sort of equilibrium. Thus, the very first of the five rules affecting pricing and output set out by the Economic Section in its 1945 memorandum to the Socialisation of Industry Committee was that the price mechanism should be used to equate supply and demand: 'prices of finished products should be so set as to bring the demand for the products into balance with the supply'. The Section explicitly recognised that marginal cost pricing could not be introduced immediately and that their advocacy in various memoranda was 'intended to present an ideal, applicable to conditions of comparative normality, towards which we should steadily move, rather than something to be put, in its entirety, into immediate operation'. None the less, although not immediately applicable, they should not be neglected since 'the pricing problems of the transition period will be more happily solved if the longer term goal is kept in mind'.[35]

In contrast to the heightened awareness among economists of the intricacies, problems, and possibilities of employing different forms of pricing, there seems to have been a diminished awareness among ministers of the possible uses of pricing mechanisms. Certainly, in the early years, arguments for a greater use of pricing mechanisms were dismissed or ignored by Morrison. His ability to do this may have been strengthened by the outbreak of arguments among economists over the respective merits of average and marginal cost pricing, even though a broad church of leading economists such as Meade, Fleming, Wilson, Coase, Little, and Lewis were agreed on the general desirability of making much greater use of pricing mechanisms. The upshot of this division was that it weakened the ability of economists to resist some of the pricing policies which were introduced, a significant number of which were some considerable way from what the broad church of economists might have regarded as 'rational'. The basic function of prices, as defined by the Economic Section in terms which were unlikely to offend many economists, was 'to guide production towards those goods and services which are most needed by the community, and to

---

[34] PRO CAB 124/950, R. F. Kahn to A. Johnston, 24 July 1948.
[35] PRO CAB 124/950, GEN 98/8, memorandum by Economic Section, circulated by Morrison, 15 December 1945.

ensure that production is carried out by the most economical methods'.[36] It was by no means clear that such a function for prices was envisaged by politicians. An immediate political aim of pricing seemed to be to keep prices down, not simply for their own sake, but also as a means of increasing the accessibility of output. As far as criteria for nationalised industry pricing were concerned, ministers were happy in general to accept the view that industries should cover their average costs over a number of years. Within the Cabinet, marginal cost pricing was not given much consideration before being rejected, the suspicion being that ministers did not properly understand the issues.[37] In accepting the recommendations of the Committee on the Socialisation of Industries for average cost pricing, ministers also appeared to be willing to share the Committee's view that it was 'desirable to make as little significant change in prices as possible on the beginning of socialisation, if only to minimise disturbance'.[38]

Of particular concern to economists both in and outside the Economic Section was the danger that average cost pricing would facilitate a drift towards cross-subsidising and pooling arrangements within particular industries. This was most likely in industries such as coal mining, where such arrangements had operated during the inter-war and wartime period. More recently, cost-pooling tendencies had been implicit in the Foot proposals and in the miners' push for national wages, with the ready association in some minds between nationalisa-tion and national prices set by a single national authority.[39] As one commentator noted, on nationalisation the coal-mining industry came with an 'obsolete pricing structure' which was 'the product, not of current needs, but of fortuitous historical circumstances'.[40] Part I of the 1930 Coal Mines Act had established a cartel with statutory force among colliery owners, providing for minimum pithead prices fixed by district associations of collieries and for output quotas applied to individual mines. Price competition was checked and despite provisions

---

[36] PRO CAB 134/693, SI(O)(45)3, Cabinet, Official Committee on the Socialisation of Industries, 'The Problems of Socialisation', memorandum by the Economic Section, circulated by M. T. Flett, 4 December 1945, para. 2.

[37] PRO CAB 124/950 A. Johnston to Robert Hall (Economic Section) re. SI(O)(45)3, 8 June 1948. PRO CAB 124/950. 'The Pricing Policy of the Nationalised Industries', 1947. Rather sulkily, the Economic Section characterised this as 'a deliberate sacrifice of economic advantage for the sake of adherence to the statutory provision which Parliament has thought fit to make'.

[38] PRO CAB 124/950, Official Committee on the Socialisation of Industries, second report, SI(M)(46)18, circulated by H. Morrison, 10 May 1946.

[39] Tom Wilson, *Modern Capitalism and Economic Progress*, London, Macmillan, 1950, p. 161.

[40] PRO CAB 124/950, 'The Pricing Policy of the Nationalised Industries', para. 13.

for the sale of output quotas from one colliery to another, the pattern of production which had existed before the Act was largely preserved.[41] At the outbreak of World War II, the general level of existing prices was frozen by agreement between the government and the colliery owners, although, from time to time, increases at a uniform rate per ton were permitted. This preserved the *status quo* except that, being proportionately greater for lower-quality, cheaper coal than for more expensive grades of coal, it altered the price ratios between different qualities. In the later years of the war, as coal mining costs rose still further, a levy-subsidy system was introduced by the government, under which the more profitable colliery districts subsidised the less profitable, through the operation of the Coal Charges Account. After the war, the structure was maintained by government control of prices, and buttressed by government control over the distribution of available supplies.[42] As some indication of the extent of cross-subsidisation existing within the industry prior to nationalisation, during the last quarter of 1946 financial relations between the Coal Charges Account and the Districts varied from a net contribution to the Account of 8s 9.14d per ton by the Leicestershire District, to a net receipt from the Account of 10s 5.31d per ton by the South Wales District.[43]

These long-run and state-supported cross-subsidisation and cost-pooling arrangements were objectionable to a broad range of economists.[44] Within government the Economic Section pointed to the inefficiency of obtaining output from 'high-cost plants which could be produced more cheaply by a more intensive working of low cost plants'. If the pooling principle, as exemplified by the Coal Charges Act, was permanently retained in the industry after it was socialised and the prices paid to the various mines continued to differ by more than was justified by transport costs, then this would lead to 'underproduction in the better mines and over-production in the marginal mines.'[45] It also ran the risk of sending distorted signals to those planning the development of new pits. The Economic Section emphasised the 'paramount need' for the 'relative pithead prices of different grades of coal to be

[41] PRO CAB 124/950, Working Party on the Price Policy of Socialised Industries, 'Price Policy of the National Coal Board', October 1948, para. 3.

[42] PRO CAB 124/950, Working Party on the Price Policy of the Socialised Industries, 'Price Policy of the National Coal Board', October 1948, para. 3.

[43] PRO CAB 124/950, 'The Pricing Policy of the Nationalised Industries', p. 1, footnote 1.

[44] A. Beacham, 'The Coal Industry' in Duncan Burn (ed.), *The Structure of British Industry*, vol. I, Cambridge, Cambridge University Press, 1958, pp. 131–4.

[45] PRO CAB 124/950, GEN 98/8, Cabinet, Socialisation of Industries, circulated by Herbert Morrison, 15 December 1945, memo by Economic Section on pricing, para. 19.

adjusted into line with the relative intensity of market demand for them. This done, the National Coal Board ought properly to place priority in its expansion programme on the production of those coals in those coalfields where the relative price, so determined, is particularly high compared with the relative cost of increased supply'.[46] The NCB's approach to pricing, however, was leading the industry in a direction virtually opposite to that sought by the Economic Section. What the NCB worked to establish was a system whereby after 'scientific evaluation', coal was divided into four categories. In an administrative procedure which was in many ways the opposite of how the price mechanism would have worked, there was to be an assessment of demand independent of price considerations, and then a fixing of prices at a level equal to the average costs of production of the output decided on. In the view of the Economic Section, however, output should be determined by price considerations and not vice versa.[47] Philip Chantler, Meade, and Fleming of the Economic Section were persistent in their efforts to dissuade civil servants in the Ministry of Fuel and Power from persisting with, if not augmenting, the existing pooling system in the coal industry. During 1945 and 1946, over various lunches at Peggy Joseph's flat with Quirk, de Peyer, and Hemming of the Ministry of Fuel and Power, and in two-man deputations to see de Peyer, Chantler and Meade failed to persuade the Ministry of Fuel and Power to accept their idea that 'the Coal Board should use the price mechanism to decide how much coal, what qualities and in what localities to produce'. As Meade recalled after the lunch in Peggy Joseph's flat just before Christmas 1945, 'the officials at Fuel and Power did not seem to have changed their attitude of believing that our ideas were both impractical and unnecessary'. Although Meade and Chantler were to persist in their efforts, the size of the task was becoming clear by April 1946, when, as Meade recalled in his diary, in spite of holding a 'very excellent paper' by Chantler on price policy in a socialised industry, 'to my horror Fergusson told me that they have it in mind to fix uniform pit-head prices throughout the country for the various grades of coal'.[48]

In making their case, the NCB stressed the administrative virtues of stability and quality. In contrast to the supposed uncertainty and fluctuations of the market, administrative categorisation would provide

[46] PRO CAB 124/950, 'The Pricing Policy of the Nationalised Industries', para. 4.
[47] PRO CAB 124/950, GEN 245/2 meeting, Cabinet, Working Party on Price Policy of Socialised Industries, 29 September 1948, p. 2.
[48] J. Meade, *Diary*, 6 October 1945, 23 December 1945, 27 April 1946, 15 August 1946, pp. 141, 191, 253, 312. PRO T230/21, EC(S)(46)17 (Revise), 'An Economic Policy for the Socialised Coal Industry', 23 March 1946.

stability and consistency of quality, both of which were cited as being of importance to industry and of interest to government.[49] Price control was not only one of the many ingredients in the government's employment policy, but price and social stability were also leading objectives of government policy in general. This was an outlook which was to persist and one which the NCB was happy to share.[50] The NCB view that 'they were enjoined to have regard to the national interest and in the eyes of the Board this meant making coal available at the lowest possible cost' was viewed sceptically by the Economic Section, who suspected the NCB of favouring the physical rationing of coal and of using inflated demand as a political weapon in its drive for an expanded investment programme.[51] To those seeking stability and uniformity, average cost pricing had more to offer than marginal cost pricing. Marginal cost pricing was seen as complicated, 'a burden on the economic life of the country', and as itself a source of inefficiency as producers operating in industries 'fixed their selling price as equal to the marginal cost of the marginal firm and so kept in production inefficient and high cost firms'.[52]

Even as the persistence and extent of the coal shortage became clear, there remained strong opposition to a price increase which 'would correct the present anomalous position where every one says coal is precious but no-one is prepared to charge a scarcity price'.[53] As a result, an economy short of coal had some of the lowest coal prices in Europe with the average pithead price of coal in the UK in the first half of 1950 being $6.61 per metric ton, compared with $7.92 in West Germany, $8.71 in the Dutch state mines, $9.64 in the Saar, $10.0 in France, and $13.7 in Belgium.[54] Resources were sunk into producing coal at a

[49] PRO CAB 124/950 NCB/CCC(48)6, Marketing Department, 'Progress in the Designing of a Coal Price Structure', Report to the Consumers Council, 1 July 1948, para. 12.

[50] LPA RD 1 'A Labour Policy for Private Industry', September 1945. 'Direct control of prices, and of profit margins, at least of necessities, has proved essential during the war. Price control will play an important part in a policy of full employment.' H. Gaitskell, *Socialism and Nationalisation*, London Fabian Tract, p. 20. Reviewing the first nine years of nationalisation, Gaitskell noted that coal prices at the pithead rose by 44%, while over the same period the average charge per unit of electricity by only 21%.

[51] D. L. Munby, 'The Price of Fuel', *Oxford Economic Papers*, n.s. 6, (1954), pp. 226–42. PRO POWE 14/555, DCFP, 11th meeting, Committee on National Fuel Policy, meeting with representatives of the National Coal Board, 25 January 1952, question 20.

[52] PRO POWE 14/551, EL 219/3, A. Farquhar to M. P. Murray (Electricity Division), 1 February 1952. PRO POWE 14/556, DCFP, 195(Annex), 'Aide-Memoire: the Case For and Against Increasing the Price of Coal', 21 May 1952.

[53] PRO POWE 14/556, DCFP 195(Annex), 'Aide Memoire: the Case For and Against Increasing the Price of Coal', 21 May 1952.

[54] PRO CAB 134/692, SI(M)(51)41, Cabinet, Socialisation of Industries Committee;

financial loss. In 1948, the Ministry of Fuel and Power estimated that more than 12 per cent of the 1947 output was produced at a loss of 10s a ton or more, with a loss of at least £1.00 per ton being incurred on a further four or five million tons.[55] By 1952, the NCB had a cumulative deficit of £14 million.[56] In August 1951, the postwar movement of nationalised fuel and power industry prices was surveyed by the Minister of Fuel and Power, Philip Noel-Baker. As Noel-Baker informed the Cabinet Committee on the Socialisation of Industries Committee in 1951, while 'by June 1951, the Board of Trade Wholesale Price Index increased by 216 per cent above the level of 1938, the figure for coal included in that Index had advanced by 176 per cent'. More striking, however, was the difference since the NCB began its operations; between December 1946 and June 1951, the Wholesale Price Index advanced by 79 per cent, while the Index for coal increased by only 39 per cent. Thus, 'it is still true, as *The Economist* noted in February this year that "coal in terms of other commodities is today cheaper than it was before the war"'.[57]

As with coal, so too with electricity prices, which were low in real and historic terms. Not only did electricity prices not adequately reflect the fact that it cost more to supply at the peak than at other times but compared with the general rise in costs and prices since 1938, the average increase in electricity charges was modest. In the decade prior to nationalisation, electricity tariffs had hardly increased at all in money terms, and the average domestic price of electricity had fallen faster than in any other decade in history, both in real terms and relative to the price of its major competitors, gas, and coal. Moreover, by 1948, while the average price per unit for power units had risen by 0.22d, the average price per unit sold for lighting, heating, and cooking had gone down by 0.138d.[58] On average, domestic electricity supplies were cheaper in January 1948 than they had been in 1938. By 1948, the average domestic consumer was using twice as much electricity as in

Price Increases by Nationalised Fuel and Power Industries; memorandum by the Minister of Fuel and Power (Philip Noel-Baker), 29 August 1951.

[55] PRO CAB 124/950, GEN 245/2, Cabinet, Working Party on Price Policy of Socialised Industries, 'Price Policy for the National Coal Board: memo by the Ministry of Fuel and Power', 1 July 1948.

[56] Little, *Price of Fuel*, p. 1.

[57] PRO CAB 134/692, SI(M)(51)41, Cabinet, Socialisation of Industries Committee, 'Price Increases by Nationalised Fuel and Power Industries; Memorandum by the Minister of Fuel and Power' (Philip Noel-Baker), 29 August 1951. Sir Norman Chester, *The Nationalisation of British Industry, 1945–51*, London, HMSO, 1975, p. 1054.

[58] PRO T228/308, memorandum on 'Electricity Policy' by Hugh Gaitskell, Ministry of Fuel and Power, to Stafford Cripps, Chancellor of the Exchequer, 23 January 1948.

1938 but paying only half as much for it per kilowatt-hour (kWh) in real terms. Similarly, by June 1951, gas prices had risen on average by 76 per cent above their 1938 level, compared with 216 per cent for all goods in the Board of Trade Wholesale Price Index, and during the first two years as a nationalised industry, gas prices increased by no more than 9 per cent. Ministry of Fuel and Power estimates suggested that while average prices paid by households for all the goods and services doubled between 1938 and mid-1951, the average price of fuel and light to the domestic consumer had increased by only about 80 per cent. As Noel-Baker noted, 'this was less than the average increase in retail food prices (despite the heavy subsidies); still less than the price of clothing; and very much less than the average price of household goods'.[59]

The modest price increase in gas and electricity prices was in part facilitated by low coal prices, which formed a large proportion of variable costs.[60] Gas and electricity received as much coal as they wanted (though often not the grade they wanted). Thus while there had been a reduction of 24 per cent (11 million tons) since 1938 in the direct consumption of coal by households, this was almost entirely offset by the increased use of gas and electricity. In the face of stark evidence of coal shortages, financial losses on imported coal and historically low coal prices, the government persisted in its efforts to keep coal prices down. Low coal prices were presented as being in the 'national interest'.[61] Indeed, the whole purpose of Noel-Baker's survey of fuel and power prices was not to urge a shift in pricing policy, but rather to assure colleagues that nationalised-industry prices were not too high and that there was 'no evidence for accusations of inefficiency, extravagance, or profiteering'.[62]

Many of the political and economic arguments over pricing were rehearsed in the meetings and the report of the Ridley Committee, which was established in 1951 to consider the use and development of national fuel and power resources.[63] During the committee's proceedings, few, if any, of the arguments made were new, but it did provide an opportunity for economists to build on the previous efforts of such

[59] PRO CAB 134/692, SI(M)(51)41, Cabinet, Socialisation of Industries Committee, 'Price Increases by Nationalised Fuel and Power Industries; Memorandum by the Minister of Fuel and Power' (Philip Noel-Baker), 29 August 1951, paras. 3, 8, 12.
[60] I. Little, *Price of Fuel*, pp. 2–3.   [61] D. Chester, *Nationalisation*, p. 710.
[62] PRO CAB 134/692, SI(M)(51)41, Cabinet, Socialisation of Industries Committee, 'Price Increases by Nationalised Fuel and Power Industries; memorandum by the Minister of Fuel and Power' (Philip Noel-Baker), 29 August 1951, para. 13.
[63] *Report of the Committee on National Policy for the Use of Fuel and Power Resources*, Cmd 8647, 1952. The Ridley Committee was first known as the 'Investigating Committee on Fuel and Power Policy', and later as the 'Committee on National Policy for the Use of Fuel and Power Resources'.

committees as Clow's, and attempt to persuade industrialists and politicians to give greater consideration to the merits of the pricing mechanism. Not that Gaitskell's experience of the proceedings and outcome of the Clow Committee made him particularly keen to establish another such committee. Ever since the fuel crisis of 1947, calls for such an independent inquiry had come from the FBI and the TUC, this request gaining in volubility following renewed concern with coal stocks in the autumn and winter of 1950. In the spring of 1951, even some ministers began to speak of the need for a 'positive national fuel policy'.[64] Scarred by his experience of the Clow Committee and inclined to regard such talk of a 'fuel policy' without adequate prices as largely special pleading for extra resources, Gaitskell's initial instinct was to refuse the requests from the TUC and the FBI. He was certainly doubtful of the ability of ministers, given their thinking on pricing mechanisms, to foster any sharp sense of opportunity cost in their discussions of 'co-ordination'. His suspicions were generally shared by the Minister of Fuel and Power, Philip Noel-Baker, who reminded the Chancellor that he had recently established a small Fuel Efficiency Advisory Committee, which could be expected to look at the whole problem of improving fuel use. However, following a meeting between the Chancellor, the Minister and representatives of the FBI and the TUC, Gaitskell relented and advised Noel-Baker that the appointment of a Committee on National Fuel Policy might at least provide an opportunity for some of the current 'ill-founded notions' about a 'national fuel policy' to be 'exploded', as well as allowing some new contributions to be made to a difficult subject.[65] Learning from his experience with the Clow Committee, Gaitskell refused all requests from the nationalised fuel and power industries that representatives of their industries should be included on the committee. Instead, Gaitskell opted for a small committee of independent members, charged with examining the use and not the production of fuel and power.[66] This

---

[64] PRO POWE 14/557, Ministry of Fuel and Power, Economic Advisers Branch, 'Committee on National Fuel Policy: General Notes in Retrospect' by P. Chantler 22 August 1952.

[65] PRO POWE 14/557, Ministry of Fuel and Power, Economic Advisers Branch, 'Committee on National Fuel Policy: General Notes in Retrospect' by P. Chantler 22 August 1952.

[66] The other members were Lincoln Evans (General Secretary of the Iron and Steel Trades Confederation and member of the TUC General Council), the FBI nominee Neil Gardiner (technical Director of Huntley & Palmers Ltd and Chairman of the Southern Region Fuel Efficiency Advisory Committee), Sir Claude Gibb (Chairman and Managing Director of C. A. Parsons and Co. Ltd, and a member of the Minister's Scientific Advisory Committee), Mrs M. McIntosh (tutor in Sociology, Bedford College, London, and a member of the London County Council), and Miss M. R.

committee was headed by Viscount Ridley, a member of the former Fuel and Power Advisory Council, which in 1946 had produced the 'Simon Report' on Domestic Fuel Policy, and included among its membership Professor W. R. Hawthorne (Professor of Applied Thermo-dynamics, Cambridge University), and Professor W. A. Lewis (Professor of Political Economy, Manchester University).

Close observers of the workings of the Ridley Committee regarded W. A. Lewis as 'undoubtedly the most constructive member of the Committee'.[67] Like Gaitskell, Lewis was sceptical of fashionable talk of 'co-ordination', regarding it as 'one of those words which it is usually better to avoid, since it has no precise meaning. Other such words in economics are "balanced", "ordered", "planned"; they mean no more than "nice"'. For Lewis, 'if co-ordination meant anything then it revolved around the two ideas that relative prices should reflect relative costs of supply and that industries' investment policies should take some cognisance of those of others, whether in relation to quantities to be supplied, or in relation to the location of plants'. Lewis saw no reason to think that, even if a national board were established on which each industry was represented, there was any reason to expect that 'any more would emerge from this but a policy towards each other of "live and let live"?'[68] Like Douglas Jay, Lewis thought that rather than establishing committees to discuss 'co-ordination', much more would be gained by addressing such immediate issues as the shortage of labour in the coal mines. Indeed, Lewis argued to the Ridley Committee that it should be abolished and the real issue of labour shortages be tackled:

I find it scandalous that responsible people in this country resign themselves to the opinion that it is impossible to increase the labour supply in the mines, to the extent of 0.3% of the working population, when this would solve most of our economic problems. I trust that the first act of a new Minister of Fuel will be to disband our committee, and to appoint instead a committee to advise him on how to get another 50,000 men into the mines since this problem is far more important than the problem with which we are charged.[69]

Lewis reiterated the view of many economists that coal prices should be increased, and that greater use should be made of price relativities. If

Schofield (Housing Manger, Stoke Newington) who was 'able very effectively to show the Committee the approach of the local authority housing expert'.

[67] PRO POWE 14/557, Ministry of Fuel and Power, Economic Advisers Branch, 'Committee on National Fuel Policy: General Notes in Retrospect', by Chantler, Kelly, and Watts, 22 August 1952.
[68] PRO POWE 14/554, DCFP(48), paper on 'National Fuel Policy: Approach to the Subject', by W. A. Lewis, 23 October 1951, paras. 72–3.
[69] PRO POWE 14/554, DCFP(48), paper on 'National Fuel Policy: Approach to the Subject', by W. A. Lewis, 23 October 1951, para. 95.

governments wished to avoid profit-making by nationalised industries, then price increases could be effected by taxing coal. If government was concerned about the 'inflationary' effects of this tax, then industries such as steel and railways, which used about 17 per cent of the coal supply, could be exempted from the tax. If anything, such a coal tax could reduce domestic inflationary pressure, by reducing disposable incomes and releasing more goods for export. If this was politically unacceptable, then the Chancellor could use the revenue from a coal tax to remit other taxes, so that the public's purchasing power would remain unchanged.[70] That the inflationary impact of higher coal prices would be as large as imagined by politicians seemed doubtful, the Ridley Committee estimating that a £1 per ton increase in the price of coal would increase the average costs of industrial production by 2 per cent and the interim index of retail prices by two points.[71] The political objection that price increases would encourage demands for higher wages and threaten the controlled stability of price–wage arrangements raised the important issue of whether such stability was hiding relativities which needed to be flushed out.[72] As Lewis argued 'if gross distortions of the structure of prices cannot be removed without some general inflation, then we may just have to regard some general inflation as a necessary cost of getting the price structure right'.[73]

Given the influence of Lewis, and the absence of industry representatives, it was perhaps unsurprising that the Ridley Committee emerged firmly in favour of increased competition between the fuel and power industries, with greater use being made of pricing mechanisms. Similarly, it did not propose any centrally organised control of all the fuel and power services, as had frequently been suggested by groups such as the TUC (Trades Union Congress).[74] Professor Lewis' support for a price increase of £1 per ton for coal was based on his estimate that the cost of the marginal 10–15 million tons was 15s 0d above the selling price, that the price of imports was twice that of the pithead price of coal, and that exports were sold at £1 above pithead prices while at the

---

[70] PRO POWE 14/554, DCFP (48), paper on 'National Fuel Policy: Approach to the Subject', by W. A. Lewis, 23 October 1951.

[71] PRO POWE 14/556 DCFP 195 (annex), 'Aide-Memoire: The Case For and Against Increasing the Price of Coal', 21 May 1952.

[72] I. Little, *Price of Fuel*, p. 36. The Ridley Committee estimated that the rise in the cost of living index from even a 40% increase in the price of coal would be between 1 and 2% only. PRO POWE 14/555, DCFP, 11th meeting, Committee on National Fuel Policy to representatives of the NCB, 25 January 1952.

[73] PRO POWE 14/554, DCFP (48), paper on 'National Fuel Policy: Approach to the Subject', by W. A. Lewis, 23 October 1951.

[74] PRO POWE 14/557, memo by P. Chantler, Economic Advisers Branch, 21 August 1952. *National Policy* Cmd 8647, para. 291.

same time there was unsatisfied demand for UK coal exports of 15 million tons.[75] Arguing for the price to be increased to the export price, Lewis noted that 'my guess is that raising the price to the consumer by 25% would reduce the demand by at least 5% or ten million tons (a guess based on the fact that few elasticities of demand are less than 0.2). This would not add ten million tons to exports; it would merely eliminate the current shortage of that amount, and permit rationing to be greatly relaxed, or discontinued.'[76]

During its deliberations, the Ridley Committee was unable to avoid becoming involved in its own wrangles over whether marginal or average cost prices should be set.[77] The £1 recommended increase was described as the marginal cost, but this concern with appellation was a little academic, since marginal cost pricing could not operate until the market was cleared. What mattered, however, was that the government effectively refused to implement the recommended £1 increase in the price of coal.[78] Nor was it prepared to consider the suggested use of tax as a means of raising prices in other industries. In 1948, even Gaitskell when pushing for higher peak-hour electricity prices, accepted that 'political objections rule out anything in the nature of a tax on consumption. For if this is to be effective, it must result in a substantial increase in the total bill for large consumers of electricity and many of these – often not from choice – belong to the lower incomes groups.'[79] Of particular concern to Gaitskell were those living in pre-fabs. That local authorities should have placed people in all-electric pre-fabs, where, with cheap electric fires, they could avoid the worst strictures of coal shortages while adding to the capacity problems of the electricity

---

[75] PRO POWE 14/556 DCFP, Ministry of Fuel and Power: Committee on National Fuel Policy, 19 meeting, 26 March 1952, minutes of meeting held on Sunday 23 March 1952.

[76] PRO POWE 14/554, DCFP(48), paper on 'National Fuel Policy: Approach to the Subject', by W. A. Lewis, 23 October 1951. PRO POWE 14/556 DCFP 19 meeting, 23 March 1952. In investigating the effects of price changes on coal consumption, Lewis drew on inter-war evidence which suggested than a price increase of 1% was associated with a saving of coal of between 0.1% and 0.2%. Thus, an increase in the price of coal of £1.00 a ton would save between 5–10 million tons a year. Some allowance should probably be made for the currently suppressed demand in the domestic field, but not a great one.

[77] While agreeing that prices should not be less than cost (para. 59) the Ridley Committee divided (para. 60) over what was the relevant cost. Professor Hawthorne, Professor Lewis, Mrs McIntosh, and Miss Schofield supported the use of marginal costs, while Lord Ridley, Mr Lincoln Evans, Mr Gardiner and Sir Claude Gibb preferred the use of average costs.

[78] A. Cairncross, *Years of Recovery: British Economic Policy, 1941–51*, London, Methuen, 1985; university paperback 1987, p. 491.

[79] PRO T228/308, memorandum on 'Electricity Policy' by Hugh Gaitskell, Ministry of Fuel and Power, to Stafford Cripps, Chancellor of the Exchequer, 23 January 1948.

industry, seemed to Chantler 'monstrously bad planning'. Even here, although politically unacceptable, had prices been raised one effect might have been that 'the householders who find their bills substantially increased pour such coals of fire as they can get on the head of their local councillors [that] it may check similar faults in the future and help us to ease our problem of the squeeze on electricity supply'.[80]

As the unwillingness of politicians to address the issue of pricing became apparent, and as the community of interest which they shared with the nationalised industries on this issue became evident, calls began to be heard for pricing decisions to be removed to an independent body. It was not just that the coal and electricity industry boards were refusing to release information on such subjects as price elasticities, while continuing none the less to argue that price elasticities were exaggerated, but also that they were exploiting splits over pricing among economists to muddy any further discussion of pricing.[81]

It was in this context that, in April 1950, M. P. Murray, in the Ministry of Fuel and Power, began to explore the scope for a minister to intervene directly and change the tariff structures of the electricity boards. Similarly, in 1952, the Ridley Committee recommended that an Independent Tariffs Committee be established to advise and report on pricing policies in the fuel industries.[82] By 1952, what was causing increasing concern was the continuing tendency of politicians to favour administrative and hortatory approaches to restricting demand in preference to price increases. By the end of the Attlee governments, Professor Lewis was by no means alone in regarding the politicians' preferred option of broadcasting 'appeals to the individual to act against his own financial interest' as bankrupt, 'six years of planning having demonstrated amply that this is of limited value'. Worryingly, ministers began to drift towards more bureaucratic methods of securing fuel efficiency, which were beset with a range of legal, administrative, and civil-liberty complications. The concern was that 'where the Government wishes individuals to do what it does not pay the individual to do', government would move administratively and legally to compel desired behaviour. As Lewis warned, down this route lay 'administrative orders', which would make it 'an offence to have an unlagged hot water pipe, to burn coal in an open grate, to use an open electric fire, or what

---

[80] PRO POWE 14/320, note from Chantler to Watkinson, 13 October 1947.
[81] PRO POWE 14/555, DCFP 11th meeting, Committee on National Fuel Policy to representatives of NCB, 25 January 1952, question 21.
[82] PRO POWE 14/319, note by M. P. Murray (Electricity Division) on Minister and tariffs, 6 April 1950. Little, *Price of Fuel*, pp. 149–53.

you will. The railways will be ordered to use oil or to electrify, even if this raises their money costs. And so on.'[83]

Among various administrative approaches to promoting efficiency in fuel use was a scheme to award efficiency pennants to qualifying firms, along similar lines to the American 'E' pennant system. With firms fully pennanted, cuts would be made in the allocation of coal to industry, from which the pennanted firms would be exempt. Such cuts were thought likely to be more effective than price increases in encouraging economy in coal use by firms where fuel costs formed a small proportion of their total costs. Yet, for such a scheme to work, a clearly defined and legally defensible standard of 'fuel efficiency' would need to be established, and an appeals procedure provided to hear complaints from the aggrieved. The experience of the 1947 crisis indicated that even a small cut in supplies produced a very large number of appeals, some of which went to civil law, and the suggested 10 per cent cut was not a small one. Given shortages of skilled staff, it was suggested that only the 3,150 large firms who burned three-quarters of the industrial allocation of coal should be inspected. However, if only coal was rationed, then consumers might switch to gas and electricity, the inclusion of which would add to the administrative difficulties.[84]

An alternative and complementary approach to the visits of inspectors was to provide users with more information on how fuel efficiency might be improved. For its own purposes, government calculated the comparative efficiency of burning coal in power stations, which released about 20 per cent of the heat in coal into the generated electricity, and the average thermal efficiency of gas-making, which approached 50 per cent.[85] This was then set against the end-use in which, while an electric fire gave out as heat all the heat in the current supplied to it, an ordinary gas fire only supplied as useful heat 50 per cent of the therms which it

[83] PRO POWE 14/554 DCFP 48, paper on 'National Fuel Policy: Approach to the Subject', by W. A. Lewis, 23 October 1951, paras. 46–8.

[84] PRO POWE 14/556 DCFP 196 (annex) 'Aide-Memoire: the Arguments For and Against Industrial Fuel Rationing', 21 May 1952.

[85] The most modern stations released just under 30%, the least efficient below 10%. It is necessary to distinguish between (1) the thermal efficiency of the carbonisation process, and (2) the coal cost of making gas – the thermal efficiency of gas-making. The thermal efficiency of carbonisation may be measured by the ratio of the heat in all the useful products of carbonisation to the heat in the coal carbonised. It is about 75% on the average, or 85% for modern plant.

The coal cost of making gas may be measured by the ratio between the heat in the gas produced to that in the coal carbonised less the heat in the useful by-products (coke and tar). In figures this is, taking one ton of coal used at a gas works:

$$\frac{75 \text{ (terms of gas)}}{300 \text{ (terms in coal carbonised} - 150 \text{ (therms in by-products)}} = 50\%$$

consumed.[86] Information was also gathered on the comparative merits of different heating appliances, although even here the effects on fuel use were disputed. Professor E. V. Simon's recommendation that radiant heat-producing open fires should be abolished in favour of convecting closed fires, which were twice as efficient, was contested by the Ministry of Fuel and Power, which argued that Simon had ignored the psychological, visible, and direct warmth of the open fire. Given that closed stoves cost five times as much to buy than open fires, only a large increase in coal prices seemed likely to make them attractive to consumers. Whether their use would reduce coal consumption was doubted by Sir Donald Fergusson, who thought that the net effect of any use of more efficient appliances would simply be to raise the temperature and comfort of homes.[87] Where Fergusson thought there was more scope for fuel-saving was in insulating factories with materials which were in fairly easy supply. In this and other energy-saving schemes, as the Ridley Committee acknowledged, their interest was not 'in fuel efficiency as such', but rather 'in those sources of efficiency which yield more than they cost. In this sense the true addressee of our report is not the Minister of Fuel but the Chancellor of the Exchequer, since it is the latter who has to be persuaded that the labour and materials saved by fuel conservation exceed the labour and materials used up in the process.' Persuading the Treasury was likely to be difficult, not only because the Treasury was attempting to reduce the subsidy bill, but also because, given cheap money and price controls, any cost-benefit analysis would need to be 're-worked at "true" rather than controlled prices so that future savings and capital costs could be compared'.[88]

Faced with excess demand for coal, one further administrative response was to switch large coal-burners from coal to oil, even though this might reduce dollar-earning oil exports. The outstanding example of this approach was the coal–oil conversion programme launched in April 1946, and given priority status by the Prime Minister on 21 June 1946. As coal shortages worsened, so the conversion programme gained momentum. During the fuel crisis, the railways were urged to begin construction of 57 fuelling depots to service 1,229 locomotives, saving well in advance of 20,000 tons of locomotive coal per week. Elsewhere, industrial conversions had been completed with an annual oil burn of

[86] PRO POWE 14/552, EL 219/3, Philip Chantler, 'Ideas about National Fuel Policy', 4 June 1952.
[87] PRO POWE 14/555, DCFP 11th meeting, Committee on National Fuel Policy, questions to representatives of National Coal Board, 25 January 1952.
[88] PRO POWE 14/554, DCFP 48, paper on 'National Fuel Policy: Approach to the Subject', by W. A. Lewis, 23 October 1951.

689,000 tons, one-quarter of these early conversions being made in the steel industry. By the end of 1947, 93 locomotives were using oil at a rate of about 5,000 tons per month, and practically all of the materials for both locomotives and depots had either been delivered or been manufactured, and most of the depot work had been completed. However, by May 1947, the forward price of oil was beginning to tighten as doubts grew about the ability to guarantee delivery of the requisite oil, not least because of the difficulty of obtaining tankers. In early April 1948, the British Transport Commission lost any enthusiasm for the programme and requested government reimbursement of £3,000 per annum for each converted locomotive that they ran. On 6 May 1948, the Cabinet abandoned the programme and agreed on 30 July 1948 that the ninety-three oil-burning locomotives should be reconverted to coal, and that the depots should be kept on a care-and-maintenance basis pending a decision about their utilisation for other purposes. Needless to say, the oil position then improved and fuel stocks became sufficiently high for the Anglo–Iranian refinery at Abadan to consider 'recycling' fuel oil back into the ground.[89]

The difficulty attending administrative approaches to easing coal shortages once again begs the question of why the government was so unwilling to use pricing mechanisms to help solve such problems as coal and electricity capacity shortages. It also begs the question of why economists failed to persuade politicians of the merits of some basic economic principles. The Attlee governments both employed and were advised by leading economists, with James Meade, the Director of the Economic Section until 1947, going on to win the Nobel prize. Why were economists unable to force first-year undergraduate economics into the formulation of pricing policies?

Part of the explanation would appear to be that economists were often talking to government in a language which few within government understood. The disparity between an immediate post-World War II world in which economic issues were rapidly moving to the centre of government policy and the presence within government of a largely pre-war generation of politicians and civil servants who came from a world and training in which economics was not so important, formed an important fundamental problem and characteristic of the Attlee governments. As Cairncross and Eichengreen have noted, what was striking about the technical discussions preceding the 1949 devaluation of sterling was the manner in which the final decision-making fell upon the shoulders of the younger generation of ministers, Gaitskell, Jay, and

[89] PRO CAB 134/221 EPC (49)25 Cabinet, Economic Policy Committee. Coal–oil conversion; memorandum by the Minister of Fuel and Power, March 1949.

Wilson, all of whom, to varying degrees, had some training in economics.[90] Indeed, Gaitskell's proficiency in economics in a Cabinet which was largely uneconomic was to see him rise rapidly to become Chancellor of the Exchequer in 1950, five years after first being elected to Parliament. With the notable exception of Cripps and Dalton, many of the senior Cabinet ministers came from a background which made them better suited to considering issues of foreign policy, or social and working conditions rather than the economic issues of the post-1945 period. Nor was this dearth of technical economic talent simply a feature of Cabinet and political circles. Within the highest ranks of the Civil Service, the absence of civil servants with formal economics training was striking. As Keynes had discovered in the 1930s, it remained difficult for economists to infiltrate their ideas into government quickly, and in the 1940s Keynes continued to think that within government and the civil service: 'Economics was not yet taken as a serious subject.'[91] As a consequence, when new national-income accounting techniques were being developed by some of the wartime import of economists, communication and discussion of new ideas and techniques proved difficult. When, in November 1944, James Meade and Richard Stone distributed copies of a pamphlet on national income and expenditure, Meade received a letter from Eady 'saying that he had no training in economics but was trying to master the subject'. As Meade noted 'when one looks at it objectively, what a state of affairs it is when the man chiefly responsible for internal and external financial policy has had no technical training. I am sure that in our grandchildren's days this will be considered very odd.'[92] Robert Hall, Meade's successor as Director of the Economic Section, thought it simply 'absurd that a Government of professed planners should not only have no one who understands planning, but also no one who understands monetary policy and the theory of international trade. I do not say that it is essential that these should be left to theorists, but at least there ought to be more than one person who is capable of appreciating the theoretical considerations.'[93]

In fact, there was to be no separate class of economists in the civil

[90] A. Cairncross and B. Eichengreen, *Sterling in Decline; the Devaluations of 1931, 1949 and 1967*, Oxford, Blackwell, 1983, pbk, p. 142.

[91] D. Winch, 'Keynes, Keynesianism and State Intervention', in P. Hall (ed.), *The Political Power of Economic Ideas*, Princeton, NJ, Princeton University Press, 1989, pp. 107–27. Meade, *Diary*, p. 26, 7 January 1945.

[92] J. Meade, *Diary*, 19 November 1944, p. 6. J. Meade and R. Stone, *National Income and Expenditure*, London/Oxford, Oxford University Press, 1944. Wilfred Eady was Joint Second Secretary at the Treasury, 1946–52.

[93] A. Cairncross (ed.), *The Robert Hall Diaries*, London, Unwin Hyman, 1989, 26 August 1949.

service until the 1964 Wilson government, governments until then continuing to rely on importing economists, from universities and elsewhere, as and when they felt that they were needed.[94] Not that persuading economists to stay in government service was easy. As Directors of the Economic Section, both Meade and, to a lesser extent, Robert Hall, regularly experienced difficulties in dissuading academic economists in particular from forsaking government service for the groves of academe.

Given the dearth of ministers and advisers within government with a formal economics training, the successful transmission of economic ideas required the main principles and their application to be delineated in a clear and accessible manner. In retrospect, it was perhaps unfortunate that the disputes over marginal and average cost pricing should have dominated the Economic Section's advice and memoranda on pricing in the early postwar years. Marginal cost pricing and the associated tolerance of loss-making by some nationalised industries was a very difficult idea to explain to politicians and civil servants. Avoiding financial losses was more important to them than the wider and more esoteric concerns of economists with optimising resource allocation. As Meade himself foresaw, to the 'hard-headed and distinguished public servants' on the Official Committee on the Problems of Socialisation the principle of marginal cost pricing would 'inevitably look a very long-haired and academic thesis'. Once the Committee began discussing pricing policy, Meade was able to confirm that his ideas 'appeared rather lunatic to most members of the Committee'.[95]

Meade persisted with his advocacy partly because of his genuine belief in its importance, but also because this immediate need to frame the statutory provisions for the long-term pricing policy of the socialised industries forced him to advocate the merits of marginal cost pricing in postwar conditions of excess demand when its use was not immediately relevant. The early arguments over marginal and average cost pricing may also have confirmed to many non-economists within government that the economists were irrevocably divided over the issue, and that the arguments were also in such a state of fluidity and contention as to make them inaccessible to the intelligent lay person. Probably the most important casualty of this within the civil service was Alec Johnston, Chairman of the Working Party on the Price Policy of the Socialised

[94] L. Hannah, 'Economic Ideas and Government Policy on Industrial Organisation in Britain Since 1945', in M. Furner and B. Supple (eds.), *The State and Economic Knowledge*, Cambridge, Cambridge University Press, 1990, p. 361. In 1964, the economist class of the civil service numbered 22, but by 1969 there were as many as 194.

[95] Meade, *Diary*, 2 December 1945, 23 February 1946, pp. 175, 224.

Industries. In December 1948, Johnston resigned as Chairman, explaining that:

I do not think I ought to continue with this work and I have throughout been troubled about my suitability for the task, because a general background about prices and charges was very desirable in the Chairman . . . The working party consists partly of civil servants and partly of Economists, and it is difficult to keep the working party in hand without a pretty confident background on the theory and practice of price-fixing. I always feel that any of us ought to be able to acquire this knowledge, and it was in that spirit that I took the job on. I am bound to say that after a little experience I feel that, while it can be done, it takes a great deal of time and effort.[96]

Despite having 'spent a lot of time reading up the economic literature on price policy of Socialised Industries', Johnston had found it 'difficult to keep a grip on the economists and administrators and to reconcile their rather conflicting points of view'.[97] In particular, he had found the arguments among economists about the advantages and disadvantages of marginal cost pricing particularly unsettling. Having initially been provided with a memorandum from James Meade which 'was more or less an explanation of the point of view which he put forward in the *Economic Journal* for December 1945', Johnston had then, 'as a non-economist', been 'rather perplexed, on reading later articles and notes in the *Economic Journal*, to know where the truth lay or at any rate to know whether one had to pay attention to the rival views expressed by T. Wilson and others'.[98]

If the Economic Section's advocacy of marginal cost pricing was not easy fare for civil servants and politicians to digest, the Economic Section did not always help its cause by the manner in which their thinking was presented in memoranda and papers. Some papers were open to the broad criticism of being too academic, with no explicit recognition of the practical problems besetting the implementation of their main principles. As early as 1935, Roy Harrod warned Meade that a paper which Meade had written on 'socialisation policy' was 'rather unrealistic' because it ignored the administrative problem. Harrod stressed that the practical issues had to be tackled 'otherwise Labour leaders such as Morrison might view it as hopelessly academic'.[99] It might, of course, have suited Morrison and others to dismiss unap-

---

[96] PRO CAB 124/950, A Johnston (Office of the Lord President) to J. Pimlott, 8 December 1948.

[97] PRO CAB 124/950, A. Johnston to J. Pimlott, 20 November 1948.

[98] PRO CAB 124/950, A. Johnston to R. F. Kahn, King's College Cambridge, 12 July 1948.

[99] E Durbin, *New Jerusalems; the Labour Party and the Economics of Democratic Socialism*, London, Routledge & Kegan Paul, 1985, p. 197.

pealing ideas as 'academic', but equally one of the Section's concerns might have been to reduce as much as possible the opportunities for dismissing their ideas with such pejorative characterisation. Similarly, Johnston complained of the tendency of some economists to fail to recognise the need to sell their ideas to an often unreceptive audience. As Johnston noted in June 1948 in a paper on the 'Problems of Socialisation':

I quite see that it is for economists to say 'here are the general principles' and that it is for the various boards to say how far they can apply them but I feel that we ought to make a greater endeavour than has been done hitherto to indicate how any general principles can be applied in practice. We have to face tremendous mental inertia in the practical men and a great level of thinking on their part derives from the time when they were engaged in exploiting a monopoly.[100]

Matters were not helped when the exposition of the principles themselves by the Economic Section were not expressed clearly. In June 1948, Johnston again complained to Robert Hall, Meade's successor as Director of the Economic Section from mid-1947, that, having read a memo by Mr Jefferies on pricing policy:

I confess that I do not understand exactly what Mr. Jefferies means when he says that:
  'the course for it to adopt which would be most in the general economic interest would be to retain at any rate the proportionality between the relative prices of its different products and the strength of demand for additional supply of them on the one hand, and between the relative costs of their additional supply and their relative prices on the other; but to widen the gap between average price and average costs by restricting supply all round.'

As Johnston complained, 'this was in a memorandum intended to be read by busy Ministers and whatever it may mean is expressed in far too condensed and telescopic a form'.[101] Throughout this period, ministers and civil servants were under considerable pressure of work, which at times of crisis could reach intolerable levels. Meade himself complained in his diary as early as November 1945 that 'there have been many . . . important issues under discussion', and that 'extreme pressure of work has made it very difficult to give them the attention which they deserve'.[102]

In addition to the problems of addressing a non-economic audience with some of the finer details of pricing cost structures, the Economic

---

[100] PRO T230/28, Economic Section of the Cabinet Secretariat, Discussion Papers 1948. Paper by A. Johnston, 'Problems of Socialisation', 8 June 1948.
[101] PRO CAB 124/950, A. Johnston to Hall, 8 June 1948.
[102] BLPES, Meade papers, 1/4, diary, 3 November 1945.

Section also experienced early problems in gaining adequate and sympathetic access to the centre of policy-making. The immediate postwar period was marked by a power struggle for control of the Economic Section between the Lord President, Herbert Morrison, and Stafford Cripps, the President of the Board of Trade. Cripps' aim was to absorb both the Economic Section and the Central Statistical Office into the Board of Trade, and by so doing make himself responsible for Employment Policy. Cripps' ambitions were resisted by Morrison in August 1945, who, as Meade noted, regarded himself 'as the central economic co-ordinator and is not going to give up the Economic Section'. The resolution of the struggle in Morrison's favour was initially welcomed by Meade. He saw Morrison as the man most likely to become the leader of the liberal–socialist approach to planning with its operation of large-scale monopolies on 'market principles of pricing and cost', and in opposition to Cripps, who Meade perceived as leading the Gosplan school with their belief 'in the quantitative planning of the economy commodity by commodity'.[103] Ironically, it was Cripps who later, as Chancellor of the Exchequer, was to support Gaitskell in his efforts to cajole the electricity industry into making greater use of peak-hour pricing. By contrast, Morrison appeared if anything to grow more attached to the use of administrative controls and more suspicious of Meade and Chantler's efforts to increase the use of price mechanisms. Chantler and Meade's suggestion to Morrison in April 1946, that 'true co-ordination between rail and road transport meant fixing road and rail charges at levels equal to marginal cost and then letting the users of transport choose what types of transport they would use', prompted a heated argument in which Morrison dismissed Meade's and Chantler's thinking as 'competition, not co-ordination'.[104] Morrison was much more responsive to Meade's re-presentation of the argument in terms of 'industrial efficiency', in which there would be 'a straightforward waste of labour if goods were taken on a system on which the marginal cost was higher instead of on one where the marginal cost was lower'.[105]

Morrison's resistance to the pricing ideas of the Economic Section, combined with Morrison's more sanguine view of controls, which Meade regarded as 'negative' and 'restrictive', became a growing source of tension between Morrison and the Economic Section. The more Morrison exhibited growing scepticism and suspicion of Meade's ideas, the more Meade would return to his room and write 'Morrison a

---

[103] BLPES, Meade papers, 1/4, diary, 26 August 1945.
[104] J. Meade, *Diary*, pp. 234, 254, 17 March 1946, 27 April 1946. This partly echoed his earlier response to similar arguments: 'But that is not socialisation, it is competition.'
[105] J. Meade, *Diary*, p. 254, 27 April 1946.

minute on the general theory of the subject', something which was unlikely to have endeared him to the Lord President.[106] The serious consequences of this fundamental difference in thinking between the Economic Section and the Lord President was to constrain the impact and currency of the Section's ideas. It also reduced the Section's direct access to the increasingly important Treasury, although Dalton as Chancellor of the Exchequer did encourage Meade in September 1945 and January 1946 to 'take the initiative and brief or visit him' whenever Meade thought that there was anything on which Dalton should be advised.[107] Although attracted by the idea, Meade recognised the difficulties that this would cause in his relationship with Morrison, as well as with Treasury officials who might well resent such advice from outwith their department. Recognising the political difficulties, Meade was left to regret the inability to exploit such access: 'The Chancellor told me to go and see him whenever I wanted to bring anything to his attention . . . My God, would that it could really be so! What could I not do with access to the Chancellor as free as my present access to the Lord President!'[108]

The relationship between Morrison and Meade deteriorated during 1946. The Section's proposals on socialised industry pricing were not adopted and possibly not fully understood by Morrison, who was, if anything, becoming increasingly resistant and obtuse in response to suggestions that a greater use be made of pricing mechanisms in general. Meade for his part was becoming increasingly frustrated and exasperated at the unwillingness of planners in general to even think in terms of pricing as an allocative mechanism. This exasperation was evident not just in issues of co-ordination in fuel and power and transport and communication, but also in such distant areas as agriculture. The outburst in his diary of 16 April 1946, recalling a recent discussion between representatives of the Ministries of Food and of Agriculture, captures both his increasing despair and his genuine political concern as a liberal economist as to where planning without market mechanisms might lead:

Here was a first-rate economic issue being discussed and it was all done in terms of administrative machinery and responsibility without any reference to or appreciation of the market mechanism. On both sides there was a general agreement that somehow the Ministry of Food had to decide what amounts of commodities they wanted and for what purposes and the Ministry of Agriculture had to decide what amounts should be produced and how. The idea that

---

[106] J. Meade, *Diary*, p. 130, 16 September 1945.
[107] J. Meade, *Diary*, p. 196, 13 January 1946.
[108] J. Meade, *Diary*, p. 137, 23 September 1945.

consumers decided or should be enabled to decide how much they wanted of various things at various prices and that the producers could follow or should be encouraged to follow this lead was totally absent. The idea that the Government could intervene, not to destroy, but to improve the workings of the price mechanism was not present because no one was aware of the existence of any such animal. It reminded me of a meeting of medieval doctors discussing how to deal with an epidemic before the existence of bacteria was discovered. It made me feel (i) what dangerous seas we are sailing into when the state is taking on more and more economic functions while those responsible for them are, quite frankly, not properly trained technically and (ii) what an important long-run contribution the economist in government has to make. But I fear one must stress the words 'long-run'.[109]

Meade resigned in mid-1947 as Director of the Economic Section, being replaced by Robert Hall from the Board of Trade, initially on a part-time basis from 1 June 1947 and then on a full-time basis, from 1 September 1947.[110] Hall devoted considerable attention to easing what he saw as some of the Section's principal difficulties. Although the Section had always experienced difficulties in recruiting and retaining first-class staff, Hall was able to engineer changes in the Section's personnel.[111] Concluding that he had 'inherited a very poor lot from James Meade', by November 1948 the staff had 'changed quite a lot', and in December 1948 Bretherton joined the Section as Joint Deputy Director.[112]

Concerned to improve the influence of the Section, Hall sought to make its ideas more accessible to non-economists. Some simple improvements could be made, such as dissuading the Section from continuing to write 'briefs that are too long. No wonder Morrison could not understand them'.[113] Accepting that marginal and average cost pricing had 'been considered by a large number of economists and that you would not get from anyone of them a view which would be accepted in detail by others', Hall sought to improve both the presentation of the Section's arguments and to reduce their perception as being a gathering of merely academic theorists. Emphasising 'the points on which there is substantial agreement' rather than the irreconcilable differences, Hall also attempted to get the economists and industrialists to meet one another. On the specific issue of socialised industries' pricing policy, Hall thought that in future

[109] J. Meade, *Diary*, pp. 318–19, 16 August 1946.
[110] R. Hall, *Diaries*, 1 September 1947. 'James Meade . . . had to resign because the strenuous life gave him stomach ulcers. I think he took everything too seriously.'
[111] R. Hall, *Diaries*, 14 October 1947.
[112] R. Hall, *Diaries*, 27 August, 18 November, 23 December 1948.
[113] R. Hall, *Diaries*, 9–10 October 1947.

the ideal arrangement would be to bring together a few economists who have studied the matter with the people who are actually concerned with price fixing in the socialised industries themselves. Until they have some discussions, it is unlikely that they will understand one another, but I have usually found that after a little fencing they come to terms quite quickly. The economist is always in danger of talking about a situation which he has imagined and which does not represent reality at all, while the practical man is often put off by the language of the economist and, indeed, often by the name itself.[114]

Not only would this help to break down the suspicion of 'the practical man', but would also encourage economists to address the issue of how exactly their ideas were to be applied in practice. It might also dissuade the economists from floating theoretical but impracticable ideas. In part, there was a natural gap between the rate at which the academics could produce and the government absorb ideas. As Meade noted, when working on the paper on 'Economic Forecasting and Employment Policy' in April 1945, as 'a pure academic, one can have an idea, publish it – and next year have a new idea which supersedes the first and publish it in turn without a blush. But once the Whitehall machine has been well and truly put into motion on these lines, it is no good one's having a totally fresh idea next year.'[115]

Hall also sought to rein in some of the excesses of academics. As he observed in April 1948 of Marcus Fleming, the future deputy director of the International Monetary Fund, he 'has fits of academic conscience in which he feels that the truth as he sees it is more important than anything else. This would be all right if he took the trouble to check his facts and his reasoning but like all economists he is an escapist and thinks he is being virtuous in taking a high line when he really hasn't done enough to justify any line.'[116] By November 1948, things had improved, with Hall noting that 'Fleming has been doing some very good work lately', although Hall was later to be asked by Gaitskell to use his good offices to stop Kaldor and Balogh 'pestering him continually with ill-informed ideas'.[117] However, while improving the accessibility and practicability of the Section's papers, Hall also recognised that to be of any use the Section had to remain a technical unit. Here, Hall was fortunate in that the appointment of Cripps as Minister of Economic Affairs at the end of September 1947 and then subsequently as Chancellor provided him with a more willing and realistic audience than Meade had enjoyed in Morrison. Hall thought

---

[114] PRO CAB 124/950 R. Hall to A. Johnston, 10 June 1948.
[115] J. Meade *Diary*, p. 69, 27 April 1945.   [116] R. Hall, *Diaries*, 16 April 1948.
[117] R. Hall, *Diaries*, 1 December 1948, 9 March 1950.

that this 'ought to be good for the Section, as I am very doubtful if Morrison could understand the long briefs we gave him'.[118]

Assisted by the changes made to the structure and aims of economic planning in the autumn of 1947, Hall was able to strengthen the Section's relations with the Treasury. The prolonged prelude to devaluation gradually increased the influence of economists on at least this aspect of economic policy-making, with Hall himself enjoying direct access to Cripps, Chancellor of the Exchequer.[119] While there was still considerable hostility to and suspicion of 'reactionary (laissez-faire or liberal) officials and economists', none the less, drip by drip, the influence of economic principles and techniques did appear to be seeping into government.[120] In fuel and power, both the Clow and the Ridley Committees encouraged ministers to make greater use of pricing mechanisms. Yet, the political and industrial resistance to such thinking proved strong. The reluctance of politicians to address the issues of pricing and resource allocation became quite apparent. Both Oliver Franks and Robert Hall concluded that Ministers were 'incapable of taking painful decisions', while Bridges was 'discouraged by the weaknesses of politicians'. Moreover, while Franks thought that among politicians 'the 40s should replace the 60s – at least the former had some ideas and some knowledge of how to carry these out', until that happened there was likely to be a continuing lack of sympathy for a move towards market mechanisms in a government lacking senior personnel with economic training.[121]

Ultimately, it was the Treasury which began to take steps to rein in the nationalised industries. In 1953, the Economic Section was transferred to the Treasury and there was some movement to establish sharper relative prices.[122] In February 1952, Sir Bernard Gilbert began to suggest that greater control over the nationalised fuel and power industries might be secured by exerting tougher control over their borrowing activity, although it was recognised that 'given personalities in electricity . . . a good deal of perseverance will be required'.[123] Steadily, moves were made towards dismissing awkward chairmen, Walter Citrine being a leading target. As John Boyd Carpenter noted in 1953 in a memorandum on nationalised industry pricing: 'I am quite

[118] R. Hall, *Diaries*, 30 September 1947.   [119] R. Hall, *Diaries*, 6 April 1949.

[120] R. Hall, *Diaries*, 11 July 1949. Cairncross and Eichengreen, *Sterling*, p. 133.

[121] R. Hall, *Diaries*, 27 September 1947, 22 April 1948.

[122] Little, *Price of Fuel*, p. 159. Relative prices of different coals were adjusted in 1953 and there was some subsidisation of more efficient firms.

[123] PRO T229/483, extract from Sir Bernard Gilbert's minute to the Chancellor of the Exchequer on 'Price Policy in the Nationalised Industries', 18 February 1953. Sir Bernard Gilbert was Joint Second Secretary at the Treasury, 1944–56.

sure that Lord Citrine has outlived whatever usefulness he may have had . . . If we want these two industries (gas and electricity) to adopt a more prudent financial policy, I think we ought at least to try and see that people are appointed to these Boards who are inclined to pursue such policies.'[124]

What could happen when, in more propitious circumstances, heed was paid to economists became apparent in both the French and the British electricity industries. In France, criticism by the economist Marcel Boiteux of the structure of electricity prices eventually culminated in the introduction of the green tariff in 1957, which helped to reduce the ratio between peak demand and average demand from 1.37 in 1954 to 1.21 in 1963 and 1964.[125] In Britain, the appointment of the economist Ronald Edwards as Chairman of the Electricity Council allowed him to exploit changes among the leading personnel in the industry so as to cajole the industry into introducing a price structure which better reflected the true costs of peak and off-peak supply.[126] In general, during the course of the 1950s the Treasury's mounting concern with nationalised industries' loss-making in the coal and railway industries and with 'crowding-out' of private fixed capital-investment projects by expanding industries such as electricity provided the background for a significant reappraisal of pricing.

In the two seminal White Papers in 1961 and 1967 on the economic and financial obligations of the nationalised industries marginal-cost pricing did finally elbow its way into nationalised-industry pricing policies, along with the requirement that rates of return nearer to those in comparable private-sector projects be earned.[127] The 1967 White Paper, in particular, was strongly influenced by the influx of able university economists recruited on secondment by the new Labour

---

[124] PRO T229/687, memorandum by John Boyd Carpenter, 'Pricing Policy in the Nationalised Industries', 25 February 1953. John Boyd Carpenter was Financial Secretary to the Treasury.

[125] J.-J. Carré, P. Dubois, and E. Malinvaud, *French Economic Growth*, London, Oxford University Press, 1976, p. 447. M. Boiteux, 'Le tarif vert d'Electricité de France', *Revue française de l'energie*, January (1957). R. Janin, 'Convergence des pratiques technico-économiques à l'électricité de France, 1946–1985' in H. Morsel (dir.), *Histoire de L'Électricité en France*, Paris, Fayard, 1996, pp. 408–9. M. Boiteux, 'La tarification des demandes en pointe: application de la théorie de la vente au coût marginal', *Revue générale de l'Electricité* (1949), pp. 321–40.

[126] L. Hannah, *Engineers, Managers and Politicians*, London, Macmillan, 1982, p. 216. Ronald Edwards was Professor of Industrial Organisation at the London School of Economics.

[127] *Financial and Economic Obligations of the Nationalised Industries*, London, HMSO, Cmnd 1336, 1961. *Nationalised Industries: A Review of Economic and Financial Objectives* London, HMSO, Cmnd 3437, 1967.

government.[128] Yet, even these papers were not well received by politicians, one possible reason being that the economists 'were riding professional hobby horses without having established a political market for their ideas'.[129] Such criticism had considerable resonance with the experiences of the Attlee governments. So too did the reaction of politicians to proposals for the greater use of pricing mechanisms. The Ridley Committee's 'excellent proposal' for an Independent Tariffs Committee was never implemented, and price interference was to continue during both the Wilson and the subsequent Heath governments.[130] Notoriously, the Cabinet discussion of the 1967 White Paper on Nationalised Industries, as recorded by the Lord President, Richard Crossman, was peremptory, if not dismissive:

We had exactly twenty minutes to consider it . . . As I got up from the table I said to Callaghan, 'This is a very poor paper.' 'What does it matter?' he said. 'It's only read by a few dons and experts.' 'Well, I'm one don,' I said, and he replied, 'You're a don who knows nothing about the subject. Personally as Chancellor I couldn't care less. I take no responsibility and I took no part in composing it.' Here was a key issue of socialist strategy and the Chancellor of the Exchequer washes his hands of it.[131]

In retrospect, what might be taken as short-term, immediate postwar difficulties in gaining acceptance of rational pricing principles appears to have heralded the emergence of some long-term and fundamental political aversion to pricing mechanisms. With pricing, as with the monopoly form of nationalisation, problems which emerged during the Attlee governments' period in office were still concerning students of political economy decades later.

[128] M. V. Posner, *Fuel Policy: a Study in Applied Economics*, London, Macmillan, 1973. W. Beckerman (ed.), *The Labour Government's Economic Record, 1964–70*, London, Duckworth, 1972.

[129] L. Hannah, 'Economic Ideas', in M. Supple and B. Furner (eds.), *The State and Economic Knowledge*, p. 372

[130] W. Robson, *Nationalised Industry and Public Ownership*, first edn, 1960, second edn, London, George Allen & Unwin, 1962.

[131] Richard Crossman, *The Diaries of a Cabinet Minister*, vol. II, London, Hamish Hamilton and Jonathan Cape, 1976, p. 524, 8 October 1967.

6   Appraising investment

Among the nationalised industries, the largest in terms of fixed capital investment were the electricity and the railway industries, which accounted for 8 per cent and 2.5 per cent respectively of gross domestic fixed capital investment in 1951.[1] Of gross domestic fixed capital formation in plant and machinery, electricity accounted for 15.4 per cent, and as such was the largest single area of industrial investment in this category. Of gross domestic fixed capital formation in vehicles, ships, and aircraft, railways accounted for 12.8 per cent, less than the 23 per cent in shipping and 22 per cent in distribution and other services, but again the largest single industry investing in this category. Like most nationalised industries, these were capital intensive, especially electricity whose capital–labour ratio was extremely high. The plant choices made by managers in each industry were clearly important, affecting as they did the efficiency of the current use of scarce resources and the subsequent productivity of each industry. It was specifically on this issue of raising the quality of plant choice that some economists saw improvements being facilitated by nationalisation in monopoly form.

In a monopoly, it was argued, managers would be free of the supply-side uncertainties which arose in competitive markets from ignorance of the fixed capital investment intentions of competitors.[2] Given such hopes, the subsequent academic criticism of the plant choices made in a number of nationalised industries in this period is striking.[3] In particular, the plant and locomotive choices made in this period by the nationalised electricity and railway industries have been described by

[1] Central Statistical Office, *National Income and Expenditure, 1946–1952*, London, HMSO, August 1953, Table 43.
[2] G. B. Richardson, *Information and Investment*, Oxford, Clarendon Press, 1990. First published in 1960. James Meade, 'The Socialisation of Industries: Memorandum by the Economic Section of the Cabinet Secretariat', in S. Howson (ed.), *The Collected Papers of James Meade: vol. II, Value, Distribution and Growth*, London, Allen & Unwin, 1988, pp. 51–77.
[3] R. Pryke, *Public Enterprise in Practice*, London, MacGibbon and Kee, 1971. C. Harlow, *Innovation and Productivity Under Nationalisation*, London, Allen & Unwin, 1977.

several commentators as having been extremely conservative and technically backward, with detrimental consequences for productivity in the industry throughout the 1950s and into the 1960s.[4] If valid, such criticisms raise questions about why such plant choices were made and encourage wider speculation as to whether fundamental sources of inefficiency were contained within either the nationalised monopoly industries or economic planning, or both.

After the war, both industries were required to maximise output from a depreciated capital stock. In electricity, the war had slowed the rate of capital formation, while depreciation of the capital stock had continued.[5] Capital growth slowed from 9.9 per cent in 1924–37 to 2.0 per cent in 1937–51, with the peak pre-war rate of plant installation of 1938 not being exceeded until 1950.[6] During the three years from 1946 to 1948, only 1,200 megawatts (MW) of new capacity came into use, an average of 400MWs per annum, compared with some pre-war rates of investment of 800MWs per annum.[7] Output growth slowed from 10.8 per cent (1924–37) to 6.6 per cent (1937–51), and, while demand in general approximately doubled between 1936 and 1946, generating plant capacity grew by only about 50 per cent.[8] Government restrictions on station construction operated from April 1942, and, in the face of rising demand, the rate of plant outage rose from 5.6 per cent in 1938–9 to 19.6 per cent in 1943–4. Capacity shortages were aggravated by the failure to choke off some peak-hour demand, which was calculated to exceed capacity by 10–15 per cent at the time of nationalisation, and by the acceleration of the growth of demand to 9.5 per cent between 1947 and 1948, against an annual rate of 6.5 per cent across the 1940s.[9] Time-lags between the ordering and commissioning of plant, arising from long construction times, limited the scope for the immediate relief

---

[4] L. Hannah, *Engineers, Managers and Politicians*, London, Macmillan, 1982, pp. 104–5. R. Pryke, *Public Enterprise in Practice*, p. 383. C. Harlow, *Innovation*, p. 66.

[5] G. Dean, 'The Stock of Fixed Capital in the United Kingdom in 1961', *Journal of the Royal Statistical Society*, Series A, 127, 3 (1964), pp. 327–51. W. B. Reddaway and A. D. Smith, 'Progress in British Manufacturing Industries in the Period 1948–54', *Economic Journal*, 70, 277 (March 1960), pp. 17–37. P. Redfern, 'New Investment in Fixed Assets in the UK, 1938–1953', *Journal of the Royal Statistical Society*, Series A, Part II (1955), pp. 141–92.

[6] R. C. O. Matthews, C. H. Feinstein, and J. C. Odling-Smee, *British Economic Growth, 1856–1973*, Oxford, Oxford University Press, 1982, pp. 400–1. Part of the higher growth of inter-war capital growth was attributable to the construction of the grid, although this was completed by 1932.

[7] Harlow, *Innovation*, p. 65. A megawatt is 1,000 kilowatts. A kilowatt is 1,000 watts.

[8] R. C. O. Matthews, C. H. Feinstein, and J. C. Odling-Smee, *British Economic Growth*, pp. 400–1. Harlow, *Innovation*, p. 65.

[9] Ministry of Fuel and Power, *Peak Load Committee*, Cmd 7464, London, HMSO, 1948. Harlow, *Innovation*, p. 65.

of excess demand. In 1946 and early 1947, only 647MWs of new plant was commissioned out of the two-year programme of 1,962MWs.[10] Unlike in industries with a larger inherited capacity, such as iron and steel, and spinning, the 'patching' strategy was not available to electricity managers, whose demand had long pushed up against capacity limits.[11] Excess demand, plant shortages, long construction times and, following the fuel crisis of 1947, increased political pressures on electricity managers to increase output quickly can all reasonably be combined to present a picture of managers working in a highly pressurised environment in which rapid additions to output were the outstanding priority[12]

In these circumstances, it would not have been surprising if managers had chosen to opt for smaller plant of known reliability which could make a quicker contribution to output, in preference to some of the larger, less well-known sets. In the short-term, rapid increases in output might be bought at the expense of some larger improvements in productivity. Such analyses of managerial decision-making in the electricity industry during this period are plausible and quite common.[13] Implicitly, electricity managers are depicted as decision-takers, rather than decision-makers, reacting to an existing environment, rather than acting to reshape it to suit their own preferences. In fact, archival evidence suggests that a more robust view can be taken of managers in the nationalised electricity industry in this period. The archival evidence shows that they did make much greater efforts to improve their operating environment, particularly on the supply side, than they are usually given credit for, and that it was the combination of government and the plant and machinery manufacturers who should bear a larger share of responsibility for the ordering of conservative plant.

The greatest supply-side problem confronting electricity managers was that of securing an adequate quantitative and qualitative supply of capital equipment. While the industry's 'priority' status meant that it

---

[10] PRO POWE 24/14, CP 81, Ministry of Fuel and Power, Committee of Inquiry into the Electricity Supply Industry, Standardisation of Generating Plant (S.R. & O. of 1947, No. 2386), note by the Ministry of Fuel and Power, 17 June 1955.

[11] D. Heathfield, 'Capital Utilisation and Input Substitution', in K. D. Patterson and K. Schott (eds.), *The Measurement of Capital*, London, Macmillan, 1979, pp. 226–45.

[12] *Report of the Committee of Inquiry into the Electricity Supply Industry*, London, HMSO, January 1956, Cmd 9672, para. 423. As was noted in 1956 by the Herbert Committee of Inquiry into the Electricity Supply Industry: 'We have seen how demand for power was rising rapidly at that time [1948], and how the Authority was sorely pressed to meet the ever increasing load and dominated by the need to put in generating plant as quickly as possible.'

[13] They are implicit to varying degrees in C. Harlow, *Innovation*, R. Pryke *Public Enterprise in Practice*, and L. Hannah, *Engineers, Managers and Politicians*.

received a larger share of the domestic residual of plant and machinery than many other industries, the industry still argued that export-driven plant and machinery manufacturers were exploiting the virtually captive position of an import-restricted domestic electricity industry.[14] Given government exhortations to export, the allocation of steel linked to export quotas, the devaluation of sterling in 1949 designed to encourage exports to hard-currency dollar economies, and the higher returns available on exports, plant and machinery suppliers were keen to export. Manufacturers preferred the profits available on supplying export, often Empire, markets with plant of inter-war technological standard, to the distraction of coping with the higher technological demands of the larger, modern sets which might be sought by an unconstrained domestic electricity industry. Export profits peaked in 1951, when the differential between a profit rate of 14.4 per cent on domestic sales of turbines, condensers, and alternators and the 25.6 per cent on export sales was clear.[15]

In addition to the practical difficulties of operating in this seller's market, the nationalised electricity industry mangers also became increasingly concerned at the assistance which these conditions gave to the operation of rings among firms supplying turbo-alternators, boilers, cables, steelworks, and high-pressure pipework.[16] These rings were often of long-standing, but were held to have gained added postwar rationale as one means of countering the monopsonist purchasing power of the nationalised electricity monopoly. Of particular concern was the perceived ring activity amongst pipework manufacturers, for whose output there was fierce competition among the electricity, coal, chemical, and oil industries.[17] Shortages of pipework slowed the entire electricity construction programme in 1950 and 1951. Electricity managers also alleged that the classic association of restricted output and price agreements was common, prices being held to reflect a weighted average among ring makers, rather than the price of the most

[14] PRO POWE 24/2, Ministry of Fuel and Power, Committee of Inquiry into the Electricity Supply Industry, Notes of a meeting held on 3 June 1955, p. 46. Of the 2,400MWs of turbo-alternators over 100MW manufactured in Britain in 1954, just under 800MWs were exported. However, the electricity industry took almost all of the remaining two-thirds. The Monopolies and Restrictive Practices Commission, *Report on the Supply and Export of Electrical and Allied Machinery and Plant*, London, HMSO, 1957, para. 155. In 1952, 94% by value of all machinery supplied in the home market was supplied to the electricity industry.

[15] The Monopolies and Restrictive Practices Commission, *Report on the Supply and Export of Electrical and Allied Machinery and Plant*, London, HMSO, 1957, Appendix 11.

[16] PRO POWE 24/2 Ministry of Fuel and Power, Committee of Inquiry into the Electricity Supply Industry, notes of a meeting held on 3 June 1955, p. 41.

[17] PRO POWE 14/116, GC/115, 'BEA: Causes of Delays in Commissioning Plant'. Paper by Generation Construction Department, 28 May 1949, p. 3.

efficient.[18] In a BEA-initiated series of meetings in 1950 and 1951, the efforts of accountants representing the plant and machinery manufacturers and the BEA to determine 'fair' prices and profit rates foundered on the refusal of plant manufacturers to reveal information on their cost structure, such that the Central Electricity Authority were later to complain to the Monopolies and Restrictive Practices Commission that 'at no time was evidence of a fair and reasonable relationship between current manufacturing costs and prices produced'.[19] In particular, the Authority was unconvinced that the cost reductions thought likely to arise from standardisation and an increased volume of production were being passed on.

The need to improve the quantitative and qualitative supply of plant and machinery, and breaking the ring operations among manufacturers, became of increasing concern to the managers of the nationalised electricity industry. The initial stage of their strategy was to chivvy manufacturers into increasing their existing capacity, both Stewarts & Lloyds, the dominant manufacturer of pipework, and Aiton & Co. being encouraged to erect new works, on Clydeside and in Sunderland respectively. Greater success greeted the electricity industry's efforts in boiler-making, where, although Babcock & Wilcox had a dominant position, as Stewarts & Lloyds did in pipework, they appeared to be more amenable to petitioning from the electricity managers. Often accounting for over half of all domestic production of particular types of boilers, Babcock & Wilcox had greater control than most firms over their own levels of production, as they manufactured a high proportion of individual component parts themselves, and also produced half of their own water-tube requirements.[20] Allied to these efforts to increase capacity, the BEA also took steps to speed up the progressing of existing

[18] PRO POWE 24/2 CI 47th meeting, Ministry of Fuel and Power, Committee of Inquiry into the Electricity Supply Industry, minutes of a meeting held on 10 June 1955. In his later evidence to the Herbert Committee on the operation of rings, some of Self's most crucial evidence was given in confidence (off the record) and at his request not recorded by the Committee. The forthcoming investigations of the Monopolies and Restrictive Practices Commission may have influenced his decision. The Monopolies and Restrictive Practices Commission, *Report on the Supply and Export of Electrical and Allied Machinery and Plant*, London, HMSO, 1957, para. 156. Accompanying such common minimum prices was a range of practices, including that of each firm notifying the Group Secretary of the purchaser's requirements, and receiving compensation for tendering expenses.
[19] PRO POWE 24/2 CI, 47th meeting of Ministry of Fuel and Power, Committee of Inquiry into the Electricity Supply Industry, minutes of a meeting held on 10 June 1955. The Monopolies and Restrictive Practices Commission, *Report on the Supply and Exports of Electrical and Allied Machinery and Plant*, London, HMSO, 1957, para. 208.
[20] PRO POWE 14/115, report on 'Electric Power Plant Programme', by F. W. Smith, CEPS, 3 September 1948, p. 9.

orders by improving the distribution of orders between manufacturers.[21] The unco-ordinated placing of orders prior to nationalisation which had resulted in Babcock & Wilcox being seriously overloaded was eased by the BEA's directing orders for coal-handling plant away from Babcock.[22] Similarly, in tube manufacture, work was spread out to such firms as Yarrow, Mitchells, Bennis Combustion, Foster Wheeler, and their licensees, Richardsons Westgarth. Although spreading out work relieved some of the problems of overloading, it also created problems for smaller firms. Even when these firms had an adequate design and drawing office staff, they often required considerable guidance in taking over parts of main pipework contracts, and, where possible, the BEA attempted to minimise these and associated organisational problems by employing boiler-makers and turbine-makers in the same division.[23]

The scope for easing bottlenecks by importing was limited, imports being tightly controlled by the Treasury through a system of licences. However, the electricity industry and the Ministry of Fuel and Power were occasionally able to convince the Treasury that 'for want of an imported nail', entire construction programmes were being delayed, and on this basis, low- and high-pressure valves, pumps, boiler tubes, porcelain for insulators, and reinforcing rods were imported at various times.[24] The judicious use of such imports does appear to have had the desired stimulating effect on some domestic suppliers, as when the Authority's importing of almost £1 million of low-pressure valves from Italy in 1950–1 provoked a significant improvement in the Authority's subsequent relationship with its domestic suppliers.[25] On a grander scale, during the Korean War, proposals were floated by Sir Henry Self and W. H. Walton, a consultant to the US Embassy, for US financial and manufacturing assistance to be used for the construction of two or three stations in Britain, providing an additional 480–1,060 MWs of plant capacity at a cost of some $20 million.[26] However, the suggestion

[21] PRO POWE 14/116, 'Generating Station Extensions', Ministry of Fuel and Power's Steering Committee meeting, 22 November 1949.

[22] PRO POWE 14/115, report on 'Electric Power Plant Programme', by F. W. Smith, CEPS, 3 September 1948.

[23] PRO POWE 14/116, Ministry of Fuel and Power's Steering Committee, 'Generating Stations Extensions', minutes of meeting, 22 November 1949.

[24] PRO POWE 24/4, Committee of Inquiry into the Electricity Supply Industry, BEA, evidence to the Herbert Committee, para. 166. PRO POWE 14/115, report on 'Electric power plant programme', by F. W. Smith, CEPS, 3 September 1948, para. 11. Sir George Usher, the Chairman of International Combustion regarded the tube shortage as seriously limiting boiler production.

[25] PRO POWE 24/2, Ministry of Fuel and Power, Committee of Inquiry into the Electricity Supply Industry, notes of a meeting held on 3 June 1955, p. 40.

[26] PRO POWE 14/252, 'BEA: Notes of the 4th meeting between Representatives of the

that the engineering and construction of the projects would be under the supervision of US engineers, with beneficial demonstration effects, did not sit well with Sir John Hacking, the BEA deputy chairman with engineering expertise, who argued that if the Treasury made more finance and resources available, then the BEA could carry out the project itself.

Despite the intermittent importing of components in order to ease domestic bottlenecks, the BEA did not regard imports as any substitute for their clearly preferred option of establishing a satisfactory working relationship with domestic suppliers.[27] Financially, while such components as low-pressure valves from Italy were only a little more expensive than those manufactured in Britain, the impact of a 25 per cent import duty and additional freight charges weighed more heavily against the consideration of importing complete boilers from Italy.[28] Also, while a low price might be obtained for a single item such as a turbo-alternator, managers were not sure that they could get a low price in perpetuity for a steady supply of these items.[29] Moreover, large plant such as boilers were not produced in complete form in the factory and then transported to the site, but rather were erected on site from the complete parts made in the factory. Given the importance and difficulties of on-site construction, electricity managers were concerned that foreign firms might experience problems working with British labour on-site and that, if German and Italian firms attempted to bring in their own labour, this might cause more general and widespread labour difficulties.[30]

The limited scope for importing complete sets was also made clear to the industry by the government. The government regarded such purchases abroad by the nationalised electricity industry as damaging to the reputation of British suppliers, and thereby as harmful to their export prospects. That emergency purchases would have had such an impact seems doubtful, but it was in keeping with the government's disposition to favour exporters. The electricity industry was also

American Embassy (Industries Division), the Ministry of Fuel and Power, and the BEA', 11 May 1951.
[27] PRO POWE 24/2, Ministry of Fuel and Power, Committee of Inquiry into the Electricity Supply Industry, notes of a meeting held on 3 June 1955, p. 91.
[28] PRO POWE 24/1, CI 40th meeting, 9 May 1955. Ministry of Fuel and Power: Committee of Inquiry into the Electricity Supply Industry. Minutes of 40th meeting held on 6 May 1955.
[29] PRO POWE 24/2, Ministry of Fuel and Power, Committee of Inquiry into the Electricity Supply Industry, notes of a meeting held on 3 June 1955, p. 46. Evidence of Mr Smith.
[30] PRO POWE 24/2, Ministry of Fuel and Power, Committee of Inquiry into the Electricity Supply Industry, notes of a meeting held on 3 June 1955, p. 45.

informed through the Heavy Plant Committee that it would have to carry higher prices so as to enable manufacturers to get into export markets, although this line fell away as plant and machinery exports proved not to be as forthcoming as the government had hoped.[31] Such pressure on managers to 'buy British' and not to import was common, probably the most notable example being the government's stopping of the British Overseas Airways Corporation's (BOAC) attempts to purchase US planes during 1945–6. Instead, BOAC was compelled to operate converted bomber types, which were inefficient in public service. Only in the face of lengthening domestic delivery times was BOAC eventually allowed to make a limited purchase of US planes.[32]

The limited scope for importing, the BEA's own preference for working with domestic suppliers, and its decision not to exercise its statutory power to manufacture plant and machinery itself led the BEA to pursue increasingly aggressive tactics against domestic plant and machinery suppliers.[33] One such means of increasing output and threatening the ring operations was to encourage new entrants, and increasing resources were directed towards this strategy. John Brown Land & Co. Ltd, Richardsons Westgarth, and Daniel Adamsons Ltd were persuaded to enter the industry, and by the mid-1950s electricity managers were claiming that this expansion of production outside the boiler-makers' agreement had resulted in a substantial break in the level of boiler prices, as well as allowing the wartime and early postwar practice of allocating orders to be dropped.[34]

Even more successful were the BEA's efforts to weaken ring operations among turbo-alternator manufacturers, which had always been much more tightly organised than those in boiler-making. Substantial investments were made in small tube-manufacturing companies, but the BEA's outstanding success was in persuading C. A. Parsons & Co. Ltd to detach itself from ring restrictions and strike a one-to-one agreement with the electricity managers.[35] For some time,

---

[31] PRO POWE 24/2, Ministry of Fuel and Power, Committee of Inquiry into the Electricity Supply Industry, notes of a meeting held on 10 June 1955, pp. 48, 51, 52, 54–5.

[32] PRO POWE 24/2, Ministry of Fuel and Power, Committee of Inquiry into the Electricity Supply Industry, notes of a meeting held on 3 June 1955, p. 52. Evidence from Mr Bagnall, who had then been Permanent Secretary to the Ministry of Civil Aviation.

[33] PRO POWER 24/2, Ministry of Fuel and Power, Committee of Inquiry into the Electricity Supply Industry, notes of a meeting held on 3 June 1955, p. 93.

[34] PRO POWE 24/4, Committee of Inquiry into the Electricity Supply Industry, para. 165. John Brown & Co. Ltd was to have its first large boilers in service in 1955. PRO POWE 24/2, Ministry of Fuel and Power, Committee of Inquiry into the Electricity Supply Industry, notes of a meeting held on 3 June 1955, p. 39.

[35] PRO POWER 24/2, Ministry of Fuel and Power, Committee of Inquiry into the

Parsons had been unhappy with the unwillingness of the rings to charge the lowest prices possible, and on 1 June 1950 Parsons withdrew from membership of the large-turbine, large-alternator, and large-condenser domestic price agreements.[36] The broad lines of the agreement with the electricity industry were that Parsons would establish a large-scale pipe-fabricating shop at Newcastle, which would supply one-quarter of its own requirements, and that, in return for improved terms and prices, the Authority would guarantee to allocate a block of orders each year to Parsons, which would thereby receive a larger share of orders than it otherwise would have done.[37] Fearing that Parsons might become the Authority's principal source of supply, the incumbent firms expanded their capacity, and, after it had received sufficient orders for four years so as to secure an adequate return on its investment, Parsons gradually tailed off its work for the Authority as a more competitive market emerged.[38]

The detaching of Parsons from the ring had been important, as the capital cost of encouraging new entrants in turbo-alternator manufacturing was prohibitive. Establishing a turbo-alternator manufacturer was estimated to require some £20 million of capital, and a labour force of 4–5,000, including 100–150 highly skilled, top-class engineers and some 2,000 highly skilled and experienced workers.[39] In time, as international competition increased, the electricity managers were gradually able to agree improved terms with most of their capital-equipment suppliers. The practice of allocating contracts to manufacturers, with prices being determined subsequently, was abandoned and by 1954 tendering for contracts was being reintroduced. None the less, the turbo-alternator side remained difficult, with competition remaining very limited.[40] Moreover, not all rings were easy to break. Particularly difficult was that organised by the steel work contractors. While prices

Electricity Supply Industry, notes of a meeting held on 3 June 1955, p. 44. The first generator of 1MW size was built by Parsons, the inventor of the turbo-alternator, in 1900 for a public utility in Germany. See Harlow, *Innovation*, p. 59.

[36] The Monopolies and Restrictive Practices Commission, *Report on the Supply and Exports of Electrical and Allied Machinery and Plant*, London, HMSO, 1957, para. 213.

[37] PRO POWE 14/116, 'Generating Station Extensions', Ministry of Fuel and Power Steering Committee, meeting, 22 November 1949.

[38] PRO POWE 24/2, Ministry of Fuel and Power, Committee of Inquiry into the Electricity Supply Industry, notes of a meeting held on 3 June 1955, p. 40.

[39] PRO POWE 24/2, Ministry of Fuel and Power, Committee of Inquiry into the Electricity Supply Industry, notes of a meeting held on 3 June 1955, p. 44, Mr Smith.

[40] PRO POWE 24/2, Ministry of Fuel and Power, Committee of Inquiry into the Electricity Supply Industry, notes of a meeting, 3 June 1955, p. 91. The electricity managers complained to the Herbert Committee in 1955 about the virtual absence of competition in turbo-alternators. There then followed some evidence, given off the record.

eased by about 10 per cent between 1951 and 1953, as Authority managers felt able to allocate jobs on the basis of some private discussions with the firms concerning price, when, towards the end of 1953, the Authority switched to inviting tenders from firms, all previous gains were lost. Forced into open, collective action, the steelwork contractors raised their prices by 15 per cent and all of the tenderers refused to discuss any feature of a ring-delivered price.[41]

In its efforts to obtain improved terms and prices from its plant and machinery suppliers, the BEA experienced an ambivalent relationship with central government. On the one hand, rhetorical and legislative condemnations of restrictive practices were issued, and in 1948 the government supervised the legislative enactment of the Monopolies and Restrictive Practices Act, which began moves towards the establishment of the Monopolies and Restrictive Practices Commission.[42] On the other hand, many aspects of the priorities and administrative panoply of economic planning seemed to foster the very rings and restrictive practices which electricity managers were striving to break. It was not simply that government promotion of the export drive combined with import restrictions to place the electricity industry in a nigh-captive relationship with their suppliers, but also that the administrative planning system provided the manufacturers with a flow of information about the electricity industry's predicament. Within the central planning machinery, suppliers and the industry came together in the Heavy Electrical Plant Committee, which had been established in 1944 for the purpose of agreeing postwar programmes for the CEB.[43] One consequence of the regular discussion of the plant and machinery position was to provide manufacturers with a flow of up-to-date information on the negotiating position of the electricity industry, information which was augmented further by the information flows within the rings. The information base enjoyed by the suppliers made it extremely difficult for the electricity industry to attempt to bluff suppliers into providing better delivery times and improved technical specifications, especially when the plant and machinery suppliers included men such as Sir George Nelson, Chairman of the English Electric Company, who 'has been on

---

[41] PRO POWE 24/2, Ministry of Fuel and Power, Committee of Inquiry into the Electricity Supply Industry, notes of a meeting held on 3 June 1955, p. 41.

[42] H. Mercer, *Constructing a Competitive Order; the Hidden History of British Anti-trust Policies*, Cambridge, Cambridge University Press, 1995, ch. 6. *Employment Policy*, Cmd 6527, Parliamentary Papers, 1943–44, vol. VIII, para. 54.

[43] Persistent shortages of heavy electrical plant led to a widening of the committee's terms of reference in 1946, to include consideration of the utilisation of the production capacity of the machinery manufacturing industry for overseas and domestic purposes.

every Government Committee for the past 25 years and knows what Government thinks'.[44]

It is arguable, therefore, that one effect of the regular meetings between government, plant suppliers, and the electricity industry, allied with the government's keen prosecution of its export-maximising/ import-saving programme, was to intensify the difficulties facing the electricity industry in securing improved supplies and terms from its main suppliers. The administrative structure of planning also provided the conduit for the most conspicuous example of the ability of the manufacturers to influence government policy towards the electricity industry. This outstanding case concerned the government's decision to issue a Standstill Order in November 1947, which effectively froze the ordering of advanced technology and restricted the production of steam turbo-alternators for the domestic market to two standard types, either 30MW capacity taking steam at 600 pounds per square inch (psi) at 850 degrees Fahrenheit, or 60MW capacity taking steam at 900 psi at 900 degrees Fahrenheit.[45] The 30MW set had made its debut in 1929 (Hams Hall A), with a 60MW set first appearing in 1936 (Fulham). Seventy-five MW sets were installed at Barking B in 1933, and 69MW and 105MW sets at Battersea A in 1933.[46] The choice of standardised specifications was based on the belief that no postwar station would have an installation of less than 30MW, that 60MW was the maximum output capacity suitable to existing standards, and that these steam conditions could be met by available boiler designs which required only low-alloy steels. The issuing of the Standstill Order marked the culmination of a stream of discussions between the government, manufacturers, and electricity managers which had their origins in the aftermath of the fuel crisis of February 1947. It was in the intense atmosphere of those days that the manufacturers first raised the possibility of a Standstill Order in their post-fuel crisis meeting with the

---

[44] PRO POWER 24/2, Ministry of Fuel and Power, Committee of Inquiry into the Electricity Supply Industry, notes of a meeting held on 3 June 1955, p. 48.
[45] The Control of Turbo Alternators (No. 1 Order) dated 7 November 1947. F. P. R. Brechling and A. J. Surrey, 'An International Comparison of Production Techniques: the Coal-Fired Electricity Generating Industry', *National Institute Economic Review*, 36 (May 1966), pp. 30–42. PRO POWE 24/14, Ministry of Fuel and Power, CP 81, 17 June 1955. Committee of Inquiry into the Electricity Supply Industry, Standardisation of Generating Plant (S. R. & O. of 1947, No. 2386), note by the Ministry of Fuel and Power. PRO POWE 24/2, Ministry of Fuel and Power, Committee of Inquiry into the Electricity Supply Industry, notes of a meeting held on 3 June 1955, p. 51. Mr Noddings argued that standardisation at 900 pounds was a jump forward at the time, there being no experience in this country of that. However, Harlow, *Innovation*, pp. 65–6, regarded these steam conditions as 'by no means advanced for the time'.
[46] Harlow, *Innovation*, p. 65.

Prime Minister on 10 March 1947.[47] Subsequent discussions with the CEB, the Electricity Commission, the Ministry of Fuel and Power, and the Ministry of Supply saw the recitation of the standard litany concerning the benefits likely to accrue from the standardisation facilitated by a Standstill Order.[48] The standardisation of plant and sizes of boiler drums, tube dimensions and other components was presented as facilitating savings of six to nine months in delivery times, with the possibility of initiating 'batch' production of machines for the home market offering further reductions in the production-time cycle.[49] In particular, standardisation of design was thought likely to reduce the amount of design and drawing work required, thereby easing pressures on the severely overstretched supply of engineering draughtsmen. However, it was acknowledged that it would be some time before the full benefits of this were realised, which begged questions about the decision to standardise around 30MW and 60MW sets.[50]

The restrictive nature of the 1947 Order was recognised by the industry, as was the fact that the volume of orders being placed for 30MW sets, in particular, allied to the prevailing long construction times, were likely to mean that these plant choices would have long-term consequences for the productivity of the electricity industry.[51] Some 86 per cent of the plants built in the early years of the BEA were 30MW and 60MW sets with standard steam conditions, with some orders placed before the Standstill Order as far back as November 1946 also being renegotiated to fit the conditions of standard sizes and steam conditions.[52] A snapshot from the CEB's own files provides confirmation of the dominance of set orders in the 30–60MW range and the growing problem of lengthening construction times. In 1951, of the 922MWs of capacity installation in hand, all of the sets fell within the

[47] PRO POWE 24/14, Ministry of Fuel and Power, CP 81, 17 June 1955. Committee of Inquiry into the Electricity Supply Industry, Standardisation of Generating Plant (S. R. & O. of 1947, No. 2386), note by the Ministry of Fuel and Power.
[48] For fashionable contemporary faith in standardisation, see Jim Tomlinson, 'The Failure of the Anglo-American Council on Productivity', *Business History*, 33, 1 (January 1991), pp. 82–92. Anthony Carew, 'The Anglo-American Council on Productivity (1948–52): the Ideological Roots of the Post-War Debate on Productivity in Britain', *Journal of Contemporary History*, 26 (1991), pp. 49–69.
[49] PRO POWE 24/14, Ministry of Fuel and Power, CP 81, 17 June 1955. Committee of Inquiry into the Electricity Supply Industry, Standardisation of Generating Plant (S. R. & O. of 1947, No. 2386), note by the Ministry of Fuel and Power. PRO T229/146, note from F. W. Smith to Sir Edwin Plowden, 5 January 1948.
[50] PRO POWE 14/115, report on 'Electric Power Plant Programme', by F. W. Smith, CEPS, 3 September 1948, para. 14.
[51] Harlow, *Innovation*, p. 69. He refers to a lecture by Deputy Chairman, F. H. S. Brown (Central Electricity Generating Board), British Electrical and Allied Manufacturer's Association Export Conference, 8 October 1961.
[52] Harlow, *Innovation*, pp. 66, 105.

30–60MW range. Of the new stations, only Keadby received 60MW sets, the other three (Doncaster, Barrow and Bideford, North Devon) getting 30MW. Extensions tended on average to get larger sets (average set size being 37MW), with estimated completion times varying from one to four-and-a-half years compared with three-and-a-half years for all new stations. The attraction of extensions was that they required less building labour and civil-engineering resources than new stations, as well as having lower capital costs.[53] A similar pattern is evident from the generating-station programme details for 1952 and 1952/3, except that the estimated construction period had lengthened to four and five years respectively.[54] The construction times of five years, which could well follow on from design periods of one to two years, perpetuated the impact of the Standstill Order well into the mid- and late-1950s.[55] As the industry's managers were to complain in 1955: 'we are getting a semi-obsolete design coming into commission'.[56]

Given the size of the programme, the standard range of sets still dominated the new plant being commissioned during 1958 and 1959, even though work had started on larger generating units with advanced steam conditions and reheat during 1950 and 1951.[57] In the new stations, 6,800MWs was installed as standard 30MW and 60MW units between 1948 and 1960. Another 700MWs of capacity in extensions of existing stations was ordered in general conformity to the standard set sizes. Between 1950 and 1958 the standard sets accounted for 60–75 per cent of all generating equipment installed. Of the generating sets programmed for 1955, 32.3 per cent were 30MW sets in size and 61.3 per cent were 60MW. These shares declined slowly over the 1950s, although the sets programmed for 1958 included 27.3 per cent of 30MW and 54.6 per cent of 60MW size. It was only in the programmed sets for 1959 that 30MW sets disappeared and the larger sets, namely

[53] PRO POWE 14/110, Central Electricity Board, 'Generating Stations Programme for 1951', February 1948. Although comparisons are perilous, it is of some interest that to build a new station for the CEB at Doncaster with a capacity of 1 × 30MW sets required 190 building and civil-engineering workers, while to extend capacity at Walsall in the West Midlands would require 100 additional workers. Capital costs would also be lower, Doncaster costing £1.9 million and Walsall £1.25 million.
[54] PRO POWE 14/110, Central Electricity Board; Generating Stations Programme for 1951–2, 1952–3.
[55] PRO POWE 24/4, Committee of Inquiry into the Electricity Supply Industry, BEA, Evidence to the Herbert Committee, pp. 35–6, para. 136. PRO POWER 24/2, Ministry of Fuel and Power, Committee of Inquiry into the Electricity Supply Industry, notes of a meeting held on 3 June 1955, p. 50. The Standstill Order is held to have standardised sets up to 1959, i.e. for fifteen years after vesting date.
[56] PRO POWER 24/2, Ministry of Fuel and Power, Committee of Inquiry into the Electricity Supply Industry, notes of a meeting held on 3 June 1955, p. 53.
[57] Harlow, *Innovation*, p. 66.

100MW straight (9.1 per cent) and 120MW reheat (22.7 per cent) began to make an increasing contribution. Even so, their contribution was overshadowed by that of 60MW sets, which accounted for 50 per cent of all programmed sets.[58] It appeared that the combination of war, the Standstill Order, and long construction times had frozen progress in the largest area of fixed capital investment in the UK.

The impression of an industry in a frozen, static state only seemed to be reinforced by international comparisons. On average, French turbo-alternators installed between 1948 and 1963 were 35 per cent larger, and US turbo-alternators 98 per cent larger, than the British ones. In 1955, the average size of turbo-alternators installed over the period 1948–55 was 142MWs in the United States, 75MWs in France, and 51MWs in the UK.[59] Similarly, average boiler sizes in France and the USA exceeded those in Britain by 32 per cent and 90 per cent respectively. Moreover, in Britain, steam temperature and pressures had been low in comparison with the USA, reheat had been less widespread, and the type of firing had been rather less advanced than in the USA.[60] However, by 1959, some more advanced technical specifications were being introduced, notably in the 200MW set installed in the new High Marnham (Nottingham) power station. These sets were supplied with steam at 2,350 psi at 1,050 degrees Fahrenheit, with that steam, on a reheat basis, after passing through part of the turbine being taken back into the boilers for a further reheat, coming out again at 1,000 degrees Fahrenheit. The long-term aim of engineers was to be able to go beyond a pressure of 3,200 psi where quantum is zero – i.e. where the water changes its state without any increment in heat – and then progress on to pressures of 4–5,000 psi with temperatures up to 1,000 degrees Fahrenheit. There were, however, material constraints to such developments, not the least being that at temperatures above 1,050 degrees

---

[58] PRO POWE 24/4, Committee of Inquiry into the Electricity Supply Industry, BEA, evidence to the Herbert Committee, para. 138.

[59] By 1958 the average size of turbo-alternator installed in Britain was 87MW, an average size achieved in the USA by 1951.

[60] Harlow, *Innovation*, pp. 66–7, states that it was only late in 1956 that the first 100 MW set without reheat ordered by the Authority came into use at Castle Donington, and fewer than 10 sets of 100 MW were in use in Britain before 1960. Up to 1959 reheat was employed only in the six power stations where it had been developed as a technique before nationalisation, and at the Blyth A and Ferrybridge B stations ordered by the Authority. A slightly more generous view is taken by Brechling and Surrey, who, noting that reheat appears to have been introduced as an experiment in 1949, observe that it took a further eleven years before all new units installed in Britain were equipped with reheat. By contrast, the French industry made the transition to 100% reheat in three years and the 98% level was reached in the USA within six years. This suggests that it may not have been the lack of technical knowledge which caused the technological lags, so much as slowness in appraising new techniques.

Fahrenheit metals, being critical to temperature, lose their strength very rapidly.[61] At such temperatures, carbon steel metal starts to 'flow', i.e. it 'creeps' and never returns to quite the same size as it was before the heat cycle. Better alloys needed to be developed before temperatures and pressures could be increased further. Metal 'creep' in a turbo-alternator was unacceptable, since, while boilers are static, the blade rotation was 3,000 revolutions per minute, with the tip speed of 950 miles per hour, faster than the speed of sound.[62] Just as the Standstill Order had been issued at the urging of the heavy electrical-machinery suppliers, so too was it revoked with their approval on 24 July 1950.[63] Part of the reasoning given was that with competition returning to the international market, British manufacturers needed to gain experience of manufacturing larger units.[64] However, in a reflection revealing of their attitude towards nationalisation in a centralised monopoly form, the manufacturers also argued that the Standstill Order could be revoked, as the nationalised Central Authority could be relied on to continue with standardisation without legal compulsion. A centrally organised nationalised industry was thought likely to have the means and incentive to exploit standardisation of design.[65] Not least, standardisation was thought likely to accompany centralised efforts to secure improvements in the distribution of orders through a central progressing organisation.[66] With the release of the Standstill Order, the electricity industry began to order more advanced

[61] PRO POWE 24/2, Ministry of Fuel and Power, Committee of Inquiry into the Electricity Supply Industry, notes of a meeting held on 3 June 1955.

[62] PRO POWE 14/555. Other schemes like that for the use of waste heat never really got off the ground, the costs of distribution being considered to be too high except in situations such as the Pimlico scheme. PRO POWE 14/319. While it was acknowledged that, technically, the supply of steam with electricity as a by-product was very much more efficient than the supply of electricity alone, the difficulty was that the demand was for electricity rather than steam, and building-up a demand for steam of the dimensions required was thought likely to be an extremely slow and difficult business. Moreover, while the supplied district heating was held to be cheap, local authorities and their tenants were not yet generally willing to pay its absolutely high price.

[63] It was revoked by S. R. & O. of 1950, No. 1221.

[64] PRO POWE 24/14, Ministry of Fuel and Power, CP 81, 17 June 1955. Committee of Inquiry into the Electricity Supply Industry, Standardisation of Generating Plants (S. R. & O. of 1947, No. 2386), note by the Ministry of Fuel and Power. Report of the Committee of Inquiry into the Electricity Supply Industry, Cmd 9672 (the Herbert Report) para. 423. Accordingly, the statutory order was withdrawn in 1950 'when the manufacturers of generating equipment were of the opinion that they were able to manufacture plant of more advanced design which would benefit them in their export drive'.

[65] PRO POWE 24/4, Committee of Inquiry into the Electricity Supply Industry, BEA, evidence to the Herbert Committee, para. 134.

[66] PRO POWE 24/2, Ministry of Fuel and Power, Committee of Inquiry into the Electricity Supply Industry, 17 May 1955.

designs: 100MW units with steam conditions of 1,500 psi/1,050 degrees Fahrenheit were incorporated into the station at Castle Donington, near Derby; 100MW capacity with steam conditions of 1,500 psi/975 degrees Fahrenheit, but with reheating to 950 degrees Fahrenheit, was installed in Ferrybridge B, for 1956; and then 120MW machines at 1,500 psi/1,000 degrees Fahrenheit reheating to 1,000 degrees Fahrenheit were installed at Drakelow B, Burton-on-Trent, for 1958.

What, then, were the costs and benefits of the Standstill Order? There is some evidence that the Standstill Order and the moves towards standardised boilers and turbines did quicken the delivery of plant, and that some benefits were obtained from economies of replication, the high reliability of 30MW and 60MW sets, and the time saved by not having to redesign or retool.[67] However, the spreading of orders among manufacturers in order to speed their progression reduced the opportunity to exploit the benefits of standardisation of manufacture and design as each manufacturer built to its own detailed design. Certainly, the Monopolies and Restrictive Practices Commission were doubtful of the benefits of standardisation, regarding the diversity of requirements and intricacy of the engineering problems as giving little scope for application of flow and batch production methods to any but the smallest machines. Evidence from France also suggested that success in reducing the forced outage rate of new classes of machines tended to be related more to the distribution of orders between manufacturers than to the total number of orders placed, the teething troubles experienced by one maker not necessarily being those of other makers.[68]

Whatever the benefits actually gained from standardisation around 30MW and 60MW sets, these need to be set against the costs in terms of lower fuel and capital productivity. The small size and moderate technical specification of sets had consequences for both the capital productivity and the thermal efficiency of the electricity industry.[69] In general, increasing efficiency and increasing size of generating plant were positively correlated, both capital and running costs per kilowatt (kW) decreasing with increases in the size of the generating set. This inverse relationship between increases in capacity and the capital cost per kilowatt-hour (kWh) of a generating unit at a given steam condition

[67] PRO POWE 14/115, Smith's report on construction of electric power station programme, paper to Sir Edwin Plowden, 2 September 1948.

[68] Brechling and Surrey, 'An International Comparison', *National Institute Economic Review*.

[69] Capital productivity is defined as the number of kilowatts supplied by a given plant expressed as a ratio of the cost of that plant. Fuel productivity is the number of kilowatt hours (kWh) supplied per unit of fuel input, the latter usually being expressed in millions of British thermal units (Btus).

resulted in a reduction of about 20 per cent in cost per kilowatt for every 100 per cent increase in size. It was estimated that while a 60MW unit with a thermal efficiency of about 29 per cent was likely to have a capital cost of £57 per kW, a 550MW unit with a thermal efficiency of about 36.5 per cent was expected to cost £39 per kW.[70] Newer, larger plant usually also incorporated higher steam pressures and temperatures, all of which combined to offer higher thermal efficiency on newer plant, with the reduction in capital cost per kilowatt being more than sufficient to pay for increased costs occasioned by a move to higher steam conditions.[71]

Since the construction of generating stations involved a considerable use of such scarce resources as steel, plant and machinery, and labour, while the station's subsequent operation burnt large quantities of scarce coal, both capital and thermal efficiency were of considerable importance in a resource constrained economy. While capital costs accounting for 15–30 per cent of costs were of interest to some economists, it was thermal efficiency and the related fuel costs, representing about 60–80 per cent of total costs which attracted most attention.[72] In 1948, coal costs accounted for 84 per cent of the generating costs (excluding capital costs) of the electricity industry, and coal shortages were predicted to persist into the mid-1960s.[73] The efficiency of the electricity industry's coal-burn was therefore of considerable importance, especially as the British electricity industry had a greater proportion of coal-burning sets than comparable economies. Even in 1963, coal-fired plant in Britain generated 84 per cent of the public supply of electricity in Britain, compared with 21 per cent in France and 54 per cent in the USA.[74] It was therefore of concern to the Ridley Committee, and especially to Professor Hawthorne, that the thermal efficiency of new sets did not maintain the pre-war rate of improvement (28 per cent in 1936), and that they compared badly with some US stations which had achieved efficiency

[70] F. H. S. Brown and R. S. Edwards, 'The Replacement of Obsolescent Plant', *Economica*, 28 (August 1961), pp. 297–302.

[71] Brechling and Surrey, 'An International Comparison', *National Institute Economic Review*.

[72] PRO POWE 24/2 CI 44th meeting, Ministry of Fuel and Power, Committee of Inquiry into the Electricity Supply Industry, minutes of the 44th meeting of the Committee on 20 May 1955. Coal costs were 66–70 per cent of direct costs. Brechling and Surrey, 'An International Comparison', *National Institute Economic Review*.

[73] Ministry of Fuel and Power, *Statistical Digest 1966* (1967) Table 87. Coal costs accounted for 99.4% of total fuel costs in 1948. Oil accounted for 0.6%. *Report of the (Ridley) Committee on National Policy for the Use of Fuel and Power Resources*, London, HMSO, September 1952, Cmd. 8647.

[74] Brechling and Surrey, 'An International Comparison', *National Institute Economic Review*, p. 30.

of 37.5 per cent.[75] The majority of the 30MW sets in 1946–9 operated at just over 26 per cent thermal efficiency, and average thermal efficiency was the same in 1946 as in 1939 (21.9 per cent), having fallen in some war years.[76] It proceeded to fall during much of the Attlee governments before improving slowly during the 1950s. By 1955, the best available thermal efficiency was about 35 per cent.

In partial mitigation, a complaint persistently heard from electricity, and railway managers, was that there had been a deterioration in the quality of coal being burnt in stations after World War II, thereby reducing thermal efficiency.[77] The Btu (British thermal unit) data in Table 6.1 provides some support for this view, and there may have been something in the industry's claim that in the USA, coal with a thermal content of over 12,000 Btu per pound was readily available, compared with the Btu content of 11,000 in coal supplied to the BEA.[78] Certainly, the Beaver Committee did acknowledge that there were real differences of quality and uniformity between the coals normally available in the two countries.[79] In theory, higher coal prices may have eased these problems by allowing the electricity industry to purchase higher-quality coal, providing it was then willing to pass on the costs to its consumers.

The use of new sets for base-load supply allowed them to make a contribution to the average thermal efficiency of the industry which was disproportionate to their size. However, offsetting this potential source of improvement was the need to make greater use of older sets with lower thermal efficiencies so as to meet total and peak-load requirements. Peak demand requiring the operation of a larger proportion of generating equipment for a short time often made the retention of older and comparatively unproductive equipment more attractive than investment in new equipment specifically for that purpose. The use of old

[75] PRO POWE 14/555, Ridley Committee on Fuel and Power Policy. PRO POWE 14/553, DCFP 15th meeting, 'Improvement in Efficiency of Generating Plant in UK, 1920–1950', 3 March 1952. PRO POWE 24/2, Ministry of Fuel and Power, Committee of Inquiry into the Electricity Supply Industry, notes of a meeting held on 3 June 1955. PRO POWE 14/555, Ridley Committee on Fuel and Power Policy.

[76] Harlow, *Innovation*, p. 67.

[77] PRO POWE 14/555, Ridley Committee on Fuel and Power. Less than 2.5 million tons of the coal consumed by the BEA was of the unscreened or grade types.

[78] PRO POWE 14/553, memo initialed 'A G F F' Electricity Division 20 September 1951. In his paper to the Second British Electrical Power Convention 1950, Mr J. D. Peattie described the reasons for the set-back in thermal efficiency which had taken place in the following words: 'The halt was due to wartime operating conditions calling for uneconomical operation in order to safeguard supplies, to restriction in the installation of new more efficient plant, to extended operation of older stations owing to the prolonged peak load demands, and last but not least deterioration in the quality and uniformity of fuel supplies.'

[79] Ministry of Fuel and Power, *Report of the (Beaver) Committee of Enquiry into Economy in the Construction of Power Stations*, London, HMSO, 1953, para. 23.

plant, however, did reduce average thermal efficiency, as well as contributing to a curious age-structure of plant operating in the industry. With the retention of old plant, wartime under-investment and the postwar investment response to peak-capacity shortages, the age distribution of steam-driven sets was a curious mix of veterans and infants. Measured as a percentage of installed capacity, the proportion of sets in commission over 30 years old was 1.6 per cent in 1945/6, 3 per cent in 1950, 9.1 per cent in 1955, and 14.6 per cent in 1960. This ageing stock coincided with an increase in the share of capacity being supplied by relatively newer sets, the percentage of capacity consisting of sets under 10 years of age rising over the same period from 20.4 per cent in 1945/6, 38 per cent in 1950, 49.3 per cent in 1955, to 57 per cent in 1960.[80] Thus, average thermal efficiency was the product of a complex of factors which included age of plant, system-load factor and plant-load factor.[81] The British system-load factor of 46.9 per cent in 1948 and 42.4 per cent in 1953, compared unfavourably with 69.4 per cent in 1948 and 61.6 per cent in 1953 in France, and 60.8 per cent in 1948 and 63.2 per cent in 1953 in the USA.[82] System-load factor both fluctuated and registered a slow general rate of improvement across the period from the start of World War II to the end of the 1950s. The system-load factor was itself a function of the wider loading and peak loading of the industry, and was only likely to deteriorate in the short term, as increases in plant installation and capacity decreased load shedding.[83]

Given the prevailing long construction times, in the early 1950s many of the sets ordered during the Attlee governments were still a long way from being commissioned. Indeed, it was not until 40 60MW sets had been ordered that one began to operate.[84] Opportunities arose to cancel some of the last 20 of these 40 sets and supersede them with orders for 120MW and 200MW sets. However, the electricity industry explicitly chose not to do this, in part because of the high cancellation charges and the likely disruption to the production programme, but also

[80] Ministry of Fuel and Power, *Statistical Digest, 1960*, 1961, Table 75. Also see Matthews, Feinstein, and Odling-Smee, *British Economic Growth*, Table G7, p. 584.
[81] System-load factor is the ratio of the average load supplied by the entire public-supply network during a year to the potential maximum peak load in that year. System-load factor thus measures the peakedness of the demand for electricity.
[82] Brechling and Surrey, 'An International Comparison', *National Institute Economic Review*.
[83] PRO POWE 24/2 CI 44th meeting, Ministry of Fuel and Power, Committee of Inquiry into the Electricity Supply Industry, Minutes of the 44 meeting of the Committee on 20 May 1955, evidence of Citrine.
[84] PRO POWE 24/2, Ministry of Fuel and Power, Committee of Inquiry into the Electricity Supply Industry, notes of a meeting held on 3 June 1955.

Table 6.1. *Load factors and thermal efficiency in the electricity industry,*
1922–60

Year	Plant-load factor [a] (per cent)	System-load factor [b] (per cent)	Average thermal efficiency of steam stations [c] (per cent)	Average calorific value of coal consumed (Btu/lb)
1922	16.8	27.3	10.6	—
1923	—	28.5	11.0	—
1924	18.4	29.2	11.6	—
1925	17.1	29.0	12.3	—
1926	17.0	28.7	12.8	—
1927	18.3	28.6	13.8	—
1928	18.3	30.3	14.6	—
1929	18.0	31.6	15.1	—
1930	17.9	31.5	15.9	—
1931	18.1	31.5	16.5	—
1932	18.9	32.1	17.2	—
1933	19.7	30.8	18.0	—
1934	22.7	31.8	18.8	—
1935	24.8	31.8	19.4	—
1936	27.4	33.4	20.0	—
1937	29.3	34.2	20.7	—
1938	29.3	33.3	21.7	—
1939	30.4	35.1	21.9	—
1940	32.2	36.2	21.0	—
1941	34.1	38.4	21.0	—
1942	34.8	40.5	21.0	—
1943	35.2	40.2	21.4	—
1944	35.9	40.1	21.0	—
1945	34.5	37.6	21.8	11,000
1946	37.5	40.0	21.9	10,916
1947	35.5	39.7	21.9 [d]	10,948
1948	42.7	46.9	21.1	10,952
1949	43.5	42.5	21.3	10,909
1950	45.8	42.8	21.6	10,935
1951	46.3	46.2	21.6	10,977
1952	43.9	43.6	22.6	10,882
1953	42.7	42.4	23.2	10,812
1954	43.9	44.4	23.7	10,746
1955	44.3	43.5	24.2	10,814
1956	43.9	48.3	24.8	10,687
1957	41.9	46.3	25.2	10,553
1958	42.4	46.4	25.9	10,454
1959	42.5	45.3	26.3	10,405
1960	44.7	48.4	26.7	10,247

(*Source:* Ministry of Power, *Statistical Digest 1966*, London, HMSO, 1967).

[a] Plant-load factor is the average hourly quantity of electricity sent out during the year, expressed as a percentage of the average output capacity during the year.

[b] System-load factor is the average hourly quantity of electricity sent out during the year (including purchases from other sources) expressed as a percentage of the maximum potential demand nearest the end of the year or early the following year.

[c] Thermal efficiency is the total calorific value of the electricity sent out expressed as a percentage of the calorific value (gross as fired) of the total fuel consumed.

[d] Up to 1947, installed capacity and electricity generated have been used instead of average output capacity and electricity sent out.

because it intended to use the 60MW sets as the donkey sets of the future. These sets, which were capable of being shut down at night and restarted in the morning, were considered by managers to be very necessary given the low load factor and associated high peaked demand in the UK. This was especially so given that 120MW sets were not thought suitable for speedy and safe start-up and shut-down, and it was only recently that designs of 60MW sets had been developed for quick starting.[85]

Like electricity, railways faced high demand with a depreciated capital stock, net disinvestment in railway assets during 1937–53 being estimated at £440 million in 1948 prices.[86] At the beginning of 1948, 16.6 per cent of the wagon fleet, 14.45 per cent of carriages, and 7 per cent of locomotives at main works were under or awaiting repair. Of the stock of 20,313 locomotives, 39.3 per cent were over 35 years of age and increasingly prone to breaking down.[87] With scarce steel allocated to urgent rolling-stock requirements, track investment was squeezed. On the worn rail network, speed limits were applied and ranking techniques sometimes employed, in which the most reliable locomotive headed departures from main-line terminals so as to reduce the knock-on effects of any subsequent breakdown by later express locomotives.[88]

Apart from patching the system, the main area of new investment decisions concerned locomotive design and the mix of steam-, diesel-, and electric-powered locomotives. This decision was the responsibility

[85] PRO POWE 24/4, Herbert Committee, Appendix(OE) 2, Central Electricity Authority: notes on the role of load factor in the design of the Authority's generating plant, para. 11. PRO POWE 24/2, Ministry of Fuel and Power, Committee of Inquiry into the Electricity Supply Industry, notes of a meeting held on 3 June 1955.

[86] P. Redfern, 'Net Investment in Fixed Assets in the United Kingdom, 1938–53', *Journal of the Royal Statistical Society*, Series A, 118, 2 (1955), pp. 141–76.

[87] PRO AN 85/17, Railway Executive Committee, memorandum to Minister of Transport, 'Five year plan for construction and repair of railway rolling stock for main line railway companies', 1947. J. Johnson and R. Long, *British Railways Engineering, 1948–80*, London, Mechanical Engineering Publications, 1981, pp. 38–9.

[88] PRO AN85/22, 'Steel for the Railways, 1949', 10 November 1948.

of the Railway Executive, in which Robin Riddles was responsible for mechanical and electrical engineering and Sir Eustace Missenden was chairman. Overseeing the Railway Executive was the British Transport Commission, of which Sir Cyril Hurcomb was chairman and Miles Beevor was chief secretary. Relations between the railway enthusiasts on the Railway Executive and the nationalising government-appointed British Transport Commission were not good. So suspicious was the Executive of the Commission that, until discovered in 1950, it kept a full set of minutes concealed from the Commission, sending it only edited reports of its meetings.

One particular point of difficulty in relations between the Executive and the Commission concerned locomotive design, and the future of steam and diesel locomotives. Beevor strongly opposed an apparent 'underlying assumption' in Executive thinking 'that the steam locomotive must necessarily remain the principal source of motive power on British railways for the next generation'. Concerned at a first full year of nationalisation which he characterised as one of 'little original thinking' on railway development policy, and at a tendency to argue that new design work should wait until the existing backlog of work had been cleared, Beevor proposed the establishment of a separate planning department free 'from all responsibilities for the daily problems of management'.[89]

The arguments over locomotive choice revolved around issues of cost and security. As in electricity, the availability of capital equipment was an immediate source of concern. Dollar-import restrictions made it difficult to obtain the newer diesel-engine technology from the USA, the large majority of which was manufactured by General Motors, whose Electro-Motive Division had an annual production of 2,000 units.[90] General Motors were unwilling to allow UK manufacturers to produce to their designs under licence, and diesel engines manufactured in the UK were more expensive than those made in the USA. The relative cost of diesel-electric and steam locomotives was 3:1 in the UK compared with 2:1 in the USA. Higher British production costs were attributed to the tradition of British shops making their own components, while US manufacturers tended to work with a limited number of sub-assemblies often supplied from outside their own shops.[91] The British railway industry was almost alone in the world in undertaking

---

[89] PRO AN 85/23, note from Miles Beevor, Chief Secretary, memo to the Commission, 'The Railway Executive: Major Development Schemes, 1948–1952', 17 January 1949.

[90] PRO AN 88/77, Report of the Committee on Types of Motive Power, 1951, para. 64. Johnson and Long, *British Railways Engineering*, pp. 168, 182. During the 1950s no diesels were ordered from General Motors.

[91] PRO POWE 14/555 DCFP 137, Ministry of Fuel and Power, Committee on National

itself both the construction and the repair of their own steam locomotives and rolling stock, a practice of nineteenth-century origin.[92] As early as 1900, this had been criticised as limiting the scope for standardisation and production economies of a type being exploited in the USA by independent engineering companies supplying locomotives to the railway companies.[93]

That the higher first (capital) costs of diesel locomotives were between three and five times higher those of steam meant that much of the discussion came to centre on the improvements in operating costs which were likely to follow any move towards diesels. Riddles and Missenden questioned whether the high annual mileages required by diesels if they were to exploit their greater power and almost continual availability were as available in Britain as in the USA, where diesels were being quickly adopted. While in the USA long runs meant that 1,000-mile daily rosters, 7 days a week were not uncommon, in Britain, even on the exceptional Euston–Glasgow run with a round trip every 24 hours, the maximum rostered weekly mileage of the twin-diesel was only 5,600. Similarly, an average length of haul for freight traffic in the USA was 405 miles, as against 72 miles in Britain.[94] Against this, diesel-electric locomotives were also used on shorter routes such as the 85 miles between Chicago and Milwaukee, with diesel-electric locomotives making 7 single trips a day, stopping at 4 intermediate stations. Over short distances, the higher thermal efficiency of diesels could be seen as conferring an advantage over steam locomotives, not least in shunting duties for which a diesel shunter used about 2.5 gallons of oil per hour as against 233 pounds of coal per hour for steam. With a low load factor and the avoidance of standby losses, this produced a fuel-cost saving of about 2s 3d per hour for diesel and 6s 4d per hour for steam, a saving of 64 per cent.[95] Calculations of comparative thermal efficiency were always contentious, when, as in electricity, the low quality of coal burnt reduced thermal efficiency.[96] The application of speed limits on many sections of the rail network also disadvantaged diesel locomotives, which were at their most efficient when working at full output. Making

Fuel Policy, 'The Relative Costs of Diesel and Steam Locomotives: Note by the Ministry of Fuel and Power', 13 March 1952.
[92] S. Saul, 'The Mechanical Engineering Industries in Britain, 1860–1914', in B. Supple, *Essays in British Business History*, Oxford, Clarendon Press, 1977.
[93] PRO AN 88/77, Report of the Committee on Types of Motive Power, 1951, para. 63.
[94] PRO AN 88/77, Report of the Committee on Types of Motive Power, 1951, para. 68.
[95] PRO POWE 14/554 DCFP 21, 19 September 1951, Ministry of Fuel and Power, Committee on National Fuel Policy, 'Diesel Locomotives and Electrification as Alternatives to Steam: Note by the Ministry of Transport and Railway Executives'.
[96] PRO AN 88/77, R. Riddles, The Railway Executive 'Report on Types of Motive Power', 23 January 1952.

cost-based comparisons was also made more difficult by the low, controlled price of coal. As the Ministry of Transport and Railway Executive argued to the Ridley Committee on National Fuel Policy, while a main-line diesel locomotive on passenger service used about 1.4 gallons of oil per mile as against 48 pounds of coal per mile for steam at 1951 costs, 'the higher price of oil "negatives" the greater thermal efficiency of the diesel engine' and fuel costs broke even for the two types of power at about 1s 3d per mile.[97] This was consistent with thinking in a output-maximising, capital-equipment-constrained economy in which considerations of immediate capital cost ranked higher than thermal efficiency.

In addition to considerations of first cost, capital productivity, and thermal efficiency, discussions of locomotive choice involved consideration of the security of fuel supply.[98] The rapid development from 1940 of diesel traction in the USA and a little later in Canada was attributed in part to the adequate availability of cheap oil.[99] Yet, in the UK, the dangers of relying on oil supplies were played up by Riddles and Missenden, who were quick to point out that 'the recent experience with the conversion of steam locomotives to oil burning has not inspired our confidence'.[100] Yet in general, world crude-oil production was predicted to almost double during the 1940s from 279 million tons in 1938 to 540 million tons in 1950, and then rise in the early 1950s at an annual rate of 11 per cent. Britain itself was planning to double its domestic oil-refining capacity between 1951 and 1954. While the Middle East was becoming politically tense, other sources of oil, such as Venezuela, were being developed all the time. The oil companies were happy to provide assurances that they could provide the 3 million tons per annum required by diesel locomotives, thereby reducing the railways' existing annual coal-burn of 14 million tons, which formed one-third of all coal directly used by all industry.[101]

In Europe, as visiting British engineers well knew, appraisals of

[97] PRO POWE 14/554 DCFP 21, Ministry of Fuel and Power: Committee on National Fuel Policy: 'Diesel Locomotives and Electrification as Alternatives to Steam: Note by Ministry of Transport and Railway Executives', 19 September 1951, para. 5.
[98] PRO AN 88/77, Report of the Committee on Types of Motive Power, 1951. PRO AN 88/77, R. Riddles, The Railway Executive, 'Report on Types of Motive Power', 23 January 1952.
[99] Johnson and Long, British Railways Engineering, pp. 158–9.
[100] PRO AN 88/77, R. Riddles, The Railway Executive, 'Report on Types of Motive Power', 23 January 1952. To Riddles it seemed 'clear that our motive power policy must be founded on coal, which we have, rather than on oil, which we have to import'.
[101] PRO POWE 14/555 DCFP 125 (Annex), 'The Railways', para. 1, 1 March 1952.

alternatives to steam favoured electrification.[102] Electrified lines were held to have been surprisingly immune from the consequences of enemy bombing, and ultimately, as the Ministry of Fuel and Power noted, the development of 'atomic power in an economic form in 25 years' would provide for greater self-sufficiency and increase the attraction of electrification 'in the face of other forms of energy, such as coal and oil, which will become more expensive as their getting becomes more difficult'.[103] Both the Executive and the Commission seemed to be in broad agreement that electrification was likely to be the future basis of the industry. Improving costs and efficiency underlined the long-run appeal of electrification, the post-World War II 'all-in' costs of electric operation approximating to 77 per cent those of steam, practically irrespective of density.[104] The British Transport Commission's Report on Electrification estimated that electrification was viable where traffic reached a minimum level of between 3 and 4 million trailing tons per mile of single-track running line per annum. In 1949, about 30 per cent of the route mileage of British Railways had a traffic density at or more than this minimum level.[105]

There appeared to be a broad consensus that electrification was the longer-term option. Riddles' view was that electrification would gradually replace steam as justification could be worked out route by route, and as capital could be found.[106] However, despite the attraction of financing capital projects in a period of 'cheap money', the scarcity of physical resources led the IPC to sanction only limited progress on the electrification of the £8 million Liverpool Street–Shenfield scheme, the £11 million Manchester–Sheffield–Wath line, and the £14.5 million London–Tilbury–Southend scheme.[107] In all, these three electrification schemes were estimated to save 97,500 tons of coal per annum, while increasing annual train miles from 8.3

[102] Johnson and Long, *British Railways Engineering*, pp. 159–61.
[103] PRO POWE 14/555, DCFP 125, Ministry of Fuel and Power, Committee on National Fuel Policy, 'The Railways', note by the Secretariat, 1 March 1952, para. 11. PRO AN 88/77, Report of the Committee on Types of Motive Power, 1951.
[104] PRO MT6/2777, 'Post-war Comparative Motor-Power Costs', by H. G. McClean, reprinted from *The Railway Gazette*, July–September (1944), p. 10.
[105] PRO POWE 14/554 DCFP 21, Ministry of Fuel and Power: Committee on National Fuel Policy: 'Diesel Locomotives and Electrification as Alternatives to Steam: Note by Ministry of Transport and Railway Executives', 19 September 1951, para. 13.
[106] PRO AN 88/77, R. Riddles, The Railway Executive 'Report on Types of Motive Power', 23 January 1952.
[107] PRO POWE 14/554 DCFP 21, Ministry of Fuel and Power: Committee on National Fuel Policy: 'Diesel Locomotives and Electrification as Alternatives to Steam: Note by Ministry of Transport and Railway Executives', 19 September 1951, paras. 13, 15. PRO AN 88/77, Report of the Committee on Types of Motive Power, 1951, para. 440.

million to 10.6 million.[108] The projects were attended by the usual construction problems, particularly on the Liverpool Street–Shenfield line, which, together with the very limited investment in electrification, emphasised the likely length of any transition period to electrification.[109] Thus, the resolution of the steam/diesel argument became crucial.

If steam was to precede the gradual electrification of the network, then Riddles favoured concentrating on improving the efficiency of steam locomotives. New expenditure of some £4.25 million would provide steam engines with increased efficiency of 6–8 per cent, with the additional benefit during transition 'that as the steam stock reduces in the future with the growth of electrification, so its composition consists to an increasing extent of modern units'.[110]

As with electricity, standardisation was also expected to bring improvement. There had been moves towards standardisation by the pre-war companies, but on 1 January 1948, British Railways still inherited some 20,024 steam locomotives of 448 classes. The contemporary concern to achieve standardisation was reflected in the aspirations of the 1947 Transport Act and in the establishment of the Locomotive Standards Committee almost within the first week of nationalisation's being effected. Resisting any temptation to standardise around the London Midland and Scottish (LMS) designs, Riddles and his LMS-dominated team continued in the short term to build twelve standard types of steam locomotive. In the period 1948–53, 1,487 new units were built to old company designs.[111] However, for the longer term, the team led by Riddles decided to create a new series of British Railways locomotives, in what has been fairly dubbed as 'one of the most controversial decisions in the history of railways in Britain'. Building began in 1950 and ended in 1960, when the 2–10–0 No. 92220 *Evening Star* steamed out of Swindon works. Between 1948 and 1956, a total of 1,518 steam locomotives were built of 24 different company designs.[112]

While capital was invested in this new generation of steam

---

[108] PRO POWE 14/554 DCFP 21, Ministry of Fuel and Power, Committee on National Fuel Policy: 'Diesel Locomotives and Electrification as Alternatives to Steam: Note by Ministry of Transport and Railway Executives', 19 September 1951, para. 16.

[109] PRO AN 85/21, S.44–1–1, 'Memorandum to the Commission from Miles Beevor; Electrification v. Diesel Electrification', 7 August 1948.

[110] PRO AN88/77, R. Riddles, The Railway Executive, 'Report on Types of Motive Power', 23 January 1952.

[111] Johnson and Long, *British Railways Engineering*, pp. 40, 134, 135. T. Gourvish, *British Railways, 1948–1973*, Cambridge, Cambridge University Press, 1986, p. 87.

[112] Johnson and Long, *British Railways Engineering*, pp. 41, 42, 136.

locomotives, trials with diesels seemed to slow up.[113] Cyril Hurcomb pointed to the disparity between the Executive's prolonged technical trials of both diesel-mechanical and gas-turbine main-line locomotives, and their comparative neglect of diesel-electric traction.[114] While limited experiments were to be run in the London Midland Region, Hurcomb was extremely concerned that, almost immediately after taking office, the Executive abandoned the plans developed by the London and North Eastern Railway (LNER) during the summer of 1947 to introduce 25 1,600HP units for trials on the King's Cross–Edinburgh service.[115] Hurcomb in the Commission felt strongly that the suppression of such experiments would also involve the suppression of information which might inform a discussion of the capabilities and costs of diesel-electric traction in relation to steam and other forms of traction. Here, as in electricity and pricing, a newly nationalised industry established as a monopoly was acting to suppress information generated by experiments which might provide weapons for its critics and those suggesting alternative plant decisions. Moreover, as Hurcomb noted, a more detailed consideration of the options might also serve to bring discussions around to consideration of 'the question of which prime mover and which type of fuel is likely *ultimately* to prove the most efficient and economical'.[116]

Given the prevailing long construction times and the durability of capital equipment, it was years before the plant choices made in this period had their full effect, after which their effect was felt for possibly as many as twenty years.[117] Interviewed by the Herbert Committee in 1955, electricity managers were still bemoaning the flow of small sets being delivered to them. The fact that two years of design work often preceded the actual four- to five-year construction period led electricity managers to claim in 1955 that virtually all of the stations then operating had at least been under consideration before Vesting Day.

---

[113] Within the Ministry of Fuel and Power, Neil Gardiner continued his interest in the machinery and operation of the Brown-Boveri heavy fuel oil-fired gas turbine, as used by the Swiss Federal Railways in the early 1940s, and urged that experiments with diesels should continue. The Brown-Boveri loco was delivered in 1949, and, after static and running trials, worked its first passenger train in May 1950, but without tremendous hopes for its immediate future. PRO POWE 14/556, DCFP 221, Ministry of Fuel and Power, Committee on National Fuel Policy, note by Neil W. Gardiner, 15 July 1952.

[114] PRO AN88/77, letter from Cyril Hurcomb, Chairman, British Transport Commission to Sir Eustace Missenden, Chairman, Railway Executive.

[115] Gourvish, *British Railways*, p. 88.

[116] PRO AN88/77, letter from Cyril Hurcomb, British Transport Commission, to Sir Eustace Missenden, Chairman, Railway Executive, in the Commission.

[117] Brechling and Surrey, 'An International Comparison', *National Institute Economic Review*.

Their point was that most of the stations would have been built whether or not the industry had been nationalised, and that while the managers of the newly nationalised industry felt that they had been left with a poisoned chalice of decisions, they saw little alternative other than to get the ordered plant completed as quickly as possible. Irritated by accusations of conservatism and backwardness, the electricity managers complained that 'the blame for the accusation of lack of enterprise does not rest at our door at all'.[118]

That these plant choices revealed fundamental productivity weaknesses in nationalised industries was far from clear. Whatever problems accompanied nationalisation, the nationalisation of the electricity industry appears to have facilitated moves towards a more orderly and balanced progressing of orders and an improvement on the muddle created by an un-nationalised industry prior to 1948. Subsequent research suggests that although the productivity performance of the nationalised industries might have been better, it was certainly no worse than that of privately owned manufacturing industry. While continued government interference with price and subsidy arrangements complicated the revenue performance, the data on capital productivity were respectable.[119] Moreover, the irony of the Attlee governments' period in office is that this was one of the few occasions in post-1945 British economic history in which an economically literate minister, namely Gaitskell, sought to reduce peak-hour demand and thereby improve system-load factor and capital productivity, only to have his efforts resisted by the industry.

As it is difficult to attribute a large part of the explanation of these plant choices to fundamental problems in the monopoly nationalised industries, what share might be attributed to economic planning and the early postwar conditions? The general conditions are easy to outline and applied to many other industries as well as railways and electricity. The political and market demand for rapid increases in output was very high, and at times excessive. Long construction times deterred managers from embarking on large construction projects which would take years to ease output problems. Instead, calculations of incremental capital-output returns pointed to the patching of existing plant and, when new plant was required, investment in plant which was likely to be completed reasonably quickly. The ability to opt for more modern, larger plant was also limited by balance-of-payments difficulties, which resulted in imports being strictly limited while domestic plant producers

[118] PRO POWE 24/2, Ministry of Fuel and Power, Committee of Inquiry into the Electricity Supply Industry, notes of a meeting held on 3 June 1955, pp. 26–7.
[119] Foreman-Peck and Millward, *Public and Private Ownership*, ch. 9.

followed government exhortation and international profit margins and exported significant proportions of their output. That such a listing of factors shaped decision-making goes a long way to explaining why specific plant choices were made, even before managerial idiosyncrasies are added. To the extent that pricing behaviour in key industries such as electricity, iron and steel, and coal exacerbated the problems of excess demand, then economic planning increased the attractions of a patching, incremental approach to fixed capital investment. To the extent that price controls held down the cost of using scarce coal and steel, then they may also have contributed to reducing the financial cost to managers of opting for plant of known lower productivity. In general, what appeared to be emerging under economic planning was a serious differential between the price and the value of scarce resources. This applied to the promotion of demand, the ordering of new sets and the operating of older and small sets. Operating older sets with lower thermal efficiencies, but with their capital charges exhausted, was often regarded as financially worthwhile by managers, even though it might be an inefficient station from the technical point of view. Managers were primarily concerned with their operating costs and not with the wider issue of securing the most efficient use of scarce resources. As managers operating sets in the mid-1950s were to tell the Herbert Committee: 'the loading of stations is entirely governed by economics, not necessarily thermal efficiency. The overall thing is economics, how cheaply we can generate electricity in the first place'.[120]

This brief cameo of a British 'production economy' characterised by excess demand, price controls, public exhortations to maximise output, a dollar-deficient balance of payments, and producing increased output, but at the expense of long-term productivity, is crudely reminiscent of a much longer-term experience elsewhere in the world, namely in the economic planning experience of much of eastern Europe after, and before, 1945. Whether there are wider lessons to be learnt is a matter for fireside rumination, which is beyond the intended purpose of this book. However, this limited but detailed analysis of micro-economic decision-making in Britain during this period of economic planning might provide some rationed food for thought.

[120] PRO POWE 24/2, Ministry of Fuel and Power, Committee of Inquiry into the Electricity Supply Industry, notes of a meeting held on 3 June 1955, pp. 21–2. Brechling and Surrey, 'An International Comparison', *National Institute Economic Review*.

7   Planning rationalisation

In the border country between the nationalised industries and private industry lay industries which although privately owned were subject to quasi-public efforts to improve their productivity. Perhaps the leading examples of the occupants of this hybrid territory were the cotton and iron and steel industries, the latter not being nationalised until 1951. These 'first industrial revolution' industries had long attracted the attentions of a mix of bankers, politicians, and industrialists concerned to improve each industry's productivity and competitiveness. The pessimistic inter-war diagnoses of the iron and steel industry by the American engineering consultants, Brassert and Co., and of cotton by the Clynes Committee in 1930, simply seemed to be confirmed by the wartime examination of each industry.[1] There was little disposition to challenge the crude comparisons published by Laslo Rostas in 1943, which estimated the relative productivities of steelmaking in the USA, Germany, and the UK as 168:114:100.[2] The transatlantic gap was assumed by many commentators to have widened across the war and visits by steelmen such as John Craig of Colvilles confirmed the progress being made by US managers in the use of the larger furnaces with hearths 27 feet in diameter, operating pressures of 18–20 psi (pounds per square inch) and with daily production capabilities of 1,000 tons.[3] Long before the end of the war, discussions on improving the

---

[1] Clynes Committee Report of 1930 (Cmd 3615).

[2] D. L. Burn, *The Steel Industry, 1939–1959: A Study in Competition and Planning*, Cambridge, Cambridge University Press, 1961, p. 64. L. Rostas, 'Industrial Production, Productivity and Distribution in Britain, Germany and the United States', *Economic Journal*, 53 (April 1943), pp. 39–54. Burn notes that these estimates were popularised by Sir George Schuster in an article in *The Times*, 24 June 1943. Schuster was to chair the 1946 Board of Trade Working Party on the cotton industry.

[3] BSA I/38557. Stewarts & Lloyds, chairman's address to 56th Ordinary General Meeting, 4 April 1946. BSA I/38684 John Craig, Colvilles, 'Notes on visit to America', 10 November 1947. Ominously, Craig also reported on the US use of oxygen in steelmaking, the Bethlehem Steel Company having installed a £1 million oxygen plant. BSA I/011474, BISF, 'Report by the British Iron and Steel Industry to the Ministry of Supply', December 1944.

productivity and competitiveness of each industry were well under way. Leaving each industry to sink or swim in a free market was not an option favoured by most discussants, and certainly not by the industries themselves. In iron and steel, formal plans were produced for the development of the industry, a leading feature of which was the suppression of market mechanisms. In cotton, a sporadic mix of encouragement and threats was employed, supported by working-party reports urging the benefits of modernisation. Neither taken into the care of public ownership, nor left in private to pursue their own family business, the fostered development of these industries was attempted at a distance by politicians and planners, who experienced considerable difficulties in devising incentive structures which were consistent with the achievement of their professed ambitions for each industry.

Various familiar solutions were proffered for the improvement of industrial productivity in iron and steel and cotton, the most popular being 'rationalisation'.[4] This approach had attracted intermittent support from the Bank of England in the middle of the inter-war period. The Bank had supported the establishment of the Lancashire Cotton Corporation, which had absorbed ninety-six companies, owning one-quarter of the industry's cotton spindles between 1929 and 1932. However, further schemes designed by Frank Platt, of the Lancashire Cotton Corporation, for the merger of 5 million spindles owned by 44 companies did not receive bank backing, and from mid-1932 much of Platt's energies were absorbed in saving the struggling Lancashire Cotton Corporation. Variously described by contemporaries, including Keynes, as a 'genius', Platt succeeded in saving the Corporation, discarding half of its mills between 1932 and 1937 while simultaneously giving his backing to the 1936 Cotton Spinning Industry Act for the purchase and scrapping of surplus spinning plant.[5] As wartime Cotton Controller, Platt continued his calls for the rationalisation of the cotton industry, especially its coarse-spinning section in his punningly entitled confidential paper, 'Whither the

---

[4] PRO CAB 124/336, R(44)59, War Cabinet, Reconstruction Committee, Cotton Industry, memorandum by the Secretary of Overseas Trade. Initialled 'H. J.', 13 September 1944, para. 1. In the view of one such sceptic, 'Rationalisation', as it was euphemistically called, 'is a queer animal', which was 'a crime when applied to shipyards but a blessing, apparently for cotton mills (and their employees)'.

[5] Platt was a director of the Lancashire Cotton Corporation from mid-1932 and managing director from 1933. J. H. Bamberg, 'Sir Frank Platt, 1890–1955', in D. Jeremy (ed.), *Dictionary of Business Biography*, vol. IV, London, Butterworths, 1985, pp. 716–22. BLPES, Dalton Papers, DI/30, p. 26, 31 January 1944. Quoted in J. Singleton, *Lancashire on the Scrapheap: the Cotton Industry 1945–1970*, Oxford, Oxford University Press, 1991, p. 28.

Cotton Industry?' in 1943.[6] In the following year, the Platt Report (1944) re-emphasised the labour productivity gap between British and US mills and repeated calls that the industry should completely reorganise itself along US-style vertical, rather than British-style horizontal, integrated lines establishing closer vertical co-operation between the spinning, weaving, and merchanting sections.[7] In the wartime iron and steel industry, there were similar reiterations of the interwar rationalist prescriptions of Firth of Richard Thomas, MacDiarmid of Stewarts & Lloyds, and H. A. Brassert and Co.[8]

Strictly speaking, modernisation and rationalisation were separate issues. In practice, they accompanied each other in reports on industrial improvement, whether in the Clynes Report of 1930 or the wartime Cotton Board Report. In the iron and steel industry, even firmer relationships were drawn between rationalisation of capacity and modernisation of fixed capital investment. The planned rationalisation of rail-making on the north-east coast in 5 rather than 9 works was to facilitate the coincidental installation of 3 1,000-ton blast furnaces, the importing of a wide-flange US Beam Mill, and the building of a new medium-section mill. The Beam Mill, of a type used for 40 years in the USA and in Western Europe, was the first used in Britain, while the blast furnaces at Lackenby were to approach the optimal technical hearth diameter size of 25–27.5 feet.[9] Closing smaller works in the district would provide the new furnaces at Lackenby with a British works record throughput of 22,000 tons per week, and contribute to the increase sought in the average size of works, both through the arithmetical fact of their disappearance and by facilitating the expansion of the Dorman, Long works itself.[10] Not that everyone was prepared to

[6] PRO CAB 124/338, 'Whither the Cotton Industry?', December 1943. Singleton, *Scrapheap*, pp. 13, 25.

[7] Ministry of Production, *Report of the Cotton Textile Mission to the United States of America*, London, HMSO, 1944, p. viii. C. Miles, *Lancashire Textiles: A Case Study of Industrial Change*, Cambridge, Cambridge University Press, 1968, pp. 30–1.

[8] Richard Clarke, writing as Ingot, was for the ruthless scrapping of equipment and merging of firms; Ingot, *The Socialisation of Iron and Steel*, London, Gollancz, 1936.

[9] BLPES Burn papers, 6/55, Duncan Burn, 'The Steel Industry and Planning', paper read at the British Association, Manchester meeting (Economic Section) 31 August 1962. BSA Middlesbrough 1066/00718, 'Proposed Blast Furnace Development Policy', paper by Central Engineering Department, signed E. T. Judge, 19 July 1946. BSA Middlesbrough, 'New Blast Furnaces at Cleveland Works', paper by E. T. Judge, 13 May 1947. Anglo-American Council on Productivity, *Iron and Steel*, London, Anglo-American Council on Productivity, 1952, p. 17. The council recommended that a minimum hearth diameter of 25 feet for imported ore and 27 feet for home ore for basic iron should be accepted as a normal standard in new developments.

[10] PRO CAB 134/439, IPC(48)8, Cabinet, Investment Programmes Committee, *Report on Capital Investment in 1949*, 16 July 1948, paras. 221–31. PRO CAB 134/440, IPC(49)3, Cabinet, Investment Programmes Committee, *Report on Capital Investment*

accept the easy association of rationalisation and modernisation. In textiles, John Jewkes pointed to the financial losses of the horizontally integrated Lancashire Cotton Corporation, its inability to curb the independence of managers in individual mills, its difficulties in attempting to drive smaller units from the industry, the struggle of the Fine Cotton Spinners' Association, and the formation of a price ring by the three largest amalgamations in the finishing trades to defend themselves against the smaller units, whom they sought to entice to join them in the ring. Jewkes could find little evidence of the superior efficiency of bigger spinning units than commonly existed in the cotton industry and he doubted that there was 'anyone in Lancashire who would be prepared to argue that a 100,000 spindles firm is any less efficient than a firm ten times as large. In fact the opposite is probably the case'.[11]

For the advocates of rationalisation, the central issue was how to achieve structural changes. A Platt-inspired proposal from Dalton, the President of the Board of Trade, for compulsory spinning amalgamations and the establishment of a spinning board charged with the reorganisation of the industry was rejected by the Cabinet Reconstruction Committee in September 1944.[12] Reorganisation through nationalisation was a possibility, partly in response to which the British Iron and Steel Federation (BISF) was preparing a development plan, the First Steel Plan, for the industry. The preferred option of both industries was for price management, the virtues of the stability of price management being set against the inherent instability of market mechanisms. In reports from the industry, approving references were

in 1950–52, 12 May 1949, para. 230. BSA Middlesbrough, letter to G. H. Latham of The Whitehead Iron and Steel Company from E. T. Judge, 3 May 1947.

[11] PRO CAB 124/336, 'Notes on Re-organisation in the Cotton Industry', paper by John Jewkes, 13 September 1944, p. 4. J. Singleton, 'Debating the Nationalisation of the Cotton Industry, 1918–50', in R. Millward and J. Singleton (eds.), *The Political Economy of Nationalisation in Britain, 1920–50*, Cambridge, Cambridge University Press, p. 215. L. Hannah, *The Rise of the Corporate Economy*, London, Methuen, second edn, 1983, ch. 6. Later research in the 1950s by Caroline Miles seemed to confirm much of Jewkes' scepticism. Perhaps partly because of inadequate information, it proved impossible to determine the relationships, if any, between size and labour productivity, or between vintages and types of equipment and labour productivity. Miles, *Lancashire Textiles*, p. 3.

[12] Dalton's views were strongly influenced by Frank Platt. Dalton was taught economics by Keynes at Cambridge University but relations between the two men were always cool. M. Dupree, *Lancashire and Whitehall*, Manchester, Manchester University Press, vol. II, 14 September 1944, pp. 212–14. PRO CAB 124/338, 'Whither the Cotton Industry?', December 1943. PRO CAB 124/336, R(44)152, 2 September 1944, War Cabinet, Reconstruction Committee, 'The Cotton Industry: Memorandum by the President of the Board of Trade'. Also see The Steering Committee on Post-War Employment in R(44)6.

made to the benefits of 1930s price management. The Report of the Cotton Board Committee on Post-War Problems applauded the 'key feature' of the Cotton Industry (Reorganisation) Act 1939, which had made possible 'the pursuit of a policy of managed prices, by providing for the statutory enforcement of schemes for minimum prices or margins', and pressed for the postwar continuation of price management, since not only was there 'no other policy by which the cotton industry can be restored after the war to the state of efficiency which is essential', but there was 'no prospect of implementing the plans and hopes implicit in the Report as a whole unless this part is made possible of achievement'.[13] As Raymond Streat, Chairman of the Cotton Board, informed Lancashire MPs in September 1944, what the 'discreet words' of their report really meant was that 'apart from price management we can think of no other alternative to jungle warfare, in which both capital and labour would be lost to the industry never to return or be regained'.[14] In meetings with the Cotton Board in 1944, Dalton enjoyed 'very little success' in inducing the industry to 'face up to realities', complaining that even when 'they had submitted a supplementary report paying lip service to the advantages of voluntary reorganisation, they claim that they must first have statutory minimum prices. Indeed, it is clear that they envisage reorganisation as an aid, not so much to increased efficiency, as to "price management"'.[15]

Similar noises came from the iron and steel industry. Tariff protection in the 1930s was depicted as having provided the essential conditions for the investment of over £50 million on new schemes, while, in general, pre-war experience had 'shown that Imports Duties on iron and steel are a prerequisite of an efficient industry in this country' whose continuance, assuming protection and price management in other countries, was essential for the industry's efficiency.[16] Competition within the domestic industry would be provided by Federation-devised pricing arrangements, which offered an improvement on market mechanisms in which the short-term inelasticity of prices hindered the speedy elimination of the inefficient.[17] As articulated by a leading

[13] Board of Trade, Working Party Report, *Cotton*, London, HMSO, 1946, p. 153, ch. 12, paras. 10, 48.

[14] PRO BT175/3, 'Cotton Industry Problems and Parliament', speech by Chairman of the Cotton Board, Sir Raymond Streat, at a meeting with Lancashire Members of Parliament, 6 September 1944.

[15] PRO CAB 124/336, R(44)152, War Cabinet, Reconstruction Committee, 'The Cotton Industry: Memorandum by the President of the Board of Trade', 2 September 1944, para. 2.

[16] BSA I/011474, BISF, 'Report by the British Iron and Steel Industry to the Ministry of Supply', December 1944, pp. 3–4.

[17] D. Burn, *The Steel Industry*, pp. 212–13.

proponent of such arrangements, Robert Shone, the Federation's more stable prices would place a more continuous pressure on firms to improve than the more fluctuating prices of the market, in which weak firms could restore their finances out of boom prices.[18] Federation arrangements were also held to be superior to those of freer markets in product areas in which competition was very limited, such as in sections of the heavy-plate and wide-flange-beam markets dominated by Colvilles and Cargo Fleet respectively.

Such proposals drew criticisms from economists.[19] Rather than minimum prices, Jewkes and Devons suggested that the industry be firmly told that it fate was in its own hands and that it should exploit fully the immediate postwar sellers' market and its favourable status with the central allocators of raw materials.[20] Similarly, the pleading of the iron and steel industry was objected to by Dennison in the Economic Section and by the leader writer of *The Times*, who suggested that the industry worry more about its 'development' and 'less with its protection'.[21] With economists such as Robbins and Keynes negotiating for international trade free of inter-war tariff and dumping practices, and with the fear that any tariffs would encounter retaliatory action from the USA, the arguments of the industry were out of kilter with the sense of the time. If international price differentials did prove to be a problem after any immediate postwar boom was over, then the Economic Section expressed a clear preference for making exchange-rate adjustments rather than reverting to protection. Economic Section economists were determined not to repeat the 1930s experiments with

---

[18] For details of price increases see PRO CAB 134/637, PC(48)2, Cabinet, Production Committee, 'Iron and Steel Prices', memorandum by the Minister of Supply (George Strauss), 8 January 1948, and 'Steel Prices', letter from A. F. Forbes (Iron and Steel Board) to G. Strauss (Minister of Supply), 1 January 1948. For details of domestic and international wartime cost and price movements, see PRO CAB 124/789, R(45)36, War Cabinet, Reconstruction Committee, Iron and Steel, Joint Memorandum by the Minister of Supply and the President of the Board of Trade, 6 April 1945. R. Shone, 'Steel Price Policy', *Journal of Industrial Economics*, 1 1 (November 1952), pp. 43–54. D. Burn, *The Steel Industry*, ch. 5(3d), pp. 213–14.

[19] Board of Trade, Working Party Report, *Cotton*, London, HMSO, 1946, pp. 154–5, para. 11(a).

[20] PRO BT 64/1057, 'The Future of Prices and Costs in the Cotton Industry', by Ely Devons, paper read at the Cotton Board Conference at Harrogate 21–23 October 1949. Devons was Professor in Applied Economics at the University of Manchester. PRO CAB 124/336, paper by John Jewkes to the Minister, 'Notes on Re-organisation in the Cotton Industry', 13 September 1944.

[21] PRO CAB 124/789, note from S. R. Dennison to Minister of Reconstruction, 7 October 1944, para. 4c. PRO CAB 124/789, EC(S)(45)6, Economic Section of the War Cabinet Secretariat, 'The Iron and Steel Industry: Some Reflections on R(45)36, Memorandum by Professor Dennison', 16 April 1945. Leading article from *The Times*, Monday, 26 February 1945.

either the Import Duties Advisory Committee in the iron and steel industry, or with the Coal Mines Reorganisation Commission, and they regarded BISF calls for 'substantial protection in the home market' for an initial five-year period as a likely prelude to a permanent arrangement.[22]

The BISF proposals for pricing arrangements to operate behind protective walls were also opposed. In its 'scientific price fixing', it was never clear how in 'setting maximum prices based on the costs of efficient plant', the Federation was to accommodate the variety of definitions of 'efficient' plant, how it was to counteract the tendency for industry-wide schemes to understate the efficiency of newer plant, or how it was to prevent maximum prices slipping into being minimum prices. In Dennison's view 'the only sure way of judging the "reasonableness" of prices is an appeal to competition; we ought not to burke the fact that the search for reasonable prices in an industry which can only be maintained by shutting out competition is likely to be fruitless'.[23] If free pricing was not to operate, the view of commentators outside the industry such as Duncan Burn was that in preference to operating domestically uniform delivered prices supported by cross subsidies, a move should be made towards a modified zonal basing-point system in which regional coal costs were reflected in regional ingot-production costs, in which scrap prices would equal pig-iron prices or be neglected, and, in the push to establish the marginal cost of ingot production for each area, regional home and imported ore costs should be included.[24] Burn expressed his opposition to the operation of uniform delivered prices in a letter to Morrison informing him that this was 'a characteristic monopoly device . . . which should be proscribed by central government, and some system of zonal pricing is required'.[25] Given that Morrison was actively promoting the use of uniform delivered prices in prospective nationalised industries such as electricity,

[22] PRO CAB 124/789, EC(S)(45)6, Economic Section of the War Cabinet Secretariat, 'The Iron and Steel Industry: Some Reflections on R(45)36, Memorandum by Professor Dennison', 16 April 1945. PRO CAB 124/789, EC(S)(45)9, Economic Section of the War Cabinet Secretariat, 'Report on the Iron and Steel Industry', meeting, minutes, 23 April 1945. PRO CAB 124/789 EC(S)(45)8, Economic Section of the War Cabinet Secretariat, The Iron and Steel Industry, minutes, 24 April 1945, p. 3.
[23] PRO CAB 124/789, EC(S)(45)6, Economic Section of the War Cabinet Secretariat, 'The Iron and Steel Industry, Some Reflections' on R(45)36, memorandum by Professor Dennison, 16 April 1945.
[24] BLPES, Burn papers 6/33, note from Burn to Frank Lee (Under Secretary, Ministry of Supply).
[25] Draft letter from D. Burn to Herbert Morrison, 1946 quoted by R. Ranieri, 'Partners and Enemies: the Government's Decision to Nationalise Steel, 1944–8', in Millward and Singleton, *Political Economy of Nationalisation*, p. 300.

he was unlikely to be responsive to Burn's complaints. Further BISF proposals that domestic prices be increased and preferential prices be offered to key export industries as a form of administered cross-subsidisation revived worrying memories of the inter-war Milk Marketing Scheme. Then, the use of liquid milk prices to subsidise manufacturing milk, so that the more milk was used for manufacturing the higher liquid-milk prices rose, produced a situation in which rising prices choked off the demand for liquid milk, the demand for which then had to be maintained by special government schemes.[26]

What, then, was the political response? That many economists within and outwith government were anxiously opposed was clear, but, as has been seen, governments do not necessarily listen to the serried ranks of economists. In making their presentations to government, industrialists emphasised the virtue of stability as a fundamental aim and outcome of price management. With government itself viewing its own retention of wartime price controls as one means of combating inflationary pressure and reducing inequity in scarce-resource distribution, there was a useful coincidence in the political and industrial vocabulary. However, what increasingly concerned government was an oft-accompanying feature of price controls, namely subsidies, the cost of which was rising. In early postwar negotiations between Oliver Franks, the Ministry of Supply, and the BISF, Franks made clear his determination to shed as many of the subsidies as quickly as possible.[27] In this he secured the active co-operation of the BISF, which took the opportunity to demonstrate its wish to act in the 'national interest' and in so doing to point up the ability to elicit desirable behaviour from free enterprise without recourse to nationalisation.[28] With Franks pushing for the halving of the initial price increases proposed by the industry, the omission of high-cost producers from the industry-wide cost calculations and the rapid abolition of the wartime Prices Fund and Central Fund, the agreement was that while for a temporary period the government would continue to carry certain excess freight costs, home ore and carriage subsidies, the industry would increasingly take on the burden of subsidies and the operation of equalising arrangements itself.[29] Politically keen to co-operate, the industry steadily absorbed the full cost of the freights on

[26] PRO CAB 124/789, EC(S)(45)6, Economic Section of the War Cabinet Secretariat, 'The Iron and Steel Industry: Some Reflections on R(45)36, Memorandum by Professor Dennison', 16 April 1945.
[27] Oliver Franks was Permanent Secretary at the Ministry of Supply. Subsequently he was Provost of Queen's College, Oxford, 1946–8, and then the British Ambassador in Washington, 1948–52.
[28] BSA I/01550, BISF, Executive Committee Meeting, minutes, 20 April 1948.
[29] BSA I/01550 BISF, Executive Committee meeting, minutes, 17 July 1945.

imported ore together with certain subsidies on internal transfers without increasing the price of finished steel.[30] By April 1948, after the industry had borne another reduction in subsidies costing around £2 million, the use of public funds was confined to the payment of freights on imported ore in excess of 100 per cent and in excess of the cost of imported steel over domestic prices.[31] From 1 April 1949 government steel subsides were ended, and the levies under the Industry Fund agreements between the Iron and Steel Corporation and the producers were increased.[32] One result was the largest increase in steel prices since the war.[33]

These negotiations followed a wartime strengthening of relations between the Federation and the Ministry of Supply. During the war, the Ministry's Raw Material Department had taken the place and most of the staff of the Import Duties Advisory Committee with responsibility for policy formulation, while the Iron and Steel Control had taken the place of the Federation concerned with policy administration.[34] Whereas before the war, regulation of capital expenditure had been confined to major schemes of capacity expansion, reviewed by an *ad hoc* Federation committee, during the war the Iron and Steel Control regulated all expenditure on alterations as well as extensions of plant.[35] The Federation, assisted by its newly established Economic Efficiency Committee, had moved towards assuming the role envisaged for the pre-war Import Duties Advisory Committee, as it played a greater role in planning the capital development of the industry and supervising the elimination of price competition.[36] During the war, the wartime Reconstruction Committee characterised the industry as having 'a strongly developed sense of industrial association' and in the postwar negotiations the Federation pressed for responsibility for pricing administrative arrangements to be returned by the Control to the Federation.[37]

[30] BSA I/01550 BISF, Executive Committee Meeting, minutes, 20 April 1948.

[31] BSA I/01550 BISF, Executive Committee Meeting, minutes, 20 April 1948. BSA I38129, Colvilles, Executive Directors Meeting, 27 April 1948.

[32] BSA Managing Directors Report: the Park Gate Iron and Steel Co., 1 April 1950 Report.

[33] D. Burn, *The Steel Industry*, Table 18, 'Material and Labour Costs and Prices, 1944–1949', p. 203.

[34] Peter L. Payne, *Colvilles and the Scottish Steel Industry*, Oxford, Clarendon Press, 1979, p. 258.

[35] BSA I/011472 BISF, 'Special Report from the Post-War Reconstruction Committee to the President's Committee', 19 October 1943, para. 2.

[36] Quoted in BSA I/011474, BISF, 'Report by the British Iron and Steel Industry to the Ministry of Supply', December 1944, pp. 3–4. BSA I/011472 BISF 1943, 'Special Report from the Post-War Reconstruction Committee to the President's Committee', 19 October 1943.

[37] PRO CAB 124/7789, R(45)36, War Cabinet, Reconstruction Committee, Iron and

This strengthening of the Federation's relations with government, and the strengthening of the Federation within the iron and steel industry, drew an ambivalent response from the iron and steel industry itself. In particular, it revived discussion of the issue of enabling powers which had been sought by Firth and MacDiarmid before the war. In 1934, Sir William Firth of Richard Thomas had openly advocated an Enabling Act to provide the statutory powers which he thought were necessary to enforce regional reorganisation, this call later being taken up by A. C. MacDiarmid of Stewarts & Lloyds.[38] Firth and MacDiarmid were opposed by the likes of McCosh of Bairds, who feared the domination of the industry by its heavy steel section.[39] With MacDiarmid's wartime appointment as Secretary and then, in 1944, as President of the Federation typifying a tendency for even large pre-war opponents of the BISF to come to play a stronger role in the wartime Federation, smaller firms became anxious lest powers of compulsion to 'rationalise' the industry be sought by the Federation. At its meeting on 16 November 1943 to discuss the special report from the post-war Reconstruction Committee (dated 19 October 1943), the President's Committee accepted that the Federation would not seek powers of compulsion for enforcing Federation decisions on capital-development programmes, relying instead on 'the moral sanction of loyalty to a well organised and properly equipped body supported by the Trade as a whole'.[40]

By the end of 1945, Firth and MacDiarmid were dead, although firms' suspicions of the centralising tendencies of Andrew Duncan and Ellis Hunter (Dorman, Long), respectively the new Chairman and Vice-President of the Federation, ensured the continuance of an uneasy relationship between the Federation and its more independent members, who sought to decentralise effective power.[41] This tension

Steel, joint memorandum by the Minister of Supply and the President of the Board of Trade, 6 April 1945, p. 36. PRO CAB 124/789, EC(S)(45)6, Economic Section of the War Cabinet Secretariat, 'The Iron and Steel Industry: Some Reflections on R(45)36, Memorandum by Professor Dennison', 16 April 1945, para. 4.

[38] D. Burn, *The Steel Industry*, pp. 54, 58. Duncan Burn found that enabling powers were MacDiarmid's chief preoccupation at his first meeting with him before the war.

[39] S. Tolliday, *Business, Banking and Politics: the Case of British Steel, 1918–1939*, Cambridge, MA, Harvard University Press, 1987, p. 304.

[40] BSA I/011472 BISF, 'Special Report from the Post-War Reconstruction Committee to the President's Committee', 19 October 1943, para. 5a. BSA I/011472, British Iron and Steel Federation, 'Report of the Sub-Committee Appointed by the President's Committee to Consider Control of Capital Expenditure', 14 February 1944.

[41] MacDiarmid died in August 1945. For an interesting discussion of Sir Allan MacDiarmid's thinking, see his entry written by Jonathan Boswell in A. Slaven and S. Checkland (eds.), *Dictionary of Scottish Business Biography, 1860–1960*, vol. I, Aberdeen, Aberdeen University Press, 1986, pp. 121–5. Andrew Duncan became chairman of the

between a central Federation interfacing with government and firms seeking to emphasise their independence was a leitmotif of the preparation of what eventually emerged as the First Steel Plan. Firms' submissions in response to Federation demands that they submit their postwar development plans for consideration were slow and often under-specified, E. H. Lever complaining that he was 'presented with continually varying arguments and estimates' lacking any 'finality in the presentation of the case'.[42] The hurriedly prepared report was presented to the Ministry of Supply in December 1944. The five-year plan called for by the caretaker government in May 1945 was submitted in December 1945 and published in May 1946. Although ostensibly compiled under the supervision of the Federation, the First Steel Plan was in fact little more than a compilation of the plans of individual sectors and companies. The only clear contribution by the Federation to the Plan was the imposition of two major new schemes. The Iron and Steel Control, created to supervise the activities of the industry in wartime, was superseded by an Iron and Steel Board in September 1946. The Iron and Steel Board had no powers and was simply to advise the Ministry of Supply.[43]

As with the iron and steel Federation, so too with the Cotton Board. War had strengthened its relations with its sponsoring department, the Board of Trade, as well as strengthening the Cotton Board's relations with the industry, although not to the same extent as in iron and steel.[44] Raymond Streat enjoyed good relations with Watkinson at the Board of Trade, addressing him in his letters as 'My Dear Watty', and Streat was sufficiently confident of his sway with the Board of Trade to inform Lancashire MPs in September 1944 that the Cotton Board could 'rapidly determine with the Board of Trade what the detailed legislative or statutory programme should be.'[45]

The Board of Trade welcomed these strengthening relations with the

BISF, despite the opposition of a group of steelmen led by Stewarts & Lloyds. See Aubrey Jones, 'Sir Andrew Duncan', in D. Jeremy (ed.), *Dictionary of Business Biography*, vol. II, London, Butterworths, 1984, pp. 196–200. In 1945, Sir Ellis Hunter, managing director and from 1948 chairman of Dorman, Long & Co., became Vice President of the BISF. See Charles Wilson, 'Sir Ellis Hunter', in D. Jeremy (ed.), *Dictionary of Business Biography*, vol. III, pp. 390–4.

[42] BSA 13432, letter from E. H. Lever to E. Lysaght (John Lysaght), 30 June 1947. Ernest Lever was Chairman of Richard Thomas & Baldwins Ltd 1940–59, and of the Steel Company of Wales Ltd 1947–1955. He became President of the BISF in 1956.

[43] Payne, *Colvilles*, pp. 276–7.

[44] PRO BT 64/1057, 'The Cotton Board', address by Sir Raymond Streat, Chairman of the Cotton Board, to the opening meeting of the Cotton Board Conference: 'The Cotton Industry in a Changing World', Harrogate, 21 October 1949.

[45] PRO BT 175/3, 'Cotton Industry Problems and Parliament', speech by the Chairman of the Cotton Board, Sir Raymond Streat, in opening discussion at a meeting with

Cotton Board, and also the apparently improving position of the Cotton Board within the industry. As Sir John Woods remarked 'experience has shown that in normal times it is pretty well impossible for the Board of Trade to deal with all the sections of this complex industry except through some central body'.[46] Yet, as in iron and steel, the Cotton Board was attempting to rein in a membership which contained some highly individualistic elements, to whom the Cotton Board's personnel and vocabulary were often almost anathema. Relations between Streat and Frank Platt always contained the grit of irritation, with Platt, who in the 1930s had been a keen seeker of enabling powers for a central authority in spinning, moving in the postwar period to help establish the Yarn Spinners Association, which simply added to the fractured and diverse organisation of an industry in which, even in the Federation of Master Cotton Spinners Associations, power lay with the eleven local associations.[47] Complaining that Platt had not kept him properly informed, Streat was sufficiently worried by the establishment of the Yarn Spinners' Association to write to Watkinson seeking reassurance that this unwelcome development would not reduce Streat's influence with the Board of Trade.[48] In many ways, Streat was still mentally evolving a view of the relationship of the Cotton Board to its members. In 1949 he was still uncertain as to how far the Board could and should go in 'pressing for measures which we are convinced are in the interests of the industry as a whole but which may be unwelcome', and he was worrying over what the Board should do if disputes developed over sectional price policies, re-equipment, and redeployment practices.[49] Was the Board to remain silent 'because individual sections hold strong views' or was 'it to have the moral right to table its evidence and to rally those who share its views even to the point of critical differences with some among its

Lancashire Members of Parliament, Manchester, 6 September 1944. G. L. Watkinson, Board of Trade, 1931–46; Deputy-Secretary, Ministry of Fuel and Power 1947–55.

[46] PRO CAB 127/103, TREES 55, Telegram from Woods to President of the Board of Trade, Cabinet delegation, Delhi, 2 May 1946, para. 1. Sir John Woods was Permanent Secretary of the Ministry of Production 1943–5; Permanent Secretary of the Board of Trade 1945–51. He retired in 1951.

[47] Bamberg, 'Platt', in Jeremy (ed.), *Dictionary of Business Biography*, vol. IV, pp. 716–22.

[48] PRO BT 64/420, letter from Raymond Streat to G. L. Watkinson, Board of Trade, 25 October 1946. There had not been wide consultation within Lancashire by the promoters of the Association. Platt, when Cotton Controller, had given Streat the first draft of his ideas under seal of confidence and quite informally. Since that time, there had been no exchanges on the topic. PRO BT 64/420, letter from Raymond Streat (The Cotton Board) to G. L. Watkinson, Board of Trade, 5 November 1946.

[49] PRO BT 64/1057, 'The Cotton Board', address by Sir Raymond Streat, 21 October 1949. PRO BT 175/5, CB6870a. The Cotton Board, minutes of first meeting, 20 April 1948. The Cotton Board, established under the terms of the Cotton Industry Development Council Order 1948, came formally into existence on 1 April 1948.

constituents?'.[50] It was in the context of this vacillation that Cripps took an active role and in 1946 offered a 25 per cent re-equipment subsidy to the spinning industry providing that it combined into groups of initially 500,000 spindles, later reduced to 400,000, with union agreement to double-shift working in the re-equipped mills. This re-equipment subsidy, without a levy on the industry, built on the recommendations of the Board of Trade Working Party on Cotton, led by Schuster, which had reported earlier in the same year, and to which Jewkes and others had appended their dissenting memorandum arguing that there was no need for redundancy schemes or re-equipment subsidies.[51] Yet, ultimately, little of this mattered. Without enabling powers, with the government apparently unwilling to force change through either the steel or the cotton industries, in the end nothing mattered except the individual capital-investment decisions of managers in the myriad of firms. These managers heard the exhortations from federations, politicians, and productivity teams; they also received day-to-day signals from a market in which economic planning was being practised. It was down in the firm that administrative ambitions and the market signals touched by economic planning met.

What, then, was the outlook of managers in the firm, and what was their response to the calls for rationalisation and modernising re-equipment? The archives present a world in which managers, apart from worrying about long-term demand prospects, were making one specific calculation above all others: the comparison of total and prime costs. Whatever the public exhortations to avoid 'patching' incremental investment in favour of large new schemes, the incremental capital-output return calculations seemed to point in the other direction: actively to pursue a strategy of 'patch and mend' (interestingly, as the IPC suggested) and to drive existing plant as hard as possible. This was especially the case in industries with a large stock of operating, if old, capital equipment. Unlike electricity, which was pushed hard up against its production boundary and where managers saw demand rising long into the future, cotton and iron and steel managers saw much more reason to be cautious. In the midst of the most sustained boom it had known during the century, cotton owners were keenly aware of the inevitable return of Japanese competition, and of the difficulties this could create for firms saddled with debt and depreciation charges, the

---

[50] PRO BT 64/1057, 'The Cotton Board', address by Sir Raymond Streat, 21 October 1949.

[51] PRO CAB 124/336, paper by John Jewkes to the Minister, 'Notes on Re-organisation in the Cotton Industry', 13 September 1944. Singleton, *Scrapheap*, pp. 32–3.

fickle chaperons of re-equipment.[52] Mindful of the fate of firms such as Richard Thomas, which had expanded on bank money during the last postwar boom, in the 1920s, iron and steel firms, such as Colvilles, were also wary of encouragement from others to increase their financial commitments.[53]

On capital:prime-cost calculations re-equipment in cotton appeared of dubious worth. Dominating discussions was the vintage of the existing capital stock. In spinning, between 60–75 per cent[54] of the predominant mule spindles had been installed before World War I, while 60–70 per cent of the buildings dated from before 1900.[55] Plant of such vintage had long had its purchase costs written off and was, in the words of Ely Devons, 'a free gift from its fathers and grandfathers'.[56] As Platt noted in 'Whither the Cotton Industry?', it was claimed within the industry that well-maintained and repaired plant dating from 1871 gave better production as to quality and volume than 1910 machinery.[57] By contrast, new plant came loaded with full capital costs and could also, as in the replacement of Lancashire looms with automatic looms, involve the additional costs of removing pillars and strengthening floors and roofs. As the space required by automatic looms plus winding machinery was twice that allowed for Lancashire looms, entirely new buildings could be required to accommodate the same number of looms.[58] This new machinery would then have to compete against the prime cost (excluding capital charges) of older plant.[59] Using data from the Yarn Spinners Association, Ely Devons estimated that in every case costs in new spinning mills would substantially exceed existing costs.[60]

[52] Miles, *Lancashire Textiles*, p. 38. Singleton, *Scrapheap*, pp. 35, 100.
[53] P. Payne, *Colvilles*, pp. 317–20. J. Boswell, *Business Policies in the Making*, London, Allen & Unwin, 1983.
[54] Miles, *Lancashire Textiles*, p. 28.
[55] PRO CAB 124/336, R(44)152, War Cabinet, Reconstruction Committee, 'The Cotton Industry: Memorandum by the President of the Board of Trade', 2 September 1944, para. 5.
[56] PRO BT 64/1057, Ely Devons, 'The Future of Prices and Costs in the Cotton Industry', paper read at the Cotton Board Conference at Harrogate, 21–3 October, 1949, p. 8.
[57] PRO CAB 124/338, 'Whither the Cotton Industry?', December 1943.
[58] PRO BT 64/2708 'Draft Commentary for Use of the Machinery and Plant Sub-committee of the Cotton Working Party', December 1945, p. 5. PRO CAB 124/341, Deputation to the Prime Minister from the Cotton Industry, 22 March 1948.
[59] PRO CAB 124/947, paper from R. S. Sayers to Lord President, 'The Cotton Industry', LP(46)271, 21 November 1946.
[60] PRO BT 64/1057, Ely Devons, 'The Future of Prices and Costs in the Cotton Industry', paper read at the Cotton Board Conference at Harrogate, 21–3 October 1949, p. 9.

The existing operation at 66 per cent of capacity also dampened incentives.[61]

This fundamental problem was recognised by Schuster's Working Party, which acknowledged that a mill equipped in 1906 and now with no capital charges might see little advantage in installing new plant and that 'from the mere profit-earning stand-point it might well *pay* an individual owner best to take advantage of present easy markets, work his machinery till it is worn out, and then go out of business'.[62] While acknowledging that 'such a course may appear for the moment to pay', the working party continued to urge that for the sake of the future 'the greater part of the present equipment should be replaced by equipment of modern type'.[63] Its recommendation was based on a comparison of the 'commercial results to be expected from modern equipment' which made it clear 'that it will pay to install equipment of the modern type instead of the old type'.[64] This calculation was based on conversion costs which indicated that with high draft ring spinning, automatic looms, and double-day shifts it was possible to achieve savings in conversion costs ranging in spinning from 5.7 per cent on drill to 11.8 per cent on lining, and in weaving from 6.2 per cent on drill to 8.4 per cent on cambric.[65] So as 'to have a strictly comparable basis for measuring commercial results as between different types of machinery', the capital charges' provision for interest and depreciation for both old and new types of machinery were included on the same basis, i.e. allowing for replacement costs at present values. Yet, as was admitted, while this could be said to have given a true commercial comparison it did not, of course, show the position as it actually presented itself to a mill operating with old plant written down in its books to a low figure.[66] None the less, this was the basis on which the Board of Trade acted and

---

[61] PRO SUPP 14/461, Mr MacMahon (Board of Trade), notes of a meeting on 27 August 1946 to discuss cotton-industry re-equipment.

[62] Working Party Reports, *Cotton*, London, HMSO, 1946, p. 69, para. 13.

[63] Working Party Reports, *Cotton*, p. 90, para. 73b(ii), conclusions.

[64] Working Party Reports, *Cotton*, p. 75, para. 28.

[65] Working Party Reports, *Cotton*, p. 74, para. 26:

Cloth	% Saving	
	Spinning	Weaving
Drill	5.7	6.2
Lining	11.8	7.6
Poplin shirting	–	7.8
Cambric	9.4	8.4
Haircord	11.2	–
Sheeting	10.7	7.3

[66] Working Party Reports, *Cotton*, para. 21(d).

which led, in the view of Sayers, to 'a fundamental misjudgement of the problem', reflecting the Schuster Working Party's own trouble in understanding 'the somewhat intricate economics of re-equipment'. Indeed, in long papers to the Lord President, Sayers broadened his attack to include all of the working parties (cotton, pottery, boots, shoes, hosiery), each of which had failed to compare total costs against the prime costs of existing equipment. In Sayers' words, they quite simply 'did not do the right sums' and if the total cost:prime cost tests were applied to the costs tabled in the Working Party Report on Cotton, then 're-equipment would not pay'.[67] In addition, the calculations made by almost all the working parties were vulnerable to wage increases if the government ever chose to tackle the problem of relative wages in undermanned industries, which would include most of the working party industries. While the government showed no immediate wish to tackle the relative-wages issue for fear of provoking an inflationary spiral, long-term investment decisions could not be made without accommodating the possibility of wage increases. Similarly, although government persisted with its cheap-money policy for re-equipment decisions, Devons suggested that managers work with interest rates closer to their 'natural rate', which he considered to be around 10 per cent but which could in fact be anywhere between 10 and 20 per cent.

In weaving, separate calculations made by Devons told a similar story. A comparison between the costs of Lancashire and automatic looms, once it was assumed that the Lancashire looms were already written off, showed that the effect in the case of Cloth U.34 would be 'that the reduction in costs of 51d per 100 yards between six Lancashire and sixteen automatics would be cut to 12d'. Moreover, if allowance was made for interest rates at around 10 per cent for machinery and buildings, then the advantage of automatic looms would be cut further. Devons concluded that 'the cotton industry is not one in which one can expect large scale investment to take place over the next few years at least. The reduction in costs that would result from large-scale re-equipment are not sufficiently great.'[68] This echoed remarks from Jewkes in the 'Dissenting Memorandum' to the Working Party Report that if capital costs were removed from the data for Lancashire looms, to represent the cost of producing cloth with old pre-war equipment, it would be pure folly for firms to re-equip at all.[69]

---

[67] PRO CAB 124/947, 'The Cotton Industry, LP(46)271', comments by R. S. Sayers, sent to the Lord President, 21 November 1946.

[68] PRO BT 64/1057, E. Devons, 'The Future', paper read at the Cotton Board Conference, 21–3 October, 1949, p. 9.

[69] Board of Trade, Working Party Report, pp. 69, 84, 227. Cited in Singleton, *Scrapheap*, p. 106.

The general conclusion was that re-equipment was not immediately justifiable and that a patching 'Heath Robinsonian technique may be sound economics!'. This accorded with the immediate need for output, while research indicated that more immediate gains in productivity were to be had through the better organisation of existing production. The Shirley Institute suggested that increases in output of 30 per cent per head were obtainable from improved practices in mills, far outweighing benefits from increases in working hours or workforce size, while the Moelwyn–Hughes Commission estimated that an increase in output of at least 20 per cent could be secured in weaving through the introduction of new wage systems and redeployment. The merits of 'Full Re-deployment', with the aid of industrial consultants, and 'Spring Cleaning' (to shake off the cobwebs and bring all mills up to good practice) were also being urged upon the industry.[70] If any re-equipment was to be effected, it would be better to wait for an easing of the intense demand for machinery, reflected in part in the 30 per cent rise in textile-machinery prices between 1946 and 1949. As part of the export drive, 80 per cent of the UK output of ring spindles was exported by an industry which produced 24,298 tons of ring spindles in 1948, compared with 44,773 tons in 1937.[71] Since imports were negligible, this left roughly 200,000 ring spindles per annum for distribution to the British market. In 1948, 35 per cent of British automatic-loom production was exported, and in 1949 Harold Wilson, President of the Board of Trade, set an export target of 60 per cent for textile machinery as a whole.[72] Over 90 per cent of automatic-loom production was in the hands of the British Northrop Loom Company of Blackburn, and the Board of Trade Working Party had considered domestic capacity inadequate to meet the requirements of the re-equipment drive. Given the existing pressure of orders in the textile-machinery trade, Sayers wondered 'whether the proposed subsidy would have much effect in hastening re-equipment: the effect might be mainly to swell prices and profits in machine-making'.[73] Such general postponement of investment would also accord better with the wish of economists such as Meade

---

[70] PRO BT 195/4, memo from H. T. Tizard, to Chancellor of the Exchequer, 17 March 1948. PRO BT 195/4, 'The Possibilities of Improved Utilisation of Labour in the Cotton Spinning Industry: Report by the Study Group on Cotton Productivity: Summary', paras. 3–4.

[71] PRO BT 64/1057, Ely Devons, 'The Future', paper read at the Cotton Board Conference, 21–3 October, 1949, p. 9.

[72] Singleton, *Scrapheap*, pp. 109–11.

[73] PRO CAB 124/947, 'The Cotton Industry, LP(46)271', comments by R. S. Sayers, sent to the Lord President, 21 November 1946.

and Sayers to use fixed capital investment to counteract later downturns in demand.

The total:prime cost calculations being made in cotton were also to be found in iron and steel. Here the existing fixed capital stock was not of such vintage as in cotton, but calculations of returns on investment were complicated by the varying incidence of steel-price controls. As in cotton, iron and steel managers were exhorted to maximise output and there were some general arguments made emphasising the higher productivity of capital goods and the general trend of substituting capital for labour.[74] In making the more specific total:prime cost calculations, the application of price controls to billets did little to entice firms to increase capacity to ease this crucial bottleneck. The calculations of the Federation were scrutinised by Dennison at the Economic Section. In 1945, Dennison estimated that at the existing price for billets of £12 5 0d per ton, new plant making billets at an operating cost of £8 12 0d per ton, would have £3 13 0d. per ton from which to cover depreciation and profit. The report set aside 15 per cent of capital costs to cover depreciation, profit, and obsolescence and estimated the capital costs of new plant as £20 per ton of capacity, although likely to rise. At a cost of £20 per ton of capacity, capital costs would be £3 per ton of steel. However, if plant costs rose to, say, £24 per ton of capacity, capital costs per ton of output would rise to £3 12 0d per ton, and the price needed to cover *all* costs would be £12 4 0d per ton, or one shilling less than the existing price. Should plant not work at full capacity, then both the depreciation cost (as well as the operating cost) per ton of output would rise, causing costs to exceed prices. In this light, Dennison struggled to see the basis of the Federation's estimate that re-equipment might lead to a reduction of £1 per ton in steel prices.[75]

Similar calculations with similar conclusions were being made at the level of the firm. Stewarts & Lloyds was one of the industry's largest producers of billets, little of which, apart from some pig iron, was sold on the open market, but went instead into their steel-tube production, from which, with cast-iron pipes, it made most of its profits.[76] The

---

[74] PRO CAB 134/439, IPC(48)8, Cabinet, IPC, *Report on Capital Investment in 1949*, 16 July 1948, p. 51, para. 221. BLPES, Burn papers 6/33, letter to Frank Lee from Duncan Burn, 14 March 1948.

[75] PRO CAB 124/789, EC(S)(45)6, Economic Section of the War Cabinet Secretariat, 'The Iron and Steel Industry: Some Reflections on R(45)36, Memorandum by Professor Dennison', 16 April 1945, para. 8.

[76] BSA I/05113 Stewarts & Lloyds Ltd, December 1953, report by Sir John Morison. BSA 05108, Stewarts & Lloyds, 'Notes Primarily Concerned with the Production of Commercial Tube and Pipe', by G. S. McLay, 15 August 1944.

company was quite clear in its articulation of its postwar investment strategy: it was to give 'priority to expanding capacity to take advantage of the post-war boom and after that to set out to modernise and replace out-of-date equipment to meet the competition which must inevitably develop'.[77] Stewarts & Lloyds was determined not to commit itself to basic capital expenditure on new steel capacity, but instead to look for *'ways and means of extending capacity at a sufficiently low capital charge per annual ton of output . . . provided always that prime costs of production are attractive, and that in doing so we are fulfilling our obligations in meeting the tube demand, particularly in the export markets'*.[78] As part of the consideration of their postwar development policy, in 1944 Stewarts & Lloyds calculated what it would cost if their 1930s-built iron and steel works at Corby were to be built under post-1945 conditions. Using minimum flat average rates of 5 per cent for depreciation and 8 per cent for interest or dividends, they calculated that 'the probable minimum capital investment per annual ton of strip, operating at 80% capacity, would be around £36 as against the actual investment value of £20'. At 80 per cent rates of operation, the capital charge on postwar values was around £5 per ton. In 1944, not knowing how long a postwar boom would last, Stewarts & Lloyds was extremely keen 'to ensure that our competitive position is not hamstrung by the colossal burden of capital charges on the steel works during periods of poor demand and short time operation'. In particular, they saw 'no case for mortgaging our economic and financial future for the sake of a short-term demand with, in all probability, a lean profit margin. There had never been 'any real profit in the sale of billets', and probably never would be for heavy steel.[79] The better profits and returns on capital investment were at the finishing end on tubes and most exports and it was here that firms were most willing to invest.[80] The steel-price controls, which fell heavily on billets and lightly if at all on finished products, simply compounded this incentive structure, which was at odds with the government and Federation rhetoric and exhortation. When challenged at a Nuffield Conference about this difference in the application of price controls

[77] BSA I/05113, Stewarts & Lloyds, December 1953, report by Sir John Morison.
[78] BSA 05108, Stewarts & Lloyds, 'Notes Primarily Concerned with the Production of Commercial Tube and Pipe', by G. S. McLay, 15 August 1944. This passage is underlined by McLay.
[79] BSA 05108, Stewarts & Lloyds, 'Notes Primarily Concerned with the Production of Commercial Tube and Pipe', by G. S. McLay, 15 August 1944.
[80] R. Shone, *Journal of Industrial Economics*, 1 (November 1952), pp. 43–54. Page 47 has price data for September 1952 showing British steel prices to be consistently cheaper than those of the USA and Europe across a range of products. Tolliday, *Business, Banking and Politics*, p. 321. Burn, *The Steel Industry*, p. 216. BLPES Burn papers, 6/33, letter to Frank Lee from Duncan Burn, 14 March 1948.

between basic and finished products, Helmore, of the Board of Trade, explained that this was not regarded as a problem so long as price-controlled steel went into non-price-controlled engineering goods, seemingly ignoring the fact that it did little to improve the incentive structure facing basic steel manufacturers.[81]

In practice, firms took a mix of 'good' and 'bad' orders, while remaining unenthusiastic about installing additional basic steel-making capacity.[82] However, they knew that political economy demanded some response. Quite apart from their own billet needs, firms such as Stewarts & Lloyds were mindful of the political pressure on them to engage in billet production. In August 1944, irrespective of the outcome of any future general election, the board of Stewarts & Lloyds anticipated that 'the Big Brothers of the Steel Industry will be forced to install capacity to meet the national billet demand irrespective of its lack of profit attraction' and that the political rhetoric could descend into the 'Small Man versus the Big Monopoly complex' in which 'the Heavy Steel Makers, being the monopolists, will probably get no support either from the Labour or Conservative Parties or from the Press. If this position eventuates, Stewarts & Lloyds, as important members of the Heavy Steel Industry may be called upon to subscribe to this compulsory charity.'[83] With the election of a potentially nationalising Labour government, Stewarts & Lloyds thought it prudent to appease government by absorbing reductions in subsidies without pushing for immediate price increases, and, from April 1948, making a 2.5 per cent reduction on 90 per cent of the steel tubes sold in the domestic market as part of their contribution to the government's anti-inflationary strategy.[84] Stewarts & Lloyds also bowed to periodic government pressure to restrict their direct exports to more profitable overseas markets to ease bottlenecks at home.[85] In 1947, their delivery of tubes for export fell by 27 per cent compared with 1946.[86]

More curiously perhaps, iron and steel firms also often held down

---

[81] UGA, McCance papers, Nuffield conference, 26–7 June 1948.

[82] BSA I/38160, Colvilles directors' minutes, 5 September 1952.

[83] BSA 05108, Stewarts & Lloyds, 'Notes Primarily Concerned with the Production of Commercial Tube and Pipe', by G. S. McLay, 15 August 1944.

[84] BSA I/38557, Stewarts & Lloyds, Annual Report and Statement of Accounts for year ending 31 December 1947. Chairman's address to 58th Ordinary General Meeting, 27 May 1948. Similarly, it fell in with dividend restraint, not recommending an increase in the rate of dividend in 1948 but carrying £735,000 to General Reserve.

[85] BSA I/05113, Stewarts & Lloyds Ltd, report from Sir John Morison, December 1953.

[86] Sir Richard Summers, John Summers & Sons Ltd, Annual Report 1947. A. G. Stewart, Stewarts & Lloyds, Ltd, Annual Report 1947. D. Heal, *The Steel Industry in Post-War Britain*, London, David & Charles, p. 45. In their annual reports for 1947, John Summers & Sons, and Stewarts & Lloyds claimed government had compelled them to restrict their level of exports to well below pre-war levels.

their export prices.[87] Anecdotal explanations suggested that firms feared that if they earned higher profits on exports, then domestic controlled prices would be reduced further.[88] As a result, British steel prices were consistently among the cheapest in Europe, a fact which was publicised by the Federation and companies as some form of evidence of their superior productivity. Typically, Stewarts & Lloyds decided 'not to take unfair advantage of the present seller's market to secure high premiums in export trade', since they had 'abundant evidence that this policy has been appreciated by our customers overseas and it will, we feel sure, stand us in good stead in the future'.[89] This not only reduced the contribution made by steel exports to easing the balance-of-payments difficulties, but also puzzled domestic and international observers. In 1948, Roy Harrod was examining with Dupriez of the Department of Economics in Belgium, international steel-price data showing British steel-export prices to be consistently lower than those of Belgium, France, the USA, Canada, Sweden, the Netherlands, Switzerland, and Italy.[90] Harrod was told by Dupriez that 'we cannot understand the British prices'. Asked by Harrod in turn how the Belgians could compete with the higher prices, Dupriez replied, 'Of course, it is delivery.' Not only was this of more benefit to the balance of trade, but the Belgian ability to provide immediate delivery gave them a trading advantage over British suppliers struggling with long order books.[91]

Apart from such total:prime cost calculations, firms were also making calculations of where to locate in response to the changing resource base of the industry and how to square this with the operation of equalising devices and uniform delivered prices. Wanting to shift operations nearer consumers, Stewarts & Lloyds saw that the uniform delivered prices offered no incentive to do this, although 'in the longer term this policy could not be right".[92] Colvilles, as Peter Payne has recorded in immense detail, went into virtual guerrilla resistance to fend off political attempts to get a new deep-water, hot-metal site built at Inchinnan. In this struggle, they very much saw the Federation as being

---

[87] P. W. S. Andrews and Elizabeth Brunner, *Capital Development in Steel*, Oxford, Blackwell, 1952, pp. 302–3.

[88] UGA McCance papers, Ely Devons at Nuffield conference, 26–7 June 1948.

[89] BSA I/38557, Stewarts & Lloyds, Annual Report and Statement of Accounts, year ending 31 December 1947. Chairman's address to 58th Ordinary General Meeting, 27 May 1948.

[90] UGA McCance papers, Roy Harrod at Nuffield conference, 26–7 June 1948. D. Burn, *Steel Industry*, pp. 210–11. BISF, *Statistical Bulletin*, June 1948, March 1949.

[91] UGA McCance papers, Roy Harrod at Nuffield conference, 26–7 June 1948.

[92] BSA 05108, Stewarts & Lloyds, 'Notes Primarily Concerned with the Production of Commercial Tube and Pipe', by G. S. McLay, 15 August 1944.

against, rather than for them, not least as the Technical Adviser of the Iron and Steel Control was T. P. Colclough. Colvilles perceived Colclough as approaching discussions with the 'preconceived idea' of reviving the Brassert proposals of 1929, which he had helped to prepare as a former partner of H. A. Brassert & Company.[93] Baulking at the estimated cost of £28 million for the deep-water site, Colvilles preferred their £15 million option centring on the installation of improved ore-handling plant at the General Terminus, Glasgow. Colvilles disputed Colclough's claim that operating costs at Inchinnan would be lower, and reminded him that the capital costs for them would be considerably higher. Against the calculated capital cost of the deep-water site, Colvilles saw much better and quicker returns from their comparatively lower-cost schemes and they were inclined 'to proceed with such improvements to existing plant as will realise the same output objectives'.[94] On the production side, Colvilles argued that on the basis of a comparison between the expected conversion and manufacturing costs in an entirely new plant and those realisable from an expansion of existing facilities to attain the same output, there was little or no justification whatever for the much greater capital expenditure required for an entirely new integrated works. Proud of the existing low conversion costs, Colvilles refused to admit that any new works was capable of effecting the significant cost reduction without which the case for transferring production was insupportable. This was perhaps not so surprising at a time when some economic commentators were even making a case for the retention of hand-charged furnaces. Improvisation and patching could all produce returns. By improving the feeding of mills with well-heated ingots, by using finishing mills more intensively, by using better fuels, larger ladles, better charging equipment in blast furnaces production, and by imitating the 20 per cent increase achieved in the pre-war German Ruhr through the better balancing of works, firms could increase output at minimal cost.[95]

This patching response and the slow progress of rationalisation did little to steady the nerves of the likes of Dorman, Long, who was 'planned' to build three new large blast furnaces. In 1946 Dorman, Long became involved in technical discussions not so much on the size of the new furnaces, which were to be between 25 and 27.5 feet in diameter, but rather on the weekly tonnage of each furnace. In part,

[93] Payne, *Colvilles*, pp. 293, 296, A. K. McCosh, Gartsherrie Iron Works, letter to Sir John Craig, 22 July 1947.
[94] Payne, *Colvilles*, p. 293. Colvilles Limited, 'Memorandum on Scottish Steel, 1947', section 90.
[95] Burn, *Steel Industry*, p. 197.

the issue revolved around expectations of future demand. If a demand of 24,000 tons of basic iron emerged within two years, then 1,000-tons-a-day furnaces could be installed with a minimum being spent on the existing Bessemers. However, if demand looked less propitious, then the move to 1,000-ton furnaces could be postponed for at least five years and instead the existing Bessemers opened out or rebuilt to a capacity of 5,000 tons. Opting for three 1,000-ton furnaces would introduce inflexibility in the face of possible falling demand and when the furnaces came off for relining. Acknowledging the importance of the 'time factor', the company tried to weigh the benefits of waiting five years or so, when 'we may have an entirely different picture of the big units', against the potential cost of losing a 'first-mover' advantage in the industry.[96] Not, of course, that there was any guarantee that prospects would be any clearer in five years' time. One concern expressed in discussions within Dorman, Long was that, in saying 'the time has not arrived', 'we' [Dorman, Long] could be 'dragging on with our small furnaces', and years may 'elapse before we embark on the 7,000 [per week] ton furnace because apparently it is such a bold move'.[97]

Dorman, Long's demand expectations were influenced both by the general level of demand and by the progress of planned rationalisation in the north-east district. The intention of increasing iron demand in the Cleveland/Redcar Works area from 13/16,000 tons to 15/20,000 tons per week was to provide Dorman, Long with the highest concentration of demand in the country and the throughput required for the high utilisation of the new capacity.[98] Yet, the longer it took Dorman, Long to build their plant, the longer other plant in the district scheduled for closure would make patching improvements to their plant. Not only would demand be dispersed across the region, potentially reducing throughput in Dorman, Long's new plant, but Dorman, Long's new plant with high capital costs would be left competing against largely paid-up plant.

Dorman, Long's expectations and fortunes were likely to be strongly influenced by the time which it took to install new capacity. In general, construction was to take longer than anticipated. In iron and steel, it soon became apparent that major schemes in Stage I of the Plan which

[96] BSA Middlesbrough, Dorman, Long files, 'Comments by Mr Patchett: Notes of a Meeting held at "The Grange", Eston', 12 April 1946.
[97] BSA Middlesbrough, Dorman, Long files, 'Comments by Mr Patchett: Notes of a Meeting held at "The Grange", Eston', 12 April 1946.
[98] BSA, BISF, minutes of the 12th meeting of the Development Committee, 16 September 1947. BSA 1066/00718, Dorman, Long, Central Engineering Department, report on 'Proposed Blast Furnace Development Policy', 19 July 1946.

were due for completion by 1952 would extend beyond this date.[99] As construction times lengthened, costs rose from an original estimate made in 1945 of £168 million for Stage I of the Plan to around £240 million.[100] Construction times ran at twice their pre-war length and at times twice those on the Continent. Long construction times were not peculiar to the iron and steel industry as managers grappled with the organisation of large construction projects in an excess-demand, dollar-short economy. Unused to building in boom conditions, managers attempted to complete construction projects of unprecedented size in which major industries competed for scarce plant and machinery, tubes, and turbo-blowers with long delivery times.[101] As in the electricity industry, efforts were made to strike a better balance in the distribution of orders for boilers and turbo-blowers between Parsons, who had 50 per cent of the steel makers orders, and firms such as Richardsons, Westgarth & Co., Fraser & Chalmers, and Daniel Adamson who had facilities available.[102] Despite discussions with the producers and federations on the late delivery of electric plant, delivery times lengthened for heavy electric motors (over 5,000kW), blowers, blast furnaces, and refractories.[103] There were also persistent shortages of cranes, excavators, and diggers, and here, as elsewhere, it was not unusual to see foundations being dug by men wielding spades.[104]

In conditions of plant shortage and as part of the postwar settlement, Dorman, Long, Colvilles, Skinningrove, and other firms attempted to get plant from Germany.[105] Stewarts & Lloyds was ultimately unsuccessful in its efforts to get sections of the German Salzgitter plant, which Brassert had built after completing Corby.[106] Even when plant such as the 42-inch continuous billet mill from the Hermann Goering

---

[99] Burn, *The Steel Industry*, p. 266. PRO CAB 134/439, IPC *Report*, p. 53, para. 228.

[100] CAB 134/439, IPC, *Report*, para. 229.

[101] BSA I/02433, 'Paper on Blast Furnace Programme', 11 March 1952. BISF, 'Outline of Second Iron and Steel Development Plan', 24 November 1952.

[102] BSA, BISF, Development Committee 22 February 1952.

[103] BSA, minutes of 17 Meeting of BISF Development Committee, 16 March 1948. BSA I/38129, Colvilles Executive Directors meeting, 27 May 1948. BSA, BISF Development Committee, 18 March 1947.

[104] On slow delivery of cranes see BSA I/3885, note to Andrew McCance, 19 April 1949. BSA I/3825, note on Dalzell Ironworks scheme, 4 September 1952. Shortages of cranes hampered work at Dalzell Works No. 4 melting shop; reconstruction of casting bay-ladle cranes.

[105] A. Cairncross, *The Price of War*, Oxford, Blackwell, 1986, p. 173. BSA, BISF Development Committee minutes, 19 December 1950. BSA I/38129, Colvilles Executive Directors' meetings, 6 November 1947, 3 February 1949, and 2 March 1951. Colvilles, Dorman Long, and Skinningrove jointly paid £63,000 to the Ministry of Supply for roller racks from the Hermann Goering 23-inch Mill.

[106] BSA I/012422, Stewarts & Lloyds Directors meetings, 13 January, 24 February 1948, and 8 November 1949.

Works did arrive in Britain, the Lancashire Steel Corporation was unwilling to meet its £500,000 installation cost as they were unable to supply it with the minimum 15,000 tons of ingots per week required to meet its rated capacity. Instead, firms were invited to buy any parts of the mill in which they were interested. More generally, it was envisaged that some 14,000 tons of German blast furnaces and mills would be stripped of parts by British companies, with half the tonnage going for scrap.[107] To these problems, could be added the housing, labour-recruitment, and infrastructure problems of constructing on greenfield sites, which had proved so unattractive to Colvilles.

In addition to the uncertainties facing Dorman, Long, and the general difficulties of major new construction work, there was also the abiding problem that many of the firms whose plant was 'planned' to be closed fiercely resisted what they saw as the Federation's worst intentions. The need for apparent unity in support of the plan had led much of the dissent during the preparation of the First Steel Plan to be glossed over. Firms such as Skinningrove, South Durham, and Cargo Fleet had never accepted Federation plans for their plant. Benjamin Talbot, the chairman of Cargo Fleet and South Durham, complained to the Minister of Supply about their treatment by the Federation during the various planning stages. Talbot objected to the interim report issued in April 1945 with its proposals for stopping production of pig iron, steel ingots, and heavy plates at the West Hartlepool works and, as Talbot saw it, limiting the life of the four-high light plate mill, and barring Cargo Fleet from continuing the manufacture of heavy rails which had proved one of its most profitable activities.[108] A compensating offer of participation in a co-operative billet mill with low profit margins did not appeal.[109] Warning MacDiarmid that 'this Report can only do incalculable harm', Talbot was placated for a while by MacDiarmid's assurances that the interim report was simply a 'signpost based on technical considerations alone', and that there might well be 'commercial and other considerations' which could outweigh the purely technical factors'.[110] Subsequently, such considerations were discussed among

---

[107] BSA, BISF Development Committee, 16 January 1951. BSA, BISF Development Committee, 18 September 1951.

[108] BSA 03785. See correspondence between Talbot and Duncan, 7, 12, 14, 19, 26, 29 November 1945. BSA 03785, letter from Benjamin Talbot (Chairman and Managing Director, South Durham Steel & Iron Co. Ltd) to Sir Andrew Duncan (Chairman, British Iron and Steel Federation), 26 November 1945.

[109] W. G. Willis, *South Durham, Steel and Iron Co. Ltd*, Portsmouth, Eyre and Spottiswoode, 1969, pp. 26–7. W. G. Willis, *Skinningrove Iron Company 1880–1968*, Privately printed, no date.

[110] BSA 03785, letter from Benjamin Talbot to Sir Allan MacDiarmid (President, BISF), 23 April 1945. BSA 03785, letter from MacDiarmid to Talbot, 26 April 1945.

the north-east coast steel producers (Consett, Skinningrove, South Durham, Cargo Fleet, and Dorman, Long) and a unanimously agreed district development report covering both the immediate five and the subsequent ten years was submitted to the Federation in August 1945 for inclusion in the national plan. However, the Federation's experts refused to accept the sections of the district programme concerning Cargo Fleet and South Durham, and instead insisted that the proposals contained in the interim report of April 1945 must apply. In November 1945, South Durham and Cargo Fleet repeated their opposition to the future planned for Hartlepool, but were unable to secure modification of the Federation plan, which was submitted to the Ministry of Supply without South Durham being allowed full sight of it.[111]

Their private protests having proved unavailing, South Durham appealed to local and central politicians for help. Supported by West Hartlepool Town Council, South Durham wrote to Stafford Cripps in February 1946 emphasising the local economic impact of a workforce of 2,500 ceasing to receive total wages of £755,000 per annum and the general multiplier effects of closure on the 63,000 inhabitants of West Hartlepool.[112] A series of meetings between the dissenting companies and the Federation were held on north-east sites and in the Dorchester Hotel London, but failed to produce agreement.[113] There were personality clashes between Duncan and Talbot, Talbot regarding Duncan as stubborn as himself, while there was general agreement that Talbot was 'lacking flexibility in argument' as befitted someone who had always been 'an uneasy bedfellow for his fellow iron and steel manufacturers'. Talbot felt awkward with a Federation vocabulary which called on firms to 'consider developments in the general interests', especially when on the north-east coast there were long-standing rivalries between firms.[114]

Benjamin Talbot died in December 1947, but the arguments persisted and extended beyond South Durham and Cargo Fleet.[115]

[111] BSA Middlesbrough 03785, letter from Talbot to Ministry of Supply, undated but probably December 1945. Cargo Fleet Iron Company Limited Minute Book No. 9, 6 December 1945.

[112] BSA, letter from Benjamin Talbot, Chairman and Managing Director (South Durham and Cargo Fleet) to Sir Stafford Cripps, President of the Board of Trade, 15 February 1946.

[113] BSA, Cargo Fleet Iron Company Limited, minute book, No. 9, 8 November 1945. BSA, letter to Shone from John Henry Bacon Forster, Chairman, South Durham, 1948–50, 5 April 1949. BSA, BISF Development Committee meeting, 16 December 1947.

[114] BSA, letter from A. N. McQuistan to B. Talbot, 24 January 1946. BSA, letter from Duncan to Talbot, 7 November 1945. W. G. Willis, *South Durham*, p. 35.

[115] W. G. Willis, *South Durham*, p. 34. Talbot's work on the basic open-hearth steel-making process while with the Pencoyd Steel Company in the USA led to his invention

Consett objected to Duncan's attempts to persuade them to build a Plate Mill when it preferred to build a billet mill. In this they were partly supported by the Federation 'expert', Bengston, who had advised in his original report, on which the White Paper was partly founded, that Consett should have a plate mill. In October 1949, however, Bengston decided that circumstances in the industry had so diverged from the intentions of the Plan that Consett should be allowed a billet mill.[116] When Duncan pressed the Consett chairman to support the next White Paper Plan for the north-east coast, the chairman sharply told him that since all north-east coast makers had departed from the White Paper and, that, for all the talk, Dorman, Long's Beam Mill had not materialised while South Durham and Skinningrove had become permanent fixtures, he had little intention of complying. As had previously been suggested in January 1947 by John Craig of Colvilles, wearing his Federation hat, all the north-east plans should be re-examined, since 'the conditions as they *now* exist were not those that existed at the time the report was drafted'.[117] By 1949, relations between the Federation and the dissenting firms were not good. Like South Durham, Cargo Fleet, and Colvilles, Consett objected to their treatment by the Federation, who they viewed as trying to make them 'the bad boys of the North East Coast'.[118] More generally, the Federation men were commonly criticised for being too distant from the firms, too unfamiliar with individual works, and short of experience and knowledge of technical and production issues.[119] While it was conceded that Colclough had technical, though not production, expertise, he was seen as having too large a remit and of receiving an insufficiently critical reception in the Ministry of Supply.[120] The government request that he evaluate the Federation's Plan, when he was also the Federation's chief adviser, was held to be particularly cosy.[121] In general, critics argued that the government was limited to one, largely Federation, source of

---

of the continuous method of steel-making known as the 'Talbot Process'. Benjamin Talbot died on 17 December 1947. His son, Benjamin Chetwynd Talbot, became Deputy Chairman of South Durham following his father's death. G. Boyce, 'Benjamin Talbot', in D. Jeremy (ed.), *Dictionary of Business Biography*, vol. V, London, Butterworth, 1986, pp. 433–6.

[116] BSA, Consett Iron Co. Ltd, Minute Book, 4 October 1949.
[117] BSA, letter from J. H. B. Forster, Cargo Fleet Chairman, to R. M. Shone, Secretary, BISF, 5 April 1949.
[118] BSA, Consett Iron Co, minutes, 4 October 1949.
[119] BLPES, Burn papers, 6/30, letter from Duncan Burn to Herbert Morrison, 8 March 1948.
[120] BLPES, Burn papers, 6/13 'Notes on the Steel Federation Plan: Administrative Problems'.
[121] BLPES, Burn papers, 6/30, paper on 'Steel'.

information and advice, with little opportunity or ability to choose between alternative strategies.[122]

Yet, while it might dominate the planning process, there was little that the Federation could do if firms chose to ignore the Plan's prescription. By 1950, not a great deal of what had been planned had happened. Stewarts & Lloyds and Colvilles did not proceed with the Federation-planned new developments at Corby and at Inchinnan. Small firms survived; Dorman, Long was to wait several more years to install its Beam Mill. South Durham evaded controls and rebuilt its No. 3 Plate Mill using resources obtained from its annual maintenance licence. It then presented the Ministry with a *fait accompli*, for which the Ministry issued a licence to legalise the work.[123] Plant destined for closure, such as the Hartlepool Works, continued, with South Durham upsetting Dorman, Long by making announcements in the local press that the Federation had agreed to the West Hartlepool works' being continued.[124]

While no immediate change to the British–US productivity gap had been expected, there were not many signs that in the longer term that the gap would narrow. American works remained 2.5–3 times larger than those in Britain, and in heavy bulk steel production the average size of the 40 British works in 1950 was 325,000 tons per annum.[125] By the mid-1950s, firms and plants with capacities of 5 million tons or above were significant features of the US industry and their importance increased substantially during the ensuing decade and a half. In 1951 the common view was that all integrated steel works should aim at a minimum standard size of 750,000–1,000,000 ingot tons per annum. In 1951, a new series of draft Federation plans continued to emphasise the benefits of rationalising and concentrating production.[126] As usual, in British economic history, there was considerable agreement on what ought to be done; the problem lay in devising an incentive structure which would effect the move from the existing to the desired. Certainly, the Cripp's 25 per cent re-equipment subsidy incentive in cotton failed to make much impact. Faced with high demand and construction problems, the immediate attractions of a patching, output-maximising

---

[122] BLPES, Burn papers, 6/30, letter from Duncan Burn to Herbert Morrison, 8 March 1948.
[123] BSA, BISF Development Committee, 18 February 1947.
[124] BSA, I/02433 BISF Development Sub-Committee, North East Coast and South Wales, details of meeting of 18 January 1950.
[125] BSA, fourth draft of BISF, second development plan, 25 January 1952. In heavy steel production in 1950, the average size was approximately 785,000 and 325,000 tons per annum for US and British works respectively.
[126] BSA, fourth draft of BISF, second development plan, 25 January 1952.

approach to fixed capital investment were reinforced by a mix of cost and pricing signals sent from the economic planning system which provided few incentives to undertake radical and fundamental restructuring of the industries. Moreover, decision-making was ultimately located in the individual firms and as such Federation talk of planning industries was always somewhat specious, unless the issue of ownership was to be addressed, either through nationalisation or through the granting of enabling powers to the Federation.

Both industries had long contained advocates of compulsion, if not of outright nationalisation; Platt and Schuster in cotton, MacDiarmid and Firth in iron and steel.[127] In cotton, some viewed Schuster's Working Party Report as containing an implicit threat of compulsion if there had not been a move towards groupings within three months. In the Wood/ Trees telegram exchanges it was suggested that although Streat doubted 'both the wisdom and the need for compulsion in the matter of amalgamations' he had 'no objections of principle to compulsion, after voluntary methods have clearly failed'.[128] Even Streat conceded that a Labour government could 'prove more bold and thorough in certain vital matters than a Tory Government', since it was 'not so afraid of justifiable interferences with property rights and old established vested interests'.[129]

However, compulsion and nationalisation were separate, if related, issues. Streat regarded nationalisation as 'plainly out of the question'.[130] The Cabinet was divided over the issue, not wishing to let this sword of Damocles hang over the industry but wishing to retain the ability to intervene should the industry, and the spinning section in particular, fail to set its house in order.[131] As Cripps told the industry on his visit to Manchester on 3 December 1946, while it was not 'part of the present Government's programme to nationalise the Cotton Industry provided that the industry . . . carries through with expedition the measures necessary for its reorganisation', the government reserved the right to

[127] Singleton, *Scrapheap*, p. 27.
[128] PRO CAB 127/103, TREES 76, Board of Trade to Cabinet Delegation, Dehli, 17 May 1946, paras. 4–5.
[129] M. Dupree (ed.), *Lancashire and Whitehall*, vol. II, p. 274. Quoted by M. Dupree, 'The Cotton Industry: a Middle Way between Nationalisation and Self-Government?', in H. Mercer, N. Rollings and J. Tomlinson (eds.), *Labour Governments and Private Industry: the Experience of 1945–51*, Edinburgh, Edinburgh University Press, 1992, p. 144.
[130] PRO BT 175/3, 'Cotton Industry Problems and Parliament', speech by Chairman of the Cotton Board, Sir Raymond Streat, at a meeting with Lancashire members of Parliament, 6 September 1944. p. 5.
[131] PRO SUPP 14/461, CM(45) 18th Conclusions, extract from conclusions of a meeting of the Cabinet held on 7 August 1945.

review its position in the light of the industry's performance.[132] In the
end, Cripps may well have come to regret not having nationalised the
industry. By March 1947 he regarded it as too late to change course,
but by then he had little but contempt for the 'ridiculous fools' among
the Cardroom Workers and the Federation of Master Cotton Spinners
Associations, who jointly and religiously opposed any attempt to bring
the industry up to date. As Streat noted, 'it was alarming to see his
mind turning to nationalisation – to anything that would rid him of
these endlessly tiresome people'.[133] Cripps, like Dalton, Keynes, and
Platt before him, was concluding that 'Lancashire must take the
consequences of putting such men in office'.[134]

The iron and steel industry was nationalised in 1951, only to be
denationalised or 'privatised' by the incoming Churchill government.[135]
Throughout most of the Attlee governments, the question of whether or
not the industry should be nationalised grumbled away like a trouble-
some ulcer. The opponents of nationalisation emphasised its disruptive
effect, its potential in delaying the adoption of major schemes of
development, thereby leaving the field to patchwork additions and
modifications of existing plant.[136] In resisting nationalisation, great
weight was laid on the industry's ability to 'plan' its own efficient future.
In seeking to persuade dissenters such as Talbot to co-operate with the
planning process, Duncan had urged that it was 'of the greatest national
importance that the industry should itself answer up to the government's requirements in furnishing this plan, rather than have a plan
forced upon them'.[137] If such planning by the industry proved to be
successful, then perhaps the threat of nationalisation might be averted.
Yet, ironically the Federation's own keenness to 'plan' the industry had
raised the persistent issue of enabling powers. In doing so, it may have
weakened the Federation's ability to argue with government against
nationalisation. In a meeting on 21 May 1947, Andrew Duncan and
Ellis Hunter experienced some sticky moments in seeking to persuade
Attlee, Morrison, and the Minister of Supply, John Wilmot, of the folly
of nationalisation. They could not invoke the sanctity of private
property, since one of their main arguments against nationalisation was

---

[132] PRO SUPP 14/461, statement of government policy on the cotton industry made by
the President of the Board of Trade, Sir Stafford Cripps, to a conference attended by
representatives of the leading spinning, weaving, finishing, merchanting, and operative
organisations in the cotton industry, on 11 August 1945, para. 3. PRO SUPP 14/461,
'President's Visit to Manchester, 3 December 1946'.
[133] Quoted by Singleton in Millward and Singleton, *Political Economy*, p. 226.
[134] Dupree, *Lancashire and Whitehall*, vol. II, 31 March 1947, p. 398.
[135] K. Burk, *The First Privatisation*, London, The Historians' Press, 1988.
[136] BLPES, Burn papers 6/30, notes for lunch on 27 April 1945.
[137] BSA, letter from Duncan to Talbot 7 November 1945.

that a privately owned iron and steel industry, supervised by a permanently established Steel Board, could wield 'powers to acquire or participate in shareholdings in cases where they thought it was necessary'.[138] In addition to controlling prices, the Steel Board would have the ability to compulsorily acquire, without compensation, any company it so chose. It was perhaps with a twinkle in his eye that Morrison remarked to Duncan: 'You are almost convincing me that you are more unscrupulous in confiscating and dealing with capital than the Labour Government has ever even thought of being'.[139] The issue of ownership concerned not so much any sanctity of private property rights, but rather the material point of who did the owning. There seemed no reason to think that a privately owned steel industry, headed by a Steel Board concerned to perpetuate pooling and pricing arrangements, offered any significantly different solution to the industry's problems from those likely to be advocated by a nationalised industry. The evidence of both publicly owned monopolies and federation-dominated oligopolies was that both would work for a mix of protection, pooling, and subsidies. These ambitions had been articulated by both industries during the Attlee governments and had been encouraged in part by the mixed signals being sent out in economic planning. For all of the disruption of war and the arguments over nationalisation, the abiding sense was of a continuity of practice stretching back to long before the war. The arguments over nationalisation had strong continuities with the pre-existing arguments over enabling powers; the government and federation attitudes towards price controls and pooling had strong resonance with the practices of the 1930s; while the contradictions between the rhetoric of government and the incentive structures produced through economic planning reflected continuing conflict between the aspirations of politicians and economists.

[138] PRO CAB 124/791, notes of a meeting between Attlee, Morrison, Wilmot, Duncan, and Hunter, 21 May 1947, p. 3.
[139] PRO CAB 124/791, notes of a meeting between Attlee, Morrison, Wilmot, Duncan, and Hunter, 21 May 1947, p. 15.

8   Return to the market?

As with guests who have outstayed their welcome, a question increasingly asked about postwar controls was, when would they be gone? The immediate postwar presumption that they were merely short-term measures to ease the reconversion from a wartime economy had tended to discourage any wider philosophical discussion of the duration and extent of controls. As Ronnie Tress noted in June 1947, there seemed to be a reasonably wide assumption in the civil service that 'the controls are just to tide us over *the transition period* and we must use what machinery we have, we can't have any new controls and it isn't worthwhile rationalising the whole construction'.[1] When, in 1947, persistent excess demand and balance-of-payments problems prompted fundamental changes in the structure of economic planning, there was an associated increase in discussion of the purpose and philosophy of planning. It was then, while working on the draft Economic Plan, that Edwin Plowden turned to Alec Cairncross and asked 'the question which has been troubling all of us for some time. What is the general philosophy behind the Plan? What is it we are trying to do and what system of controls is needed to do it?'[2] The subsequent debates within Whitehall between Hall, Cairncross, Gaitskell, Meade, Robinson, and others were complemented by discussion in other fora such as the 24th Nuffield private conference on 'The Government's Controls of Industry and Trade' on 26–7 June 1948 attended by academics, civil servants and industrialists.[3]

Faced both with the prospect of some controls surviving for longer

[1] PRO T230/25, letter to A. K. Cairncross, Board of Trade, from R. Tress, 21 June 1947. PRO CAB 124/1200, 'Personal Covering Note to Memorandum on "The State and Private Industry" (Revised)' by Harold Wilson, 1950, para. 2.

[2] PRO T230/25, letter to R. Tress (Economic Section) from Alec Cairncross (Board of Trade), 19 June 1947.

[3] UGA, McCance papers, 24th Nuffield Private Conference, on 'The Government's Controls of Industry and Trade', 26 and 27 June 1948. The conference was chaired by Henry Clay and its themes were 'The Relation of Controls to the Use of the Price Mechanism', Saturday 26 June and 'The Present Position of Controls', Sunday 27 June.

than originally anticipated and with regular allegations that controls impaired efficiency, central government initiated a review of the kaleidoscope of controls. On 26 February 1948 Laurence Merriam was appointed by the President of the Board of Trade for twelve months to examine the controls (excluding location of industry, price controls, investment control, and clothes rationing) in the Board of Trade, and in March 1949 he was asked to continue the work on a part-time basis until the end of 1949.[4] The specific relationship between controls and efficiency was examined by the Cabinet 'Controls and Efficiency Committee', which was of the general, if vague, opinion that the existing system of controls encouraged inefficiency and a tendency to monopoly, both through the operation of price controls and by virtue of the administrative preference for dealing with concentrated industries and trades. More specifically identified as a common source of inefficiency was the practice of allocating resources, especially steel, on the basis of previous, often 1938–9, patterns of consumption.[5] Considerations of 'fair shares' strongly influenced this historic basis of allocation, but a common view was that fairness was bought at the cost of freezing the industrial structure. In 1948, Sir John Woods thought that these controls had produced 'a kind of freeze, a twilight sleep, a *rigor mortis*'.[6] In 1950, in his memorandum on 'The State and Private Industry', Harold Wilson criticised the effect of quota schemes in excluding new entrants, penalising the efficient, and cushioning the inefficient from competition. Wilson saw a continuity with the past, arguing that 'the quotas have exactly the same effect as those pre-war cartels and rings which fixed quotas on supply and in every way operated to keep prices up and the inefficient in production, except that the arrangements are statutorily enforced, and that any consequent unpopularity can be

---

[4] PRO T230/319, LPB Merriam, 'Final Report to the President on the Examination of Controls'. Mr Bovenschen was appointed for the War Office. Sir Laurence Merriam was seconded to the Ministry of Supply, 1940–5, and lent to the Board of Trade from 1948–50. Once he had completed his review of controls, he left the Board of Trade to return to industry in 1950.

[5] UGA, McCance papers, Henry Clay (Warden of Nuffield College, Oxford 1944–9) and Mr A. Whittaker (food industry) at 24th Nuffield Private Conference, 27 June 1948. PRO CAB 134/89, CE(48)16, Cabinet, Controls and Efficiency Committee, notes of a meeting 16 August 1948. PRO CAB 132/15, LP(50)16, Cabinet, Report of the Committee on Economic Controls, 27 March 1950, para. 23b. PRO CAB 134/89, CE (48)22, Cabinet, Controls and Efficiency Committee, note on the Report of the Joint Committee on the Working of the Steel Distribution System, 8 November 1948, para. 9. PRO CAB 134/89, CE(48)18 (Revise), Cabinet, Controls and Efficiency Committee, 'Materials Allocations: Questions for Consideration', 21 October 1948.

[6] UGA McCance papers, Sir John Woods and LPB Merriam at 24th Nuffield Private Conference, 27 June 1948.

passed on by the trade association to the Government Department concerned'.[7]

In this context, some businessmen were strongly suspected of vociferously complaining of the delays and form-filling attendant upon economic planning, but at the same time of not wishing to see a speedy end to controls in their industry.[8] In the course of his examination of controls, Laurence Merriam was 'appalled to find how much industry likes control. The senior civil servants with whom I have had to deal are only too anxious to get rid of controls; they are all overworked and would be only too glad to get rid of them, but I must say that resistance has come from industry. They do a great deal of talking about getting rid of controls but they mean any control but their own, and it is a deplorable thing.'[9] Sir Hubert Henderson also suspected of trade associations that 'although they may join in general denunciations of controls, they will not really want to get rid of control in their own industry, which does have its effect of assuring minimum profit in every firm'. By 1948, H. A. Benson wanted the government to end profit and allocation protection and 'to force industry out into the hard world of "survival of the fittest".' Isaac Pitman, the MP, with interests in the paper industry, thought that

the time has come for the Government and the Civil Service to do a bit of 'dirty work' and to put the responsibility of controls more fairly and squarely on the shoulders of the industries concerned. I am sure that a great many of the controls are welcomed by industries and that they are now sheltering behind a 'phoney' reluctance which might well be shown up.[10]

Moves towards the scrapping of controls were generally welcomed by the civil servants who were charged with operating a system of sometimes quite labyrinthine complexity. The Board of Trade's guide to raw material controls ran to ninety pages, with Merriam doubting that 'there is any one man in the Board of Trade who knows what is

---

[7] PRO CAB 124/1200, 'The State and Private Industry', memorandum by Harold Wilson, President of the Board of Trade, 4 May 1950, para. 22 (a).
[8] PRO CAB 132/15, LP(50)33, Cabinet, Lord President's Committee, 'Government Controls and the Public', Memorandum by the Lord President of the Council, 8 May 1950, para. 1.
[9] UGA McCance papers, LPB Merriam at 24th Nuffield Private Conference, 27 June 1948.
[10] UGA McCance papers, Sir Hubert Henderson, Mr H. A .Benson, and Mr I. J. Pitman at the 24th Nuffield Private Conference. Isaac Pitman was a Conservative MP, 1945–64. Previously, he had been Director of the Bank of England, 1941–5 and Director of Organisation and Methods at the Treasury, 1943–5. Henry Benson was Controller of building materials, Ministry of Works in 1945. Sir Hubert Henderson was Professor of Political Economy, Oxford, 1945–51, and Chairman of the Statutory Committee on Unemployment Insurance 1945–8.

controlled'.[11] Civil servants frequently stressed the sheer pressure of work and time under which they worked, and were naturally interested in ideas such as that for raising the licensing figure for private building work to £100, which was hoped to produce a saving of six million forms. While attracted by practical, detailed changes of this sort, they tended to be more wary of, and irritated by, some of the more fundamental reforms suggested by economists. It was the disparity between the daily grind experienced by civil servants and the clarity of economists' brighter ideas which often jarred with civil servants. What annoyed James Helmore of the Board of Trade about the academics of the 'long-haired front' was 'a certain irresponsibility'. While agreeing that 'it would be very nice to see what would happen if the price mechanism were allowed to work, or any of the other "long-haired" remedies were adopted', what he felt was missing was 'the feeling one has, at a desk in Whitehall, that what one does is not the answer to an examination paper, or an article in the *Economist*, or somewhere else; it really is going to affect the future of the particular industry and that particular industry's contribution to balance of payments, or any other of the national objectives one is thinking of'.[12]

Partly as a consequence of two interim reports delivered by Merriam, as well as of a general easing of shortages, the lighting of two 'bonfires' of controls was announced by Harold Wilson, the President of the Board of Trade, on 4 November 1948 and 22 March 1949. In general, there was a drift away from controls. While in 1947, 1 million export licences were issued, by 1949, this was 550,000. In 1947, 973,000 raw-material permits were issued; in 1949, 520,000. In total, in 1947 2,580,000 licences and permits were issued by the President of the Board of Trade; in 1949, 1,118,000. As controls fell, so too did the control staff. Personnel at the Board of Trade fell from 14,200 in 1947 to 10,450 in 1949.[13]

If this drift away from controls as a corollary of the progress of reconversion from a war economy were continued, then ultimately controls would disappear, being replaced with market mechanisms. Under-impressed with the operation of pre-war markets, and attached to a set of policy objectives which were thought unlikely to be wholly secured by market mechanisms, politicians began to address the issue of

[11] UGA McCance papers, LPB Merriam at 24th Nuffield Private Conference, 27 June 1948. PRO T230/319, EC(S)(47)18, Economic Section, Note by Mr. Butt on 'Controls', 27 May 1947, p. 3.
[12] UGA McCance papers, Sir John Woods, Sir James Helmore, and Henry Clay at 24th Nuffield Private Conference.
[13] PRO T230/319, LPB Merriam, 'Final Report to the President on the Examination of Controls', para. 13.

just which controls they wished to retain on a longer-term basis. Thus, politicians having almost taken the retention of many controls for granted in 1945, and having been forced in 1947 to begin to develop some rationale for the purpose and practice of planning, by 1950 the most fundamental issue of what controls government should operate in a peacetime economy forced itself to the fore of discussions of economic planning.

Decisions on what, if any, controls to retain on a long-term basis needed to be preceded by a clearer articulation of what longer-term social and economic objectives the government was pursuing. Arguing with Meade and Robinson in June 1948 on the pace of decontrol, Robert Hall observed that there was

a very great multiplicity of controls, most of them inherited from previous stages, and established for a great variety of reasons. Some of the reasons are no longer valid, many of them are in connection with social or political objectives about which we are not, even today, altogether clear. And the result of that is, I think, as in the old story, that we have got the bear by the tail and the problem is to know where and when to let go.[14]

While it was probably prudent to let go of the bear at some point, discretion suggested that it should not be left to run entirely loose. Morrison was all for relaxing controls which were no longer required, but he did so in the hope that 'the public will be much readier to accept the controls which are necessary for long-term planning if we can show that we are not wedded to controls for the sake of controls'.[15]

What, then, were these longer-term controls which the government was interested in maintaining? While the electoral defeat of the Attlee government in October 1951 ultimately means that this question of which controls would have been retained, and for how long, will always be a matter of speculation, some indication of the emergent thinking of the next generation of Labour Party leaders and senior personnel can be gleaned from the discussions on the future of controls which took place towards the end of the Attlee governments' period in office.[16] The rising generation of Douglas Jay, Hugh Gaitskell, Aneurin Bevan, and Harold Wilson were all to the fore of discussions of what controls a future

---

[14] UGA McCance papers, Robert Hall at 24th Nuffield Private Conference, 26 June 1948.

[15] PRO CAB 132/15, LP (50)33, Cabinet, Lord President's Committee, 'Government Controls and the Public', memorandum by the Lord President of the Council, 8 May 1950, para. 5.

[16] N. Rollings, '"The Reichstag Method of Governing?" The Attlee Governments and Permanent Economic Controls', in H. Mercer, N. Rollings, and J. Tomlinson (eds.), *Labour Governments and Private Industry: the Experience of 1945–51*, Edinburgh, Edinburgh University Press, 1992, pp. 15–36.

Labour government might wish to retain. At the turn of 1949/50, in a paper on 'Controls and Economic Planning', which was welcomed by Robert Hall as 'a real attempt, one of the first I have seen, to state the economic policy of the government', Hugh Gaitskell posed the central question of 'what controls are needed in the full employment economy?'.[17]

Gaitskell identified three broad areas which he thought should concern future policy-makers: (1) securing a stable balance of payments; (2) maintaining nearly full employment; and (3) pursuing certain distributive objectives. This last concern was, for Gaitskell, the fundamental defining feature of socialism. Gaitskell was impressed with the redistributive and equity aspects of the Attlee governments' use of direct controls, urging in January 1950 that 'it cannot be too strongly emphasised that it is the use by the government of direct controls – whether rationing in order to secure fair distribution or industrial controls in order to expand exports – which has been the distinguishing feature of British socialist policy'.[18] The pursuit of full employment was an important associate of wider redistributive ambitions, and balance-of-payments stability was an important concomitant of the pursuit of full employment. Thus, for Gaitskell, 'in an economy, where it is desired to plan the level of employment and the distribution of income, two forms of control will always be indispensable whatever else is dismantled; exchange control and control over imports.'[19]

Although imports were to remain heavily restricted until 1953, import controls were not to be as important as Gaitskell seems to have hoped.[20] Indeed, Gaitskell's views on imports were not as liberal as one might expect of someone who was broadly in favour of competitive mechanisms. Gaitskell seemed to want to retain some control over what was imported, lest the population find itself having to 'refrain from buying butter from Holland because we are increasing our purchases of bulbs'.[21] Nor did Gaitskell think it right that the UK

---

[17] PRO T230/319, 'Controls and Economic Policy', paper by Hugh Gaitskell, December 1949/January 1950, para. 1. PRO T230/319, EPC(50)9 'Economic Planning and Liberalisation', Paper by Robert Hall, 16 January 1950, para. 1. PRO T230/319, 'Controls and Economic Policy', note from Robert Hall to Sir Edwin Plowden, 4 January 1950.

[18] PRO T230/319, 'Controls and Economic Policy', paper by Hugh Gaitskell, December 1949/January 1950, para. 5.

[19] PRO T230/319, 'Controls and Economic Policy', paper by Hugh Gaitskell, December 1949/January 1950, para. 10 (i).

[20] J. C. R. Dow, *The Management of the British Economy 1945–60*, Cambridge, Cambridge University Press, 1970, p. 153.

[21] PRO T230/319, 'Controls and Economic Policy', paper by Hugh Gaitskell, December 1949/January 1950, para. 10d.

should export essential goods at much cost to ourselves, in order to import inessentials from Europe. We are almost certainly to some extent now exporting coal and steel which might better have been used at home, or exported to 'hard' markets, to pay for all manner of inessentials (lawn mowers, ash trays, oysters, cosmetics) . . . If the essentials, such as coal, were not rationed except by price and the price mechanism worked freely, it might be argued that people preferred the inessentials. But the fact is that consumers do not have a real choice at present. They cannot get the coal even if they wanted it.[22]

Whatever the irrationality of the pricing of coal and steel, and whatever the aesthetic desirability of being spared many of the brasher Dutch tulips, the protective aspects of Gaitskell's thinking raised their own issues of concern. Robert Hall questioned Gaitskell's presumption that he could decide what people could and could not import, worrying that 'anyone who thinks he knows what is essential for other people (above subsistence level) is making a dangerous mistake'.[23] While Richard Clarke had 'considerable sympathy with the arguments against liberalisation of trade' he thought that the logical consequence of Gaitskell's thinking was 'that we should strive to increase trade barriers within Europe (and within the sterling area) for all we are worth. This obviously cannot be right'.[24]

While Gaitskell's perception of the role of government in securing a stable balance of payments provoked contention, there was more agreement on the need for government to retain some controls in pursuit of its employment policy. In his memorandum on 'The State and Private Industry' in May 1950, Harold Wilson made clear his unhappiness at simply relying on Keynesian demand-management techniques to counteract the onset of depression and unemployment. With the IPC's experience providing confirmation of the limited influence which the government could exert over fixed capital-investment activity in private industry in the midst of a boom, then 'how much weaker will be our powers to increase the volume of investment when we are threatened with unemployment'. Wilson worried that 'when slump conditions are in danger of setting in, there is an acute danger of Keynesian ideas dominating our thinking so much that we shall be driven into a Maginot-like dependence on purely financial methods of preventing a depression'. In these conditions, Wilson saw the haunting spectre of the financial crisis of 1931. It was at just such a

[22] PRO T230/319, 'Controls and Economic Policy', paper by Hugh Gaitskell, December 1949/January 1950, para. 10e.
[23] PRO T230/319, 'Controls and Economic Policy', note from Robert Hall to Sir Edwin Plowden, 4 January 1950, para. 4.
[24] PRO T230/319, RWBC/3523, 'Economic Planning and Liberalisation', EPC(50)9, paper by R. W. B. Clarke, 10 January 1950, pp. 4–5.

moment that government should not only order capital equipment, but should also have some powers, in addition to its budgetary and financial instruments, with which to influence private firms 'to increase the scale of their buying of capital equipment, consumer goods and working materials. So far no plans have been worked out for either.'[25]

In pushing for 'positive' powers in support of employment policy, Wilson was in step with similar arguments being made by Douglas Jay in the course of discussions with the committee under Bernard Gilbert which was considering the powers which might be identified for longer-term retention, these ultimately being collected in the Economics Powers Bill. However, the almost entirely 'negative' character of these powers drew criticism from Jay and Bevan.[26] Bevan was keen that a more up-beat preamble be attached to the bill. Jay, who initially had been inclined to wait for another year before introducing the bill, responded to Morrison's apparent keenness to see the bill included in the king's speech.[27] However, Jay was keen that such a bill should not be negative and restrictive in tone and character. The aim, as he saw it, was to remove the impression that planning is a matter of saying 'Thou shalt not'. Jay's list of the main 'positive' powers which could be included in the bill included the power of manufacture by government departments; the power to purchase domestic industrial and agricultural output; the power to lend at 'uneconomic' rates of interest to stimulate investment by public boards and local authorities; and the power to stimulate investment by private industry.[28] Following discussions with the Chancellor of the Exchequer and a meeting of ministers, the bill was revised again, the Economic Planning and Full Employment Bill being the result.[29] The bill revived earlier 'positive' powers for the stimulation of capital investment activity and provided for the purchase of capital goods on public account, as well as once more encouraging local and

---

[25] PRO CAB 124/1200, 'The State and Private Industry', Memorandum by Harold Wilson, President of the Board of Trade, 4 May 1950, p. 4, para. 11.

[26] PRO T228/241, CP(50)230, 'Economic Planning and Full Employment Bill', note from Bernard Gilbert to Mr Armstrong, 26 October 1950. The result was the Bill attached to CP(50)178, where the title had become 'Economic Planning and Full Employment', and where the preamble in the first eleven lines had appeared, but where the Bill was otherwise the same as the Economic Powers Bill.

[27] PRO T228/241, note from Douglas Jay to Chancellor of the Exchequer, 27 October 1950.

[28] PRO T228/241, note from Douglas Jay to Chancellor of the Exchequer, 27 October 1950.

[29] PRO CAB 130/65, Annex, 'Report by the Official Committee on the Economic Planning and Full Employment Bill', February 1951, para. 1. The Economic Planning and Full Employment Bill was revised in the light of the views expressed in the memorandum of 9 November 1950, by the Chancellor of the Exchequer (GEN 343/2) and at the meeting of Ministers on 10 November 1950 (GEN 343/1 meeting).

public authorities to establish a 'reserve of works'.[30] While referred to in the king's speech, the bill's enactment did not then appear to be of immediate concern. When enquiries were made to the Lord President's office regarding the timetabling of the Economic Planning and Full Employment Bill, the reply from the Lord President's Private Secretary was that 'the Lord President is not in a frightful hurry for the Bill and will not expect it to be introduced immediately after the debate on the Address'.[31] As it was, the Attlee government's days were numbered, the Conservative government under Winston Churchill being elected in the October 1951 general election.

Superficially, it might be thought that with the election of a Conservative government the whole apparatus of state economic planning would have been dismantled rapidly. After all, Churchill had warned in his first broadcast of the 1945 general-election campaign that 'socialism is inseparably interwoven with totalitarianism and the abject worship of the State' and that a socialist government faced with opposition 'would have to fall back on some form of Gestapo'.[32] As ever, of course, the outlook of the Conservative government was never as simple as this and the practical necessities of the administration of government prevented any radical immediate change. As seen, many controls and much of the machinery of economic planning had ebbed away and dissolved of its own accord. Of the remaining instruments of planning, many, like the IPC, were regarded as being of considerable use by civil servants such as Bernard Gilbert. Advantages were seen in persisting with the physical style of planning involving the IPC, not least in that it provided a means of deciding priorities and preventing overloads in particular industries.[33] The mixture of physical and financial controls that was being used to regulate investment removed some pressure from the budgetary, monetary, and credit mechanisms.[34] Certainly, to rely on financial techniques of control alone raised serious concerns about the breadth of the effects of credit restrictions and the

[30] PRO CAB 130/65, Annex, 'Report by the Official Committee on the Economic Planning and Full Employment Bill', February 1951, para. 1. PRO T228/241, CP (50)230, 'Economic Planning and Full Employment Bill', note from Bernard Gilbert to Mr Armstrong, 26 October 1950.
[31] PRO T228/241, letter from A. Johnson (Cabinet Office) to Sir Bernard Gilbert (Treasury), 27 October 1950.
[32] A. Sked and C. Cook, Post-War Britain: A Political History, Harmondsworth, Penguin Books, 4th edn, 1993, pp. 20–1.
[33] PRO T229/483, 'Control of Investment', notes of Strath, Figgures, and Hall, 4 September 1952. William Strath, Ministry of Supply 1945–7; CEPS 1947–55; Treasury 1948–55. Frank Figgures, joined Treasury in 1946; Director of Trade and Finance, OEEC, 1948–51.
[34] PRO T229/41, note by W. Strath to Sir Edwin Plowden, 8 September 1952.

hazards of monetary targets.[35] The other appeal, to civil servants at least, of retaining the IPC, was that it could be used to establish priorities 'for trying to ensure that first things get done first'. While the broader anti-inflationary role of the IPC could be subsumed within the Treasury, the abolition of the IPC was seen as reducing the opportunity for Ministers to make decisions about priorities and attempting to prevent overloads on particular industries.[36]

It was a back-handed tribute to the IPC's ability to place decisions about priorities before Ministers and Cabinet that the lead in seeking the Committee's abolition was taken by Harold Macmillan, the Minister for Housing and Local Government. Just as in 1947, when Aneurin Bevan had been the fiercest opponent of the birth of the IPC, so too now was Macmillan to dance, Salome-like, for its head. Among the tempting tit-bits passed before the eyes of watching departments was the general, if bathetic, enticement that releasing licensing restrictions on private industrial building would facilitate more building and produce productivity improvements in the building industry. This was directly contrary to the IPC's experience that the more demand was placed on the industry, the greater the risk of overload and reduced productivity.[37] While soliciting support from other departments, Macmillan also attempted to destroy the credibility of the IPC by simply ignoring it. Launching a new 'housing crusade' to build up to 300,000 houses per annum, a 50 per cent increase on the 200,000 agreed with Bevan, Macmillan's spending exceeded agreed building-expenditure targets by £40 million in 1952 and by £60 million in 1953, as he made little attempt to limit the programme to the estimate of 230,000 completions in 1952 and that of 260,000 in 1954.[38] It was not just that limits were exceeded, but that Macmillan had made it clear that he had little intention of respecting the limits on this or any other of his programmes.[39] Without strong political support and leadership, there seemed little that the IPC could do to constrain him. As Frank Turnbull complained to Sir Edwin Plowden in July 1952, 'if the Ministry of Housing and Local Government were to turn up in six months time and

---

[35] PRO T229/483, 'Control of Investment', memo by Sir Bernard Gilbert, 29 April 1953, para. 4.

[36] PRO T229/483, 'Control of Investment', notes of Strath, Figgures, and Hall, 4 September 1952.

[37] PRO T229/41, 'Investment Control', note to Mr Strath by F. F. Turnbull, 29 August 1952. Frank Turnbull, Under Secretary, Treasury 1949–59. PRO T229/483, 'Control of Investment', F. F. Turnbull, note to Sir Edwin Plowden, replying to Sir Bernard Gilbert's memorandum, 5 May 1953.

[38] PRO T229/483, 'Control of Investment', F. F. Turnbull, note to Sir Edwin Plowden, replying to Sir Bernard Gilbert's memorandum, 5 May 1953. para. 3.

[39] PRO CAB 134/776, Harold Macmillan to R. A. Butler, letter, January 1952.

say that they had authorised £15 million too much in Blitzed Cities, I do not think we could do very much about it, and I think the Ministry are aware that that is the position'.[40] The more Macmillan flouted the limits, the harder it was to keep other departments in line. As Turnbull remarked, 'it is going to be extremely difficult to say formally to Departments that they must toe the line when the line is already £64 million beyond where it ought to be. I think we shall lose the co-operation of the Departments concerned with these programmes almost entirely if we insist on them implementing the reduced programme when the housing programme is allowed to go free of restriction'.[41] Where Macmillan led, others followed. By August 1952, many officials were increasingly ignoring investment limits, knowing that they would be supported by their minister, who might then be able to get small easements by pressing the matter in the Cabinet.[42]

The basis of this system of investment control was eroding. By May 1953, Turnbull reported to Plowden that the 'foundations are crumbling'.[43] There was a growing inclination among officials to scrap a system which was neither politically liked nor respected, and which as such threatened to bring the wider system of Treasury expenditure controls into disrepute. With a sense of loss, in May 1953, at a meeting chaired by a reluctant Sir Edward Bridges it was decided to support the proposal that the IPC be wound up and that the investment operation be concentrated in the Treasury and the Economic Section, and put primarily on a financial basis.[44] Robert Hall regarded the passing of the IPC as 'a very serious misfortune'.[45] It left unsolved a range of persistent issues concerning the influence which a government with aspirations to demand management actually had over investment, both in general and in particular areas such as the nationalised industries and local government. Fiscal and monetary methods of influencing investment activity were being tried, but their impact was still uncertain. Canadian government budgetary techniques of deferring depreciation

[40] PRO T229/41, 'The Investment Programme', note to Sir Edwin Plowden from F. F. Turnbull, 29 July 1952.
[41] PRO T229/41, 'The Investment Programme', note to Sir Edwin Plowden from F. F. Turnbull, 29 July 1952.
[42] PRO T229/41, 'Investment Control', note to Mr. Strath by F. F. Turnbull, 29 August 1952, para. 6.
[43] PRO T229/483, 'Control of Investment', F. F. Turnbull, note to Sir Edwin Plowden, replying to Sir Bernard Gilbert's memorandum, 5 May 1953, para. 2.
[44] PRO T229/483, 'Control of Investment', F. F. Turnbull, note to Mr Lucas and Mr Jukes, 21 May 1953. John Jukes, Economic Adviser, Cabinet Office and Treasury, 1948–54.
[45] PRO T229/483, 'Control of Investment', Robert Hall, note to Sir Edwin Plowden, 11 May 1953, para. 3.

allowances for particular projects were watched with interest, and efforts continued to improve the government's statistical base.[46] With the IPC gone, an alternative form of surveying departmental investment activity would be required. As Hall pointed out, ministers were no more likely to accept an arbitrary monetary limit arrived at through a financial approach than an equally arbitrary monetary limit arrived at through a physical approach.[47] The demise of the IPC was in keeping with the general dismantling of the postwar system of economic planning. Although some building and import controls lingered on, and domestic coal rationing survived until 1958, by 1954 most of the remaining vestiges of economic planning had gone. Certainly, in the 1950s few spoke of planning as they had in the 1940s. Its time had gone and it was quietly buried.

Buried, but not dead. By the start of the 1960s planning was becoming fashionable again. As Britain was enjoying its highest ever level and rate of economic growth, there was increasing concern with relative economic decline. Across the Channel, the French economy was growing more quickly and flaunting the apparent benefits for growth of indicative planning. Encouraged by this example, the Wilson government of 1964–6 established the Department of Economic Affairs, which duly published the National Plan in September 1965. Growth targets approaching 4 per cent per annum were set, in the pursuit of which George Brown at the Department of Economic Affairs was to use his political weight to resist Treasury attempts to sacrifice growth to the copy-book gods of price and balance-of-payments stability. Particular emphasis within this growth strategy was given to raising the share of national income devoted to fixed capital investment. Higher investment would promote economic growth; or was it *vice versa?*

In fact, Britain's investment performance continued to disappoint the supporters of investment-led growth models, and years later Harold Wilson was to look for the institutional financial obstacles to higher investment in Britain. His conclusion was that Britain did not suffer from some perverse distaste for investing in its own industries, but rather that rational investors eschewed projects with relatively low returns. If anything, it was almost arguable that investment had actually been a little higher than might have been expected, as during the

---

[46] PRO T229/325, EC(S)(51)20, Economic Section of the Cabinet Secretariat, 'Full Employment and the Control of Investment', paper by Mr Atkinson, 1 June 1951, paras. 9, 10.

[47] PRO T229/483, 'Control of Investment', notes of Strath, Figgures, and Hall, 4 September 1952.

postwar period capital investment had grown faster than output. As the capital–labour ratio had risen, so too had the capital–output ratio, with an associated decline in the profit rate.[48] The capital–output ratio was unattractive, especially when compared with other returns available in an increasingly international market. While from 1963–72 the crude capital–output ratio was 3.4 in the UK, it was 1.5 in West Germany.[49] In manufacturing industry from 1963–73, the ratio was 7.2 in the UK, and 2.5 in West Germany.[50] No matter which measures of output and investment were taken, the relative picture was similar. In terms of net output per unit of investment, the West German level was 1.9 times that of Britain from 1958–72, and 1.7 from 1973–9.[51] At the margin, in terms of incremental capital–output ratios, that for Britain was 4.88 over the period 1956–62, compared with 3.05 for West Germany, 3.26 for France, 2.34 for Italy, and 4.17 for the USA.[52] Given these relatively lower and falling returns on capital investment, there was a relatively lower demand for investment. As the Wilson Committee was to conclude in 1980, low investment was the result of poor output and low financial yields and profit rates, rather than any peculiar difficulties in providing external finance.[53]

If we leave aside the extractive industries, the structures of most modern economies were not wildly dissimilar, and yet their capital–output performance clearly diverged. What Britain had was a straight-forward productivity problem. While the postwar relative growth performance of the West German and Japanese economies is usually instanced, in many ways, the problem is seen most clearly in the postwar comparisons with France. Over the period 1950–73, the quantitative and qualitative contribution of capital and labour to annual GDP growth were roughly similar. By far the largest contribu-tion to the difference between the 5.13 per cent annual growth of French GDP and the 3.02 per cent of the UK came from the total

[48] R. C. O. Matthews, C. H. Feinstein and J. C. Odling-Smee, *British Economic Growth 1856–1972*, Oxford, Clarendon Press, 1982, Table 13.1, p. 378.

[49] National Economic Development Office (*NEDO*), *Finance for Investment*, London, HMSO, 1975. Cited in A. Cairncross 'The Postwar Years, 1945–1977', in R. Floud and D. McCloskey (eds.), *The Economic History of Britain Since 1700*, vol. II, Cambridge, Cambridge University Press, 1981, p. 380.

[50] Confederation of British Industry, *The Road to Recovery*, London, CBI, 1976. Cited in A. Cairncross, 'The Postwar Years, 1945–1977', in R. Floud and D. McCloskey (eds.), *The Economic History of Britain Since 1700*, vol. II, p. 380.

[51] N. Crafts, 'Economic Growth', in N. Crafts and N. Woodward (eds.), *The British Economy Since 1945*, Oxford, Clarendon Press, 1991, p.277.

[52] W. Beckerman, *The British Economy in 1975*, Cambridge, Cambridge University Press, 1965, p. 30.

[53] *Committee to Review the Functioning of Financial Institutions*, Wilson Committee, Cmd 7937, London, HMSO, 1980.

factor productivity of 3.11 per cent in France compared with 1.53 per cent in the UK.[54]

Consideration of the issue of productivity during the 1940s was dominated by comparisons with the USA. The general opinion was that, as in World War I, the productivity gap with the USA had widened across the war, although in estimates made soon after the war Rostas doubted that the gap was quite as wide as some feared.[55] In comparison with the productivity gap with the USA, there was less concern with the UK–West German productivity position. Although roughly at parity with Germany in 1937, a slight productivity gap in the UK's favour seems to have opened during the war, before being closed again in the 1950s.[56] Specifically in manufacturing, the widening of the wartime gap was quite marked, later estimates placing (West) German manufacturing productivity at only three-quarters that of the UK in 1950, although one-fifth higher by 1965.[57] In the comparisons with both the USA and West Germany it was heavy industries which gave most concern. Certainly, the impression of steelmen in Britain that their US counterparts had moved even further ahead of them during the war was confirmed by later estimates which put the relative US/UK productivity ratio of blast furnaces at 3.62 in 1937/5 and at 4.31 in 1947/8.[58] Elsewhere, other industries which had also concerned the Attlee government continued to operate at relatively lower rates of productivity. In 1968, comparative US/UK productivity ratios in construction were 2.06, and 1.72 in West Germany/UK comparisons.[59] While the gap with the USA was to narrow to 2.06 in 1977, that with West

[54] N. Crafts, 'Economic Growth', in Crafts and Woodward (eds.), *British Economy Since 1945*, Table 9.4, p. 265.

[55] PRO CAB 134/191, ED(48)3, 'Change in Productivity in British Industries', paper by L. Rostas. S. N. Broadberry, 'The Impact of the World Wars on the Long-Run Performance of the British Economy', *Oxford Review of Economic Policy*, 4 (1988), pp. 25–7. A. D. Smith, D. M. W. N. Hitchens and S. W. Davies, *International Industrial Productivity*, Cambridge, Cambridge University Press, 1982, p. 93. S. N. Broadberry, 'Technological Leadership and Productivity Leadership in Manufacturing Since the Industrial Revolution: Implications for the Convergence Debate', *Economic Journal*, 104 (March 1994), pp. 291–302.

[56] S. N. Broadberry, 'Technological Leadership and Productivity Leadership', *Economic Journal*.

[57] Bart van Ark, 'Comparative Levels of Manufacturing Productivity in Postwar Europe: Measurement and Comparisons', *Oxford Bulletin of Economics and Statistics*, 52, 4 (1990), pp. 343–74.

[58] S. N. Broadberry and N. F. R. Crafts, 'Explaining Anglo-American Productivity Differences in the Mid-Twentieth Century', *Oxford Bulletin of Economics and Statistics*, 52, 4 (1990), p. 378.

[59] A. D. Smith, D. M. W. N. Hitchens and S. W. Davies, *International Industrial Productivity*, Table 11.3, p. 131.

Germany was to widen to 2.37 in 1977.[60] Across the entire postwar period a stream of official reports and committees of inquiry reflected the persistent concern with the low level of building productivity. In 1983, the National Economic Development Office and others were still considering the problem.[61]

In short, industries whose productivity had been the subject of government and industrial investigations from 1945–51 continued to operate at relatively low rates of productivity long after the demise of economic planning. Factors contributing to low productivity, such as barriers to entry and exit, cross-subsidisation in public and private industries, producer rings, long construction times, deficiencies in technical training, and allocative decision-making on the basis of distorted relative prices continued to characterise the British economy for decades.[62] These were not peculiar to economic planning, although economic planning did provide an intensified example of the effects of such factors in an output-maximising economy subject to balance-of-payments constraints. All of this would have been disappointing, if not altogether surprising, to ministers such as Dalton and Cripps, who had shown a particular interest in securing long-term productivity improvements.[63] The common aspiration of a postwar reconstruction

---

[60] A. D. Smith, D. M. W. N. Hitchens and S. W. Davies, *International Industrial Productivity*, Table 3.2, p. 23.

[61] *Report of the (Wilson) Committee of Enquiry into the Delays in the Commissioning of CEGB Power Stations*, Cmd 3960, 1969. NEDO, *Report of the Working Party on Large Industrial Construction Sites* 1970. NEDO, *Faster Building for Industry*, London, EDC/HMSO, 1983. Geoffrey Briscoe, *The Economics of the Construction Industry*, London, Mitchell Publishing, 1988. p. 286. P. Trench, 'Low Productivity: High Time for a Re-think', *Building*, 10 September 1976, pp. 108–9. Slough Estates, *Industrial Investment: A Case Study in Factory Building*, Slough, Slough Estates, 1979. I. L. Freeman, 'Comparative Studies of the Construction Industries in Great Britain and North America: a Review', London, Department of the Environment, *Building Research Establishment Current Paper*, CPS, Watford, July 1981, p. 15.

[62] PRO 130/65, Annex, Report by the Official Committee on the Economic Planning and Full Employment Bill, Appendix III, 28 December 1950, para. 3. Cross-subsidies were ultimately authorised by charge orders such as that in Section 2 of the Emergency Powers (Defence) Act of 1939. Charges Orders could be used to distribute over an industry, a burden which would otherwise bear unevenly on its members, as in iron and steel. The effect of this was equalised by a system of levies imposed by voluntary agreement over the whole industry, with the Charges Order being held in reserve as a weapon with which to compel a recalcitrant firm to make its contribution. Other examples were the Fish Charges Order, which were used to equalise transport costs in that industry, and the Coal Charges Order.

[63] N. Tiratsoo and J. Tomlinson, *Industrial Efficiency and State Intervention: Labour 1939–51*, London, Routledge, 1993. Most European countries had a keen interest in productivity and many were subject to the attentions of transatlantic-crossing productivity teams. Defeated economies were often even more interested in such US practices than the British. France had many visits from US productivity teams, while in Austria, a ministerial decree of the Austrian Government of 4 April 1950 established

characterised by mutually beneficial increases in output and productivity lost its lustre as increased capacity was bought at some cost to longer-term productivity. This was much more evident in the microeconomic details of the technological choices made within industries than in the broader macro-economic policy options pursued by government. It did not arise from any wilful neglect by government of the needs of manufacturing and industrial investment, nor from a lack of interest within government in modernisation and improving productivity. There is no substantial statistical evidence to support the accusations that the Attlee governments sacrificed economic modernisation to the needs of their health and social-security programmes. More valid is the criticism that the housing programme was too large, and that in competing with industry for scarce construction resources it contributed to the problem of long construction times. In its associated school-building requirements, the housing programme also contributed to the discouragement of efforts to establish a credible and expanded programme of technical education, this impact being heightened by the determined efforts of the IPC to restrain spending on social investment. Yet, the impact of the house-building programme should not be exaggerated. Although it was proportionately larger than in some other countries which had suffered more damage to their housing stock, it was politically inconceivable that any victorious British government at the end of the total war of 1939–45 would renege once again on promises to initiate a substantial postwar house-building programme. The opportunity costs of the housing programme might be written down as costs of victory, and are arguably deserving of a kinder history than the Korean War rearmament programme, which, when coupled with the needs of the export drive, brought the postwar trend of rising investment to an abrupt halt.

That the export drive was a constant in resource-allocation discussions reflected the emergence of the altered balance-of-payments as the most important economic legacy of the war. Ever persistent, the

the Austrian Productivity Centre in Vienna with Professor Dr Wilhelm Taucher as its President. PRO BT 195/26, Memo on 'Österreichisches Produktivitäts-Zentrum', Report of Work Done. Dalton's support for the establishment of the British Institute of Management was attacked by the economists Lionel Robbins and Arnold Plant, who regarded the required government expenditure of £75,000 per annum for the first five years as sheer extravagance. Robbins, who was later to be so closely identified with the expansion of university education in the 1960s, was of the view that 'if the Government wished to get value for its money, £25,000 a year to the Universities would produce very much more than £75,000 a year to an independent institute of industrial management, with no tradition behind it and the very poor sort of personnel which experience shows tend to cluster in the neighbourhood of this complex of propaganda'. PRO CAB 124/827, paper from Lionel Robbins to A. N. Coleridge, 23 February 1945.

balance-of-payments problem was a bemusing but increasingly looming spectre hanging over planning discussions. That the successful prosecution of a substantial export drive could coexist with recurrent biennial balance-of-payments crises mystified many politicians. The technical details of dollar shortages, the capital account, or shifts in the terms of trade were matters in which the pre-war-educated leadership had no training. What was understood was that the export drive, import controls, and the need to clear domestic bottlenecks combined to produce an economy whose predominant characteristic was persistent excess demand. When the widely expected slump failed to appear, the intellectual and administrative adjustments to the new problem were painful and partial. The fuel and convertibility crises of 1947 provoked administrative changes and a definite budgetary strategy aimed at reducing the pressure of demand, but the political mentality had not changed sufficiently to allow for the greater use of price mechanisms in the struggle to constrain and shift demand.

The case for making a greater use of price mechanisms so as to assist government in the achievement of some its objectives was argued strongly, notably by Meade, Chantler, and Lewis. The intensity of their advocacy reflected their perception that the use made of the price mechanism represented the fundamental issue of economic planning. If resources were not be allocated on the basis of prices reflecting the preferences and decisions of consumers and producers, then on what basis was allocation to occur? If the distribution of resources was not to the planners' liking, how far would they be tempted to resort to administrative and dirigiste methods to achieve their ambitions? Economic planning did not involve the overthrow of the price mechanism but rather a move to a different set of prices. Persuading politicians to view planning in this light was always likely to be difficult, not simply because they often had a political commitment to low prices but also because of the general postwar distrust of market mechanisms. It was unfortunate that the immediate postwar arguments over the merits of average and marginal cost pricing in socialised industries should have been rendered irrelevant by the immediate problem of excess demand and impracticable by the dim prospect of any government ever agreeing to underwrite some of the potential losses. In terms of the development of welfare economics the arguments were of importance. In terms of their impact on economic policy, the entire episode was illustrative of the chasm which at times separated the thinking, approach, and vocabulary of politicians and economists.

The depth of the resistance to greater use of the price mechanism was evident even in the efforts of Gaitskell to increase peak-hour electricity prices. While unusual among politicians in his willingness to use price mechanisms to constrain capacity requirements, both he and Cripps were adamant that the general level of electricity prices should not be raised significantly because of its impact on lower-income groups. The political concern with prices, allied to socialist redistributive ambitions, informed the discussion of prices and the decision to nationalise industries in monopoly form. Often regarding monopoly as an inevitable consequence of the capital intensification of the economy, Labour supporters and politicians were inclined to define the boundaries and incidence of natural monopoly more widely than economic theory suggested. In establishing nationalised industries in monopoly form, there was an assumption that ownership would enhance control. If anything, ownership enhanced responsibility, which was then exploited by the monopoly to weaken control. This problem was quickly perceived by Gaitskell and Jay, and sharp consideration was given to abandoning the nationalisation of entire industries and to increasing the scope for state competition within industries. Although these ideas were to be developed by Crosland in the mid-1950s, it was to take the Labour Party and British governments decades to incorporate crucial distinctions between forms of ownership and market structures into their policy statements.

The immediate consequence of nationalisation in monopoly form was to reduce competition in an economy which had enjoyed external and internal forms of protection since the inter-war period. Externally, the inter-war protection provided by tariffs was replaced by the immediate postwar protection of import controls, world shortages, and dollar restrictions. Internally, the array of cross-subsidies, cost-pooling, and price arrangements operated in the inter-war period was not only consolidated during the war, but maintained after it. With barriers to new entrants strengthened, ring-operating incumbents could respond to the export drive while holding domestic consumers captive. Faced with excess demand stoked by price controls, managers pursued fixed capital-investment strategies which were most likely to produce rapid incremental additions to output, even at the expense of foregoing some improvements in future productivity. This often rational response to the signals sent through the system of economic planning was encouraged by disparities between the nominal cost and real value of resource inputs. The coexistence of such micro-economic incentive structures alongside quite genuine government concern to promote improved productivity may not be entirely unfamiliar to students of economic planning in other countries. While the British experience of economic planning from 1945–51 was a unique moment in its history, the struggle between market and state administrative mechanisms which lay at its heart was to continue in and beyond Britain for decades to come.

Index